IN PRAISE OF BARBARIANS

IN PRAISE OF BARBARIANS

ESSAYS AGAINST EMPIRE

MIKE DAVIS

Haymarket
Books

Chicago, Illinois

First published by Haymarket Books in 2007
P.O. Box 180165
Chicago, IL 60618
773-583-7884
www.haymarketbooks.org
info@haymarketbooks.org

Trade distribution:
In the U.S. through Consortium Book Sales, www.cbsd.com
In the UK, Turnaround Publisher Services, www.turnaround-psl.com
In Australia, Palgrave MacMillan, www.palgravemacmillan.com.au

This book was published with the generous support of the Wallace Global Fund.

Cover design by Josh On and Eric Ruder
Cover illustraion: "The Huns at the Battle of Chalons" by A. De Neuville (1836–1885)

ISBN-13: 978-1931859-42-4

Printed in Canada by union labor c
consumer waste in accordance with
www.greenpressinitiative.org

Library of Congress CIP Data is ava

2 4 6 8 10 9 7 5 3

AUTHOR'S NOTE:

To save space and a few trees, citatións are expressed as numbered references to the more important sources as listed in the bibliography at the end of the book. Many of these pieces were originally published in simultaneous versions on Tomdispatch.com (New York) and *Socialist Review* (London). I am very grateful to Tom Engelhardt and Pete Morgan and the rest of the *SR* crew for their support and collaboration.

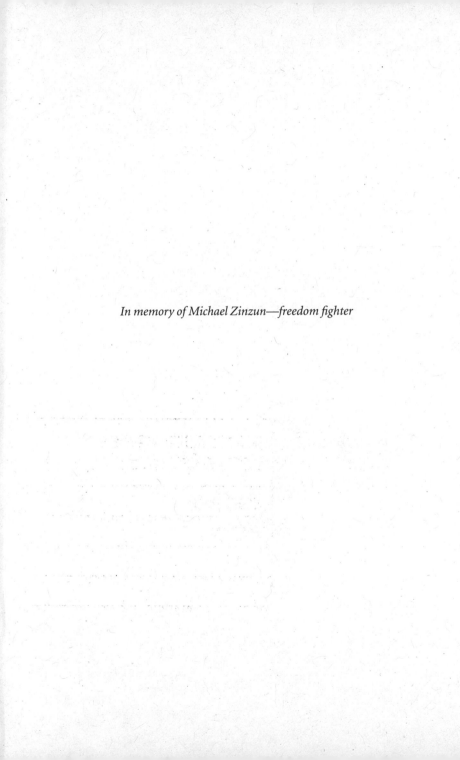

In memory of Michael Zinzun—freedom fighter

"You're a real Karl Marx, you are!" the squadron's military commissar said to him in the evening. "What the hell are you writing there?"

"I am describing various thoughts in accordance with the oath I have taken," Khlebnikov answered…

—Isaac Babel, *The Red Cavalry* (1926)

CONTENTS

PART ONE

ROMANS AT HOME

Augustus was sensible that mankind is governed by names;
nor was he deceived in his expectation, that the Senate and people
would submit to slavery, provided they were respectfully assured
that they still enjoyed their ancient freedom.

—Edward Gibbon, *The Decline and Fall of the Roman Empire*

ONE

THE END OF AMERICAN EXCEPTIONALISM

On an otherwise gorgeous morning in September, ordinary Americans suddenly became vulnerable to the consequences of the history that has been made in our name in the Middle East for the last sixty years. It was an "apocalyptic" day in the exact theological sense (according to the great Orthodox theologian E. Lampert) of a "revelation that reveals the mysterious pathways of evil."(89) Suddenly, thanks to a complex history of oil, Zionism, and CIA "ghost wars," the lives of thousands of New Yorkers were consumed in an inferno of volcanic grandeur and supernatural terror. In the most intimate and terrible way, we became citizens of a world where one atrocity is repaid with interest by another; where the price of oil is the slaughter of innocents.

No one, I think, has grasped the essence of this better than the left-wing Egyptian journalist Hani Shukrallah writing in *Al-Ahram*.(135) He focuses on what for him, as for several other writers, was the ultimate moral horror of the attack: four-year-old Juliana McCourt, cradled in the arms of her mother, as their plane careened into the World Trade Center (WTC). Who of us, he asks, could understand the anguish of her mother in those last moments? What monstrous politics uses little children as suicide weapons?

But Shukrallah also reminds us of another terrified and helpless child: twelve-year-old Mohammed al-Dorra. On a car-buying expedition with his father, this Palestinian sixth-grader was trapped in a gun battle with the Israeli Army. For almost an hour he cowered next to his father, before an Israeli sniper—with deliberate precision—shot and killed him. "How many tears were shed or candles lit," wrote Shukrallah, "in Britain, the U.S., or Germany—for Mohammed al-Dorra and the thousands of other Palestinian children killed or maimed during the past year alone? Where was the sense of horror when Mrs. Albright, responding to a question about the five hundred thousand children that have died in Iraq as a result of U.S.-imposed sanctions, gruesomely stated that 'the cost, we think, was worth it'?"(135)

Shukrallah's point, obviously, is not to justify one child's murder by another; but to remind all his readers, Arabs as well as Americans, that empathy—"that innate capacity that makes us worthy of the self-designation 'human'"—must be a consistent principle. Crimes against humanity are no less and no more terrible when they occur in a New York skyscraper, a Palestinian refugee camp, or an obscure Kurdish village. And "a world," he warns, "in which our choices are limited to Bush and bin Laden is a damned and doomed world of madness."

This is a world, of course, in which most ordinary people of both the Middle East and North America are little more than pawns. Despite what both Bush and bin Laden aver, the people and the empire are not synonyms for each other; I do not buy the claim, for example, that "Americans have reaped what they have sown." The victims of the WTC massacre—the secretaries, accountants, deli delivery guys, window cleaners, stock analysts, and firefighters—were not the ones who designed and implemented our secretive, antidemocratic, and criminal policies in the Muslim world.

They did not overthrow the elected government of Mossadegh in Iran; support the genocide of eight hundred thousand leftists in Indonesia; intervene on behalf of the fascist Phalange against the Palestinians in Lebanon; fight a dirty war against Dhofarian insurgents; underwrite absolute monarchies like Saudi Arabia, the shah of Iran, Morocco, and the Gulf Emirates; build with billions of U.S. tax dollars the golden throne upon which Mubarak sits like a modern-day pharaoh; arm Saddam Hussein in the 1980s and turn a blind eye to his genocide against the communists and Kurds; then kill seventeen thousand Iraqi civilians in bombing raids during the Gulf War, including more than four hundred women and children incinerated in the Amariyah bomb shelter. Nor did they stir the Shias of southern Iraq into revolt, then abandon them to Saddam Hussein's executioners because George Bush senior calculated that the total destruction of the regime would create an impermissible power vacuum that Iran might rush to fill.

Ordinary New Yorkers, likewise, did not blow an Iranian passenger jet out of the sky or kill Qadaffi's baby daughter; secretly sell arms to Iran in order to fund mass murder in Central America; pin medals on Ariel Sharon, the butcher of Beirut; turn a blind eye to Israel's continuing expropriation of Palestinian land; smile when Kuwait and other Gulf autocracies expelled four hundred thousand Palestinians; give Stinger missiles to Bulddadin Hikmatyar, a sadistic fanatic who made Afghanistan the world's leading exporter of heroin; condone one military dictatorship after another in Pakistan; romance the Taliban in 1995–96 because Union Oil wanted to build a pipeline across Afghanistan; or blow up the pharmaceutical plant that was Sudan's only source of antimalarial drugs.

Nor did three thousand missing New Yorkers partake in the sixty-year feast that U.S. oil giants, construction companies, and aerospace manufacturers have enjoyed in the Arabian peninsula. They did not bribe sheiks, wine and dine torturers, sell arms to murderers, sponsor terrorists in the name of combating terrorism, or subsidize religious bigots as long as they promised to kill secular leftists. Nor, in order to preserve their control over the world economy, have they prostituted the name of freedom to support the rule of billionaires over paupers.

Yet all this was done, and much more, in the name of American people. "Made in the USA" is the label on some of the most sinister episodes in the recent history of these ancient lands. I am not claiming that the United States is the prime mover of every evil and inequality in the Muslim world, the literal "Great Satan" excoriated in the prayers of fundamentalists. No, reactionary local ruling classes, in the last instance, are the ultimate enemies of democracy, feminism, minority rights, and social justice in the Arab and wider Muslim worlds. And British, French, and Brezhnevite imperialism, along with Israel, have also helped steal the dreams of the Arab masses.

But who can deny that the principal structural obstacle to any kind of progressive socio-economic change in this region has been the unholy but seemingly impregnable alliance between U.S. oil companies and arms manufacturers, right-wing Zionism, and the superrich ruling classes of the Arabian peninsula? Who believes that the House of Said or the playboy emirates of the Gulf would survive for a month without their U.S. military shield? Or that Israel could continue to colonize the West Bank if it faced a U.S. foreign policy that was just as committed to Palestinian as Israeli self-determination?

We are now offered as responses to al-Qaeda extremist versions of the same policies that have proven so catastrophic to human rights in the past. And the principal architects of these bankrupt policies—all the aging but still crew-cut generals, CIA directors, and undersecretaries of state—now seem to live permanently on our TV screens, where twenty-four hours a day they preach virulence and fear with the aid of half-truths and grotesque simplifications. Confronted with the "blowback" of fifty years of CIA dirty tricks and secret wars, we are told that our intelligence agencies have their hands tied by "political correctness" and irresponsible liberal principles. We must unleash the men in black, let them get down and dirty, assassinate foreign leaders, and make love to torturers.

Confronted everywhere with the moral and political debris of the First Gulf War—whether it is called Timothy McVeigh or Osama bin Laden—we are harangued that war, relentless and unending, without boundaries or time limits, is our salvation. As if the anger in the refugee camps and shantytowns is not great enough, we propose to bomb the most broken and pitiful country in the world, Afghanistan. As one of Spain's leading jurists, Baltasar Garzon, recently wrote in the *Financial Times*, we are commanded to "pledge unlimited suport for the hypothetical bombardment of nothing; for the massacre of poverty; and for a breach of the most fundamental logic, which proves that violence begets violence. The spiral of terrorism is fed by the number counted among its victims."(60)

President Bush has painted a vision of the United States as a huge, gated suburb with security cameras in every tree. For the sake of our safety, the world outside must become a free-fire zone for the CIA and Delta Force. Let's "coalesce" (the president's bizarre word choice) around the flag, with our gas masks and national identity cards, and try to enjoy life as it used to be. Is this anything other than the urban, war-on-crime paranoia of the 1980s now raised to the level of world history? The city on the hill turned into a well-padded bunker?

Finally, amid so much frenetic signing of blank checks and celebrations of common purpose, we are utterly betrayed by what now consolidates itself as a one-party system in Washington. George W. Bush (elected president by a majority of the Supreme Court, not the majority of the electorate) has been given war powers—*against whomever, wherever, forever*—that have no precedent in American, or perhaps world, history. This is not the polity imagined by Tom Paine or Thomas Jefferson. In such a time, dissent—and dissent within dissent—become the most profound and responsible memorial to the dead of 9/11.

(September 2001: teach-in, SUNY-Stony Brook)

TWO

GREAT AND GLORIOUS DAYS

*On some great and glorious day the plain folks of the land
will reach their heart's desire at last, and the White House
will be adorned by a downright moron.*

H. L. Mencken (1920)

Thanks to hanging "chads," Republican goon squads, and a corrupted
Supreme Court, George W. Bush—the consummation of Mencken's
mordant prophecy—has adorned 1800 Pennsylvania Avenue for eighteen months. He is, of course, a preposterous marionette in every respect:
lacking even the charisma of Calvin Coolidge or the mental agility of
Ronald Reagan. Elsewhere in the world, lights this dim only inherit
power at the end of thoroughly dissipated aristocratic bloodlines. Their
arrival in the palace usually signals that the peasants have already sharp-
ened their pikes and that the Bolsheviks are in session in Smolny.

Yet opinion polls confirm that since his coronation as Crusader
King on 9/11, his domestic popularity has soared higher (and for
longer) than any president in American history. Indeed, the usually
sober *National Journal* believes there is simply "no historical parallel"—not even FDR after Pearl Harbor or Bush Sr. during the First
Gulf War—for the Shrub's currently stratospheric approval ratings
from Mencken's "plain folks," including a staggering 76 percent of reg-

istered Democrats. Moreover, the 1960s-era generation gap has now been reportedly inverted: Generation X and Y voters are rallying to the flag in higher percentages than their elders. (Should our new slogan be: "Don't trust anyone under thirty"?) Overall, the Democrats' commanding 46 percent to 37 percent lead in partisan identification in June 2001 polls has collapsed; the two parties are now (March 2002) dead even.

Having stolen an election and then quickly become the second most popular president in all of American history (at least according to one recent poll where George W. tied with FDR just behind Abe Lincoln) is no mean feat. In so many decisive senses, including the wholesale resort to government by executive order and presidential privilege, it has been the moral equivalent of a coup d'etat. It is also the kind of seeming historical paradox that once prompted an obscure London journalist to write a tract of almost Shakespearean grandeur known as *The Eighteenth Brumaire*.

How we might relish Marx's delicious treatment of the intrigues in Florida: the feeding frenzies among the oilmen and defense contractors, the secret government inaugurated on 9/11 (or was it earlier?), the craven sycophancies of Murdoch and Blair, the stealthy night visits of Ashcroft and the tantrums of Rumsfeld, George W.'s doglike obedience to Cheney, his unblinking declaration that his "mission is saving the world," and so on. So much dialectical irony to savor.

But are we to believe, in the last instance, that the "plain folks"— e.g., the U.S. working class—are simply a "sack of potatoes" like the witless French peasants who endorsed the thuggish dictatorship of the lesser Napoleon? (If this is obscure, I leave it to readers to make their own acquaintance with Marx's masterpiece.) Is human nature between the Mexican and Canadian borders now so Pavlovian that our rulers need only wave flags and bloody shirts to make us bay at the moon for tactical nukes and military courts? Are Americans (like French peasants stricken with nostalgia for *Le Grand Armée* or German burghers obsessed with the "treason of 1918") so cocooned within the mythology of the "American Century—Part Two" that they don't see the widening circle of imperial carnage, not to mention the destruction of their own civil liberties?

Marx, I am sure, would have placed the emphasis elsewhere. He would have, so to speak, pinned the tail on the donkey, not the elephant. The true "miracle" of this initially ill-starred administration was not the punctual arrival of a made-in-Hollywood Evil Other to pump up the national testosterone, nor even another video-arcade triumph of Pentagon technology, but the fact that all this has been politically managed without a scintilla of serious debate or opposition in Congress. If ordinary Americans seem to be fulfilling Mencken's misanthropic prophecy, it is because they have been comprehensively betrayed by the Democratic Party.

Socialists, of course, have been pointing out for generations that the Democrats are a capitalist party with some social-democratic camouflage. But the trade-union and civil rights elites have always found new excuses for their old addiction, even after the sharp rightward turn of the Carter administration in 1978 and the consolidation of power by the post-liberal Democratic Leadership Council (DLC) during the 1980s. There was always some scrap of lesser-evilism—labor law reform, Supreme Court appointments, defense of abortion rights, and so on—to justify turning another trick, buying another nickel bag of contaminated pro-business poison mislabeled as pure Old Roosevelt.

The tricks continue but there are no longer any visible scraps. The Democratic Senate majority has sold out the Bill of Rights, endorsed military courts and concentration camps, supported the militarization of the U.S.-Mexico border, and turned the other cheek as Bush jettisoned the Kyoto Protocol and the ABM Treaty. Without serious debate or traditional hearings, Majority Leader Tom Daschle has licensed the administration to escalate its intervention in Colombia's dirty war, while Bob Graham, the Florida Democrat who chairs the powerful Senate Intelligence Committee, supports the option to use "low-yield" nuclear weapons against the so-called Axis of Evil. Likewise, Joe Lieberman, Gore's former vice-presidential running mate, has screeched louder than any Republican in the Senate for Saddam Hussein's head, while Carl McCall, who as Democratic state controller in New York has invested millions of pension fund savings in Israel, promotes his current campaign for governor with lurid photos of himself firing an M-16 at an Israeli "anti-terrorist" training camp.

On the domestic front, Daschle has kept his party—those reformed spenders—on the straight and narrow path of fiscal rectitude that Herbert Hoover once practiced so famously. Daschle scolds naughty Republicans for proposing to spend their way out of the recession with "guns and caviar" (a huge weapons buildup combined with a $1.3 trillion tax cut targeted at the rich), but offers no alternative stimulus program of "jobs and schools." Yet, at the same time, he and his House counterpart, Minority Leader Richard Gephardt, refused to support Teddy Kennedy's attempt to repeal Bush's egregious upper-bracket tax cuts. (In a recent speech to the Democratic Leadership Council, Gephardt made love to the same corporate centrism he used to scorn in the Clinton administration.)

Writing in tandem in the *American Prospect* (the journal of nearly extinct "Progressive Democrats"), Robert Kuttner and Jeff Faux remind us that the current anti-Keynesianism is in the truest spirit of "Clintonism without Clinton." "Ever since economic adviser Charles L. Schultze sold Democrat Jimmy Carter on deregulation," explains Kuttner, "the resurrection of the invisible hand has been a bipartisan project."(87) "Urged on by Federal Reserve Chairman Alan Greenspan," adds Faux, "Bill Clinton had made eliminating the national debt more important than expanding investment in health, education, and other programs."(49) But then Greenspan, after convincing them that deficits were the root of all evil, did the dirty on the Dems by turning around and endorsing Bush's huge tax cut.

The Democrats, of course, are also the more fanatical free-traders. Because Bill Clinton didn't "feel your pain" in the coal and steel valleys of West Virginia, he lost Gore the critical electoral votes of a normally rock-solid Democratic state. As leading Democrats continue to fret about "fiscal deterioration" and trade barriers, Bush is on television talking jobs to heartland Teamsters and steelworkers. His 30 percent tariff on foreign steel—an inconceivable violation of globalist dogma in the days of Clinton and Rubin—may well ensure continuing Republican control of the House, if not the recapture of the Senate.

Indeed the escalation of the War on Terrorism is shrewdly designed to strengthen the Republicans' current domestic advantages. In addition to the obvious functions of legitimizing military Keynesianism and rule by executive order, the war-without-end aims to divide the Democrats. As Trent Lott's pit bull–like attack on Daschle demonstrated, the Republicans are dying to "Saddamize" any Democrat who wavers in unconditional commitment to the commander in chief.

Does this mean, as Kuttner suggests, that the Democrats are rapidly losing "their raison d'etre as a party?" Probably not. But what materially grounds partisan difference in the early twenty-first century is radically different from the idealized image most trade-union bureaucrats and Black Democrats retain of the former party of Roosevelt. Thanks to watchdog groups that monitor and analyze campaign financing, the macro-economic power structures of the two parties have become more fully visible than ever before.

In the year 2000 election cycle, for example, Republican congressional candidates received three-quarters of all contributions from energy and agribusiness, 70 percent of all manufacturing, and two-thirds of all prime defense contractors. (The presidential contributions are even more skewed: Bush got 93 percent of oil and gas and 87 percent of agribusiness.) On the other hand, the Democrats received a slight majority of contributions from the communications, electronics, entertainment, and gaming sectors that constitute the new engine of the U.S. economy. The so-called FIRE sector (financial services and insurance) was split 58 percent Republican and 41 percent Democrat with commercial banking favoring Bush and venture capital gambling on Gore.(28)

The Republicans, in other words, remain solidly grounded in the Old Economy sectors: indeed, the Bush administration is virtually an executive committee of the energy, construction, and defense industries. On the other hand, the Democrats, primarily in the Clinton/Rubin years, have made spectacular gains in the New Economy. Meanwhile, Wall Street old money veers Republican while the new money is marginally Democratic. The health care sector, which favored Clinton in 1992, remains a competitive terrain for Democratic fund-raisers. If the Bushites aren't exactly economic nationalists in the McKinleyite sense advocated by Pat Buchanan, they certainly are prepared to use military spending and the War on Terror to prop up the profits of Old Economy sectors. The Clinton administration, on the other hand, was more rigorously theological in its advocacy of an essentially Wall Street view of economic globalization and free trade.

It is always wise, of course, to "follow the money," and the current alignment of capital fractions explains much about the Democrats' timidity and Republicans' overweening aggressiveness. Clinton's historic achievement was to bring information economy billionaires into the Democratic fold and the Daschle/Gephardt/Gore leadership will do nothing that might scare away Hollywood or Silicon Valley (including pushing too hard on the Enron scandal). Conversely, the Republicans have seized the opportunity to revive the flagging fortune of oil and war, as well as raid the alienated Democratic heartlands.

Bush may be a moron, but, sure, it's a fool's paradise.

(April 2002: *Socialist Review*)

THREE

OCCUPIED AMERICA

Every night the forces of occupation fan out across the sullen, cratered landscape of the defeated enemy capital. Their objectives are to uproot, engage and, hopefully, annihilate the surviving loyalists of the old regime. It is war without pity.

The occupied capital, of course, is Washington, D.C., and, as the Bushites regularly reassure their supporters, regime change is being as ruthlessly pursued on the banks of the Potomac as on the Tigris and Euphrates. Indeed to listen to any of the right-wing demagogues who dominate the U.S. airwaves, the Democrats are an even more despised, cowardly foe than the Baathists. Just as Paul Bremer is imperial proconsul of the new American oil properties in Mesopotamia, so Grover Norquist is Bush's gauleiter for the formerly Democratic Beltway.

"Grover who?" Most Americans don't know the name either, but the former lobbyist for South Africa–backed guerrillas and the mastermind of the fanatically antigovernment Americans for Tax Reform (ATR) is the bludgeon with which the Bush administration hopes to pound the Democratic Party into oblivion. An obese rich boy from the Boston suburbs who grew up in a home with an indoor pistol range and a huge library of conservative books, Norquist was the leader of the College Republicans when he was conscripted by the Reagan White House in 1986 to run its ATR front group. Later he took a sabbatical to lobby support for right-wing terrorist groups like the

Nicaraguan Contras, Jonas Savimbi's UNITA in Angola, and the murderous Renamo guerrillas in Mozambique. He also accepted a lucrative retainer to defend the besieged empire of Microsoft in its famous antitrust battle.

In 1993–94 he emerged as Newt Gingrich's éminence grise: marshalling an unprecedented coalition of business and conservative groups to defeat the Clinton administration's modest proposed expansion of federal health care and to advance the radical agenda of Gingrich's "Contract with America." (Blame Grover directly for the soaring price of medical coverage—a larger cost component of the family car than steel—that has led Detroit automakers to shed hundreds of thousands of American jobs.) With Republicans in control of the House of Representatives for the first time in forty years, major industry groups (auto manufacture, construction, financial services, health care, and so on) that had previously split campaign contributions between parties, now massively tilted toward GOP candidates. Norquist's mission was to make sure this defunding of the Democrats was permanent and irreversible.

Every Wednesday, he presided over a disciplined strategy session that synchronized the efforts of the coalition's key players, including the National Rifle Association, the Christian Coalition, the major right-wing think tanks, the liquor, tobacco, and gambling lobbies, and the antienvironmental "property rights movement." In a parody of vulgar Marxism, Norquist's Wednesday Group (together with a parallel "Thursday Group" operating under the Capitol dome) became a de facto "executive committee of the ruling class" with industrial lobbyists and Christian extremists openly writing the legislation that Majority Leader Gingrich then presented to the House.

The grand strategy, as explained by Norquist, was to roll back the New Deal, if not the entire twentieth century, by "defunding big government." Huge tax cuts for the investor class, as well as multitrillion-dollar federal deficits for future generations, would force the privatization of what remained of the American welfare state as well as permanently disabling the Democratic Party. "My goal," Norquist boasted, "is to cut government in half in twenty-five years, to get it down to the size where we can drown it in the bathtub." The United States, as a result, would be returned to the entrepreneurial "golden age" of the McKinley era for which ATR and similar groups pine. (This was the period, circa 1898, when little children worked in mines, Blacks were lynched from magnolia trees, strikers were shot down by militia, and millionaires didn't pay taxes.)(95)

Norquist survived the fall of Gingrich to provide new éminence grise to his Republican successors, Tom DeLay and Dick Armey. In 1999 he rallied skeptical conservatives to the Bush camp and coordinated the vicious right-wing attacks on the chief Republican rival, Senator John McCain of Arizona. Shortly after the Florida presidential coup d'etat in January 2001, Grover's Wednesday Group resumed its heroic work of demolishing a century of social reform. With a typical attendance of more than one hundred, the Norquist brunch has been described as nothing less than "Grand Central Station" where corporate money and reactionary ideas are transformed into the Bush party line.

The Wednesday Group's greatest domestic conquests so far have been the 2001 and 2003 tax cuts. The windfalls to the very rich (much of which the Republicans hope will be returned to them as campaign donations) are less important than the deliberately engineered $3.6 trillion cumulative deficit: an Archimedean lever for downsizing and/or privatizing social spending. The frightening ease with which Norquist and DeLay blitzkrieged the second, larger tax cut through the supposed Maginot Line of Democratic resistance in Congress exposed the bankruptcy of the Democratic leadership's post-9/11 strategy of abdicating criticism of Bush's War on Terrorism in order (so they claimed) to take a principled stand on the economy.

But the Dems may have only begun to feel the pain. The great achievement of the Clinton presidency—purchased at the price of alienating its blue-collar electoral base—was to win support of much of the "New Economy" with its ultra-free-trade policies.

Now the Republicans, led by Norquist and DeLay, are forcibly breaking up this marriage of high-tech billionaires and New Democrats. In their view, there is only room for one capitalist party in Washington's New Order.

Thus Norquist's so-called "K Street Project" (referring to the home of most Washington lobbyists) has carefully tracked the party affiliation of the key employees of the four hundred largest trade associations and political action committees. Business groups have been told that they can continue to write Bush policy only if they purge Democrats (like Senate majority leader Tom Daschle's wife, Linda) and replace them with a loyal Republican cadre. According to the *Washington Monthly's* Nicholas Confessore, the "GOP and some of its key private sector allies...have become indistinguishable. DeLay alone has placed a dozen of his aides at key lobbying and trade association jobs in the last few years.... The corporate lobbyists who once ran the show, loyal only to the parochial interests of their employer, are being replaced by party activists who are loyal first and foremost to the GOP."(33)

"Homeland security," of course, provides a gigantic slush fund to reward Norquist's supporters as well as to further militarize and Republicanize the high-tech sectors. In the aftermath of the dot-com crash, many of the high-tech companies so ardently wooed by the Democrats in the 1990s have rushed to feed at the trough of the Bush administration's mega-billion-dollar expenditures on "net-war," surveillance, space-based weapons, and a national "Bioshield." Drowning human-needs programs in Norquist's bathtub goes hand in hand with vast federal subsidies to corporations willing to sing in the K Street Project's choir.

"Technology companies," writes Brendan Koerner in *Mother Jones*, "have been the most aggressive in marketing their wares as vital to the War on Terrorism. Software titans like Oracle and Sun, anxious to find new customers for their database programs and Web servers, are pushing for the creation of a national identity-card system. Old-line defense contractors like Raytheon and Northrop Grumman, stung by the decline in demand for big weapons systems after the end of the

Cold War, are recasting themselves as security providers, hiring 'homeland security directors' and pitching their technologies to shield nuclear plans or retrofit the Coast Guard's patrol boats."(82) Even that bedrock of the Clinton Democratic Party, Hollywood and especially its high-tech subsidiaries, is being alternately cajoled by Norquist threats and seduced by Pentagon contracts (designing war-game and anti-terrorism simulators, for example).

One result of this new cold fusion of capital and politics is that the Bush administration has unprecedented access to the market power of its allied private corporations. "During the Iraq war, for instance," Confessore continues, "the media conglomerate Clear Channel Communications Inc. had its stations sponsor pro-war rallies nationwide (a few affiliates even banned the Dixie Chicks, who had criticized Bush, from their play lists)."(33) Moreover, as the old liberal state machinery is bankrupted and sold off (national parks, big city schools, even Social Security are all currently under threat), the Republicans will cement lucrative liaisons with the new private contractors. Rumsfeld's Pentagon, already extensively privatized to the benefit of Republican donors, is the prototype for this brave new world of eternal Republicanism where the taxpayers subsidize Halliburton and Northrop, and the corporations, in turn, subsidize Norquist and his bullies.

(September 2003: *Socialist Review*)

FOUR

VERMONT'S PIED PIPER

The rapidly growing list of U.S. casualties from the invasion of Iraq now includes the names Dick Gephardt, Joe Lieberman, John Edwards, Wesley Clark, and even perhaps John Kerry. Not ordinary "grunts" but official Democratic frontrunners, they were severely wounded, if not outright killed in action, on December 9, 2003, in Harlem when Al Gore endorsed the candidacy of Howard Dean, the antiwar insurgent from Vermont. Gore's embrace of Dean, which seemingly caught the other Democrats by complete surprise, was remarkable in at least two respects.

First, the winner of the popular presidential vote in 2000 broke ranks with both sets of his political parents: the Clintons, who have played a typically Machiavellian hand by encouraging the Clark candidacy, and the right-wing Democratic Leadership Council (DLC), which fervently supports *Likudnik* Lieberman. Secondly, Gore emphasized Dean's "courage" in opposing the "catastrophic mistake" of the Iraq invasion. The former vice-president in recent months has sounded more like a Nader voter than his old centrist self. He has warned of the "police state" being constructed by the Bushites and has described the Iraq debacle as the worst U.S. foreign policy decision in two hundred years. Like Dean (another born-again DLCer), Gore clearly believes that the future belongs to MoveOn.org and the Internet nation of young anti-Bush activists.

There is rich irony, of course, in the irresistible rise of the Dean campaign. After 9/11 the Democratic congressional leadership—Richard Gephardt in the House and Tom Daschle in the Senate—abdicated any principled opposition to Republican foreign policy and the invasions of Afghanistan and Iraq. Democrats left their scruples in the gutter as they rushed to support the Orwellian "Patriot Act" and U.S. aggression against Iraq.

The leadership's strategy, endorsed by "Hillary Inc." (as the *National Journal* calls the Clinton-controlled national Democratic apparatus), conceded the War on Terror to Bush as proof of Democratic patriotism while concentrating on fighting Republican economic policies on the home front. It was a morally repulsive calculation, typical of the New Democrats, that quickly boomeranged against its authors.

Gephardt and Daschle badly miscalculated the response of Old Democratic constituencies—unions, African Americans, Latinos, and women—who, by and large, were suspicious of the Iraq adventure from the outset and, unlike their erstwhile leaders, easily made the fundamental connection between civil and workers' rights at home and limitless neo-imperialism in the Middle East. For almost two years, as a result, grassroots opposition to Bush mushroomed without a single major Democrat having the guts to side with the movement. Unlike during the war in Vietnam, there was no McCarthy, Kennedy, or McGovern to channel protest back into electoral channels or co-opt activists into the Democratic Party.

This was a dangerous moment for the Democrats and a rare opportunity for the American left. A national Green Party with a strong, class-rooted candidate might have seized the time. In the event, however, Ralph Nader was temporarily missing in action and along came Howard Dean. There are, to be sure, two far more progressive Democrats than Dean running for the nomination: economic populist Dennis Kucinich and controversial civil rights leader Reverend Al Sharpton. But they have failed to ignite their own grass roots (rustbelt unionism and African Americans, respectively) or to capture the imagination of the college students and young dot-com professionals who constitute Dean's childrens' crusade.

Dean's principal asset, everyone agrees, has been his consistent pugnacity in confronting the lies and crimes of the Bush regime. He has crafted a media persona—forthright and combative—that appears to be the opposite of the carefully hedged and mealymouthed style of the Democratic establishment. Most of all, he has embraced his young supporters and given them unprecedented leeway to organize his campaign as a New Model Internet Army, with a "certified geek," Joe Trippi, as his savvy manager.

As a result, much of the antiwar movement has rushed to Dean like an orphan greeting its long-lost father. His inverted-Bushite bombast about "taking back America" excites messianic hopes amongst a generation starved for heroes. "Al Gore's endorsement," writes an editorialist on the influential CommonDreams.org website "gives Howard Dean a unique opportunity to build a new American majority...and transform the world."

In fact, neither Dean's record as governor nor the fine print of his current pronouncements support the extravagant hopes attached to his campaign. Vermonters remember the wealthy doctor as an anti-progressive indistinguishable from other New Democrats. More recently, he hastily retreated from a vague promise to be evenhanded toward the Palestinians after the American Jewish Congress barked at him. Even his opposition to the war is compromised by his vague timetable for gradual U.S. withdrawal. More importantly, as he ventures into southern primaries and comes closer to the Democratic convention, his positions will undoubtedly shift back toward the center. The antiwar movement has been his launching pad, not his ultimate constituency. His followers see in him a populist hero, but more than anything else he resembles a postmodern version of William Jennings Bryan, the Democratic firebrand whose demagoguery derailed the People's Party in 1896.

Dean's and Gore's true project is the renovation of the Democratic

Party and a return to the happy days of "normal" multilateral imperialism circa Bill Clinton in the late 1990s. The American left, accordingly, must fight like hell against the world of illusion bound up in the popular slogan "Anybody but Bush."

(January 2004: *Socialist Review*)

FIVE

THE ANTI-BUSH COMETH?

A Letter to London

To appreciate the idiosyncrasy of the American Democratic primaries, imagine Tony Blair and Gordon Brown, clown-like smiles glued to their eroded faces, spending week after week pressing flesh and chatting up the locals in the pubs and chippers of Barrow-in-Furness. And imagine an electoral system that gives more strategic clout over the selection of the Labour leader to Cornwall and Essex than to Liverpool and Glasgow. Indeed, a system that puts London almost last in line, after the press have already anointed a winner and the punters have collected their bets.

Such, indeed, is the crazy logic of the U.S. primaries that catapult Iowa, New Hampshire (Concord equals Barrow), and South Carolina ahead of the queue of large states and deprive the big divisions of Democracy, like Chicanos in California, public-sector workers in New York, and African Americans in Illinois, of roles proportionate to their size or historic importance as voters. It is a system, to be fair, that actually forces candidates, with their robot-like spiels and carefully coiffed personas, into brief but spontaneous contact with real people. (One can imagine Emperor Blair recoiling in horror from face-to-face encounters with a lusty Labor rank and file.)

But it also a system that gives the corporate media a strategic advantage in shaping images of candidates and issues long before the primaries reach the big cities and major industrial centers. A lurid and typical example was the press gang-up on Howard Dean, the most outspoken critic of Bush's Iraq invasion, after the Iowa primary. Dean's election night yawp—variously interpreted as a crowd-pleasing holler or a nervous breakdown—was rebroadcast incessantly for several days. The *New York Times* estimated that the average TV viewer saw it twenty times. The same television networks, like Rupert Murdoch's Fox News, that have never lifted an eyebrow over Bush's idiot smirk, Rumsfeld's gloating megalomania, or Ashcroft's private conversations with God, suddenly were whispering in the public's ear that Dean was a madman.

Although Dean himself is a rather ordinary centrist Democrat with an austere record as governor of Vermont, his campaign has aroused elite fear and loathing not seen since the nomination of McGovern on an anti-Vietnam-War platform in 1972. It is a campaign—now rapidly being refashioned and moved to the right by party regulars—that originally grew up in the political and moral vacuum created by the Democratic leadership's abject surrender to Bush's War on Terrorism.

Dean became a hero to angry students and trade unionists because of his willingness to articulate what millions believe but no other Democrat had the guts to say: that the president of the United States is a war-mongering fool controlled by a cabal of oil millionaires and Christian fanatics. In Iowa and New Hampshire, ironically, Dean became the victim of his own campaign's success in forcing other candidates, particularly John Kerry and John Edwards, to speak out against the Iraq deception. Indeed Kerry, so long embalmed in compromise and hypocrisy, suddenly showed faint signs of a former self: the militant veteran who so eloquently denounced American war crimes in Vietnam before Congress in 1972. In the last days in Iowa, surrounded by Teddy Kennedy and an honor guard of veterans, Kerry reinvented himself as the "tough dove."

Without a monopoly on the antiwar issue, Dean crumbled on his domestic flank, where his policies on health care, tax reform, and welfare are indistinguishable or even to the right of the other candidates. In particular, his trademark "taking back America" appeal wilted in the face of Senator John Edwards's more militant us-versus-them contrast of "two Americas." Edwards, boasting of his mill-town origins, won unexpected second place with a rhetoric targeted precisely at the pain of Iowa's many downsized or deunionized meatpacking towns.

In this week's new crop of primaries, Edwards must win his home state of South Carolina to preserve his serious-contender status, while Kerry will attempt to fortify his lead by carrying Missouri (whose favorite son, Dick Gephardt, perished in Iowa) and Arizona. Dean, meanwhile, must grimly hang on until the big states' "super-primary" in early March at last gives voice to his hard-core support among college students and public-sector workers. The bomber of Belgrade and the Clintons' stealth candidate, General Wesley Clark, has so far proven more of a stiff cardboard cutout than a charismatic hero. Joe Lieberman, finally, whose ultra-Likud views are to the right of the White House, is now little more than an obscure cargo cult worshipped by the Democratic Leadership Council.

Unlike the upcoming re-coronation of Bush, the Democratic race will remain a tense cliffhanger for a few weeks at least. But it is drama with little substance. Despite a facade of deep debate, all the leading Democrats, including Dean, have no higher aspiration than to be the new Bill Clinton, whom they all profess to adore. None has dissented from U.S. policy in Afghanistan or unconditional support for Israel. All endorse the War on Terrorism (but want it more focused) and all vow to pour more, not less, money into Homeland Security and the promotion of national paranoia. Kerry, meanwhile, is a big-time WTO internationalist, Edwards (despite his log-cabin CV) is a wealthy trial lawyer, and Dean is a notorious fiscal conservative.

The ultimate Anti-Bush, inevitably, will be a clone of Clinton, promising rapid (but not immediate) withdrawal from Iraq and partial repeal of Bush's more egregious fiscal giveaways to the superrich.

"Freedom fries," moreover, may become French again, and allies may be occasionally consulted about bombing targets. What is slouching toward November, then, is a dispiriting choice between the Bushite "super-imperialism" and the Democratic "normal imperialist" status quo ante.

Ralph Nader, meanwhile, has bowed out of a Green Party nomination and, indeed, the Greens are bitterly divided over what to do in November. Prominent progressives are also all over the map, although none more so than Michael Moore, who has been canvassing votes for Clark. Third-party forces may still get their acts together (perhaps behind California Green Peter Camejo), but, for the moment, it looks as if the Democrats will once again succeed in stealing the thunder from the grass roots. Thank the Dean campaign for disorganizing a broadly populist antiwar movement.

(March 2004, *Socialist Worker*)

SIX

JUMPING OFF THE BANDWAGON

Is the Pentagon too small, the War on Terrorism too meek, and the Department of Homeland Security too underfunded? John Kerry thinks so. In recent days he has repeatedly attacked the Bush administration for failing to put sufficient troops in the field or move aggressively enough against al-Qaeda and North Korea. If elected, he promises to dramatically enlarge the army by forty thousand soldiers and increase spending on domestic anti-terrorism. He pledges to streamline and multilateralize the War on Terrorism (he calls it "progressive internationalism") with tougher stances toward erstwhile allies like Pakistan and Saudi Arabia. While refusing, so far, to commit himself to concrete steps for reducing the U.S. profile in Iraq, he has specifically endorsed Ariel Sharon's "right" to brutally wall off the West Bank and reiterated traditional Democratic support for ultra-Zionism. He was also the cosponsor of the recently passed "Syrian Accountability Act," which provides legitimation for future U.S. aggression against Damascus.

Hardly the platform of a "peace" candidate. Indeed, having already banked the Democratic nomination, the Kerry campaign no longer needs to woo antiwar Dean and Kucinich supporters. The rebellion on the party's left is over. The mantra now is "electability," and Kerry has turned rightward to charm conservative Democrats, independents, and dissident Republicans. Chief foreign policy adviser to the senator from Massachusetts is Rand Beers, formerly George W. Bush's chief adviser on counterterrorism. Beers reportedly deserted the White House because he felt that the neoconservative obsession with Iraq was diverting attention from Afghanistan, North Korea, and Colombia. (He was one of the architects, during the Clinton years, of "Plan Colombia"—the United States's largely clandestine intervention in the Andean country's civil war.) A Kerry administration, in the vision of Beers (as well as top Democratic national security gurus like Richard Holbrooke and Sandy Berger), would return the United States and Europe to the glory of the Clinton years, when "normal imperialism" prevailed and smiling allies bombed and invaded in unison.

Although Democrats, like AFL-CIO political chair Gerald McEntee, are hyping next November as "the most important election in our lifetime," it is clear that what will be on offer are merely modest amendments, not authentic alternatives to the core Bush agenda. Withdrawal from Iraq is not a Kerry plank, nor is the repeal of the Orwellian Patriot Act. Kerry voted for both and proposes only "kinder, gentler" versions of what Rumsfeld and Ashcroft have wrought. (We won't nuke Paris after all.) Indeed, as both the *Economist* and the *Financial Times* have noted recently, there is now substantive "continuity" between Republican and Democratic foreign policies.

On the domestic front, Kerry has explicitly reaffirmed his commitment to the "Third Way" exemplified by Bill Clinton and Tony Blair, and declared, "I really pride myself on being pro-business." Since 2001 he has reportedly visited with Silicon Valley executives at least seventeen times; his reward was a majority share of presidential campaign contributions from the communications and electronics industries.

"Anybody but Bush" thus translates into a restoration of the status quo ante and a historic, self-inflicted defeat for the antiwar forces that have now let themselves be corralled inside the Democratic Party. This is why braver and more clear-sighted elements of the American left are rallying behind Ralph Nader's "independent citizen" candidacy. Nader, who waited and wavered while Dean stole the thunder of the antiwar movement, is now running (his website explains) to "mobilize citizens behind an issues agenda...and to take our democracy back from the corporate interests that dominate both parties." To the surprise of most pundits, two recent polls by the Associated Press and the *New York Times* show Nader's seemingly quixotic campaign garnering the support of 6 percent to 7 percent of the electorate. (In 2000 Nader won about 5 percent of the vote in states where he was on the ballot.)

To the advocates of a popular front around Kerry (which includes the editors of the *Nation*, MoveOn.org, and most of the celebrity left), Nader's audacity is sheer treason. Indeed, as the *Los Angeles Times* recently reported, "to many Democrats, Nader represents an election-stealing evil just this side of the Antichrist." Conversely, Peter Camejo, the recent Green Party candidate for governor in California and one of the party's most respected spokespeople, has applauded Nader's candidacy as "the best thing he has done in his life."

Nader, to be sure, is not Eugene Debs (the beloved presidential candidate of the old American socialist movement) nor even Jesse Jackson, vintage 1984. Though surprisingly strong on labor issues during his 2000 campaign, Nader lacks street credentials in the inner cities and attracts little Black or Latino support. Still, Camejo and others argue, Nader remains the most celebrated champion of independent, anticorporate politics, and his campaign offers the best available platform for contesting the neoliberal Democratic resurgence that is addling the brains and confiscating the energy of so much of the liberal left.

But the ultimate impact of the Nader campaign will depend on the critical scope of his platform as well as his ability to win the endorsement of the national Green Party convention in June. "While it is crucial to defend Nader's right to run," one well-known socialist activist told me the other day, "the verdict is still out whether he will mount a left-wing campaign or not." Likewise, it is unclear whether the Greens, despite the heroic efforts of Camejo and others, will again mobilize behind Nader. As always, in the shadow of the monolithic U.S. two-party system, the future of an independent U.S. left hangs in suspense.

(April 2004: *Socialist Review*)

SEVEN

OEDIPUS BUSH

Ronald Reagan was notoriously shrewd at diverting public attention whenever his administration found itself in trouble. A famous example was his invasion of the tiny island of Grenada just forty-eight hours after a truck bomb destroyed the U.S. Marine barracks at Beirut airport in 1983. An unprecedented defeat for U.S. intervention in the Middle East was cunningly transmogrified into a cheap victory for counter-revolution in the Western hemisphere.

Reagan's masterstroke, however, was to synchronize his own death with the Bush administration's hour of greatest need. The timing was impeccable. At the very moment when the jaws of the Abu Ghraib atrocity seemed to be closing around the White House, the last light punctually went out in the former president's already dim brain. Voilà—the U.S. media abandoned coverage of torture and murder in Iraq in order to broadcast interminable footage of the mournful suburban crowds (minus Blacks and trade unionists) at Reagan's send-off, with a teary-eyed George W. Bush reading a soliloquy from a teleprompter. The White House flooded the universe with the conjoined images of Reagan and Bush. A *New York Times'* columnist complained that "it was difficult to tell where the 40th president ended and the 43rd began."

But few (apart from the Reagan family, who reportedly loathe the Bushes*) will contest George W.'s right of inheritance. As Kenneth Duberstein, Ronnie's former chief of staff, told the press, "Bush's name may be Bush, but his heart belongs to Reagan." The current regime has long conceived itself as Reagan III not Bush II. It is Reagan's photograph, not dad's, that hangs above George W.'s desk. More substantively, none of the elder Bush's foreign policy inner circle—including the once mighty James Baker, Lawrence Eagleburger, and Brent Scowcroft—now own a pot to pee in since Junior came to power on the wings of a stolen election. This, of course, raises some intriguing, even alarming, oedipal questions about presidential fathers and sons. Is Junior really the love child of Reagan and Laura Bush? (Poor ole 41, meanwhile, had to jump out of an airplane over Normandy during the D-Day celebrations to remind the world that he's still around.)

Veteran White House reporter James Mann is no psychoanalyst, but he provides fascinating historical background to Bush versus Bush in his new book *The Rise of the Vulcans*.(98) ("Vulcans" was the nickname adopted by Bush's neoconservative foreign policy advisers during the 2000 campaign.) Mann traces the schism in Republican ranks back to the immediate post-Watergate days when Cheney and Rumsfeld battled against an attempted coup d'état by Henry Kissinger. Kissinger who initially was both secretary of state and national security adviser—tried to grasp all the levers of foreign policy from weak president Gerry Ford. Rumsfeld (chief of staff, then secretary of defense) and Cheney (Rumsfeld's protegé), however, were fanatically opposed to Kissinger's grand strategy of détente with the faltering USSR.

From this early stalemated Republican civil war to the breathtaking hubris of their own current shadow presidencies, Rumsfeld and Cheney, according to Mann, have demonstrated remarkable fidelity to

---

* In a 2003 interview with Salon.com before his father's death, Ronald Reagan, Jr., bitterly denounced the Bush administration expropriation of the actor-president's legend. "The Bush people have no right to speak for my father, particularly because of the position he's in now.... These people are overly reaching, overly aggressive, overly secretive and just plain corrupt. I don't trust these people." (Reprinted in *Los Angeles Times*, June 15, 2004.)

the ideal of a world unilaterally ordered by U.S. military omnipotence. For thirty years they have been the unrelenting opponents of so-called foreign policy "realists," whether neo-Kissingerians (with their belief in the jujitsu of balances of power) or Democratic neoliberals (with their emphasis on economic globalization via the IMF and World Bank). In addition, Rumsfeld's frustrated presidential ambitions repeatedly conflicted with those of Bush Senior (a classical "realist"). So did the extremist fantasies of hard-core "neoconservatives" like Paul Wolfowitz, Richard Perle, and William Kristol, who found the first Bush administration lacking in the crusading zeal of Reagan's support for counterrevolution in Central America. They were particularly vexed by the elder Bush's refusal to turn the defeat of Saddam Hussein into a full-fledged Judeo-Christian jihad.

In recounting the events from 9/11 to the attack on Iraq, Mann is particularly illuminating about the roles of Condoleezza Rice and Colin Powell. Rice, although a protegé of Scowcroft (and thus indirectly of Kissinger), has repeatedly rallied to Rumsfeld/Cheney/Wolfowitz, while Secretary of State Powell (whom Mann shows to be far more reactionary than his usual avuncular image) has been forced to become more of a "realist" than he originally wished. Mann, in short, is a skillful archaeologist of the internal evolution of an imperial policy that has culminated in massive aggression against the Muslim world. Yet the greatest merit of Mann's book is undoubtedly his insistence that the real divide between neoconservatives and "realists," however rancorous, is extremely narrow. The realists differ from the fundamentalists principally in tactical nuance and rhetorical emphasis.

The proof of this, of course, is the current hawkish platform of the Kerry campaign, which promises not to withdraw from Iraq and Afghanistan, but to drastically enlarge Homeland Security and double the army special forces. The irony is that while Junior has jettisoned his dad for Reagan redux, the Democratic contender has been encouraging speculation that his foreign policy would be a return to the Camelot days of George H. W. (Even weirder, of course, has been the growing friendship between the old man and the Arkansas huckster who defeated him in 1992. Has the famously fatherless Clinton at last found Daddy? The oedipal labyrinth of the Bushes and Clintons should keep psychoanalytic historians busy for generations.)

In the *Atlantic Monthly*, Joshua Marshall recounts recent discussions with Kerry's foreign policy team. They outline a Kerry strategy that rejects "soft multilateralism and fealty to the United Nations" in favor of "skilled diplomatic management and a willingness to use force abroad. A marriage of power and values." When Marshall suggests that "what you're describing to me sounds a lot like what I'd expect from Brent Scowcroft [Bush Senior's national security adviser]," they readily agreed.(100) Kerry, now disdaining Dean voters, is pitching his campaign to disgruntled generals, national security apparatchiks, and the friends of Henry Kissinger. John Kerry, who for one magnificent moment in his youth had the guts to confront the Nixon administration with its war crimes in Indochina, is now running for president as the heir-apparent to the Nixon-Kissinger worldview. Is there any better reason to vote for Ralph Nader and Peter Camejo?

(July 2004. *Socialist Review*)

EIGHT

WHAT'S THE MATTER WITH AMERICA?

A Debate with Thomas Frank

My conversation with Thomas Frank's best-selling polemic *What's the Matter with Kansas?*(56) focuses on one point: what do the 2004 elections tell us about the crisis of class consciousness in the United States? Does George W. Bush's victory in the popular vote confirm Frank's thesis that the white working class has surrendered any rational calculation of its economic interests to hopeless, manipulated cultural rage?

At first approximation, the election does look distressingly like Frank's "French Revolution in reverse—one in which the sansculottes pour down the streets demanding more power for the aristocracy." Despite the loss of 18 percent of its industrial base over the last four years, Ohio—the universally acclaimed pivot of the national vote—remained a red state, with Buckeye voters seemingly more alarmed by images of gay marriage in faraway San Francisco than by plant closures in their backyard. Veteran Democratic pollster Ruy Teixeira claims that when the exit poll disaster is sorted out, the Democrats will discover that "Kerry got killed by the white working class." According to his estimates, the white working-class vote—defined as whites without a four-year college degree, about half the electorate— endorsed Bush by a whopping 23 percent margin: ratifying the pattern in 2002 congressional races (18 percent) and the 2000 election

(17 percent).(144) Is it time to scrap the "economic interpretation of history" and admit that culture trumps all, especially when Karl Rove is the Republican generalissimo?

1. Identity and Self-Interest

American national elections have seldom been straightforward transcriptions of economic interest: "culture war," indeed, is the default condition of U.S. politics. As political historians like Lee Benson and Walter Dean Burnham have long argued, "the American liberal value consensus on such fundamentals as economic and church-state relationships helped make possible a full articulation of ethnocultural antagonisms in party politics at a remarkably early date."(12) Religious, ethnic, and racial conflict, often disguised in a rhetoric of "values" (like temperance or state's rights), have *normally* structured the field of electoral competition. Only episodically, in the late 1820s, the 1890s, and the 1930s, have economic interests (although usually as mere cartoons of class consciousness) been the explicit terrain of partisan rivalry and then usually in a sectional disguise. The New Deal era stands out as almost unique.(19)

The primacy of "identity politics"—Puritan versus Scots-Irish, the Protestant Republic versus the Papist horde, old-line American versus new immigrant, Main Street versus Babylon, white versus Black—testifies to the volatility and constant recomposition of the American social structure. (My book, *Prisoners of the American Dream* [1985], offers a controversial account of the roles of ethnic fragmentation and white supremacism in retarding labor and socialist consciousness in American history.) There should be no need to emphasize that the fourth and largest migration in U.S. history forms the historical backdrop for the Reagan-Bush era in the same way that the great immigration of southern and eastern Europeans was both a source and ultimately the downfall of Republican hegemony from McKinley to Hoover. (We are, by the way, twenty-five years into the post–New Deal age, with the Clinton interval an odd reprise of Woodrow Wilson, with Perot as Bull Moose.) I'll return to the ethno-racial context of culture war later.

But, first, I want to question the idea of an antinomy between self-righteous identity fantasies and economic self-interest. Ethno-religious and racial identities are rarely just phantoms of false consciousness. More often than not, they correspond to the assertion or defense of perceived systems of privilege and entitlement. Identity politics almost always has a large, even dominant substrate of material self-interest. Thus, "Protestant" and "white' have usually coded for privileged positions in the marketplace, in the hierarchy of the labor process, and in the receipt of political patronage or economic paternalism.

Most of the "obvious" counterexamples in American history of passionate partisan commitments detached from rational self-interest don't completely stand up to scrutiny. It is often argued, for example, that the rank and file of the Confederate Army had no stake in slavery and instead fought so fanatically for an imaginary community, a "Southern nation." I'm enough of an unreconstructed Beardian to doubt this: the plebian white South, in fact, was hugely and variously implicated in the exploitation of Black labor, both before and after 1860. Southern nationalism was (and is) an expression of real as well as symbolic privileges of whiteness.

In general, I am inclined to believe that literal "false consciousness," in the sense of the kind of Stockholm syndrome described by Frank—of embracing purely imaginary solidarities with one's exploiter or oppressor—is not common. (Frank, for example, writes of "sturdy blue-collar patriots reciting the Pledge while they strangle their own life chances; of small farmers proudly voting themselves off the land; of devoted family men carefully seeing to it that their children will never be able to afford college or proper health care" and so on.) I am not denying the existence of symbolic wages and imaginary demons, but cultural wars rage most fiercely when they are able to mobilize material self-interest, however ignorant or shortsighted.

2. Poorest and Most Republican?

Take the startling example that begins *What's the Matter with Kansas?*—the prairie county that may be the poorest in the United States but faithfully votes 80 percent Republican. Frank writes: "When I told a friend of mine about that impoverished High Plains county so enamored of President Bush, she was perplexed: 'How can anyone who has ever worked for someone else vote Republican?' she asked. How could so many people get it wrong?"

But did they? McPherson County, Nebraska, first of all, has a smaller population than most cineplexes on a Friday night: just 533 people according to the 2000 Census. Indeed almost all the poor, Republican counties in the Sand Hills of Nebraska and adjacent parts of Kansas, South Dakota, and Colorado have rapidly diminishing populations of two thousand or less. It is unclear that these ghost towns and buffalo commons can actually tell us much about the larger relationship between white poverty, cultural rage, and Republican neo-populism. Moreover, the typical resident of McPherson County seems to be a small, drought-ridden cattle rancher whose family tax returns are covered in red ink. On the income side, to be sure, his interests seemed aligned with those of female-headed single households in Washington, D.C., or farm workers in the Rio Grande Valley.

But the asset side is a very different story. Many of these bankrupt ranchers still own large chunks of grazing land and several hundred head of cattle. I don't know enough about the local politics of cattle and drought subsidies in the Great Plains to suggest how this rationally translates into partisanship; but certainly, it doesn't automatically follow that voting Republican in McPherson County is economic self-annihilation. Nor is it a very helpful synecdoche for false consciousness in white America.

Frank's principal argument about "people getting their fundamental interests wrong" in Red America, of course, doesn't rise or fall on this infinitesimal example. Indeed, Frank seemingly has an embarrassment of riches to choose from: consider, for example, the case of West Virginia.

3. Split Voting in West Virginia

No state has undergone a more dramatic rightward shift in its presidential vote. A bastion of once powerful steelworkers' and mineworkers' unions, West Virginia was famously loyal to the national Democrats in such dismal elections as 1956, 1968, and even 1988; yet Kerry lost West Virginia by a shockingly large margin—13 percent (or more than double Gore's losing margin). Moreover, he was defeated in the Mountain State despite trends—falling industrial employment, wages, and medical coverage—that seemingly should have favored Democrats.

Without any other context, one might assume that Republicans had made huge gains in the hundreds of small-town churches where pious West Virginians still cast out Satan and fret about the legalization of sodomy. Indeed West Virginia might seem to be the "jewel in the crown" of the Rovian strategy of using cultural backlash to turn Rooseveltian Democrats into Bushite Republicans. But as Alice says in Wonderland, things in West Virginia get "curiouser and curiouser" on closer inspection. For the same voters who gave Bush a 13 percent edge also gave an enormous 29 percent margin to Joe Manchin, the Democratic candidate for governor. Manchin won despite a juicy Clinton-style sex scandal involving his Democratic predecessor; similarly, Democrats retained two of three congressional seats by authoritative two-thirds margins.(76) Paradoxically, West Virginia, while voting for Bush, remained otherwise a solidly Democratic state.

What explains such a schizophrenic vote? Well, it probably didn't hurt the socially conservative Manchin that he had endorsements from the National Rifle Association and some antiabortion groups. But Manchin, with the support of the state AFL-CIO, crusaded primarily about jobs. In every hamlet of the state he touted his "West Virginia: Open for Business" initiative, promising to reduce unemployment through a high-powered Jobs Creation Council. Manchin, moreover, defied conventional electoral wisdom by warning voters that because jobs were the highest priority, they should not count on tax breaks in the near future. So we have a local Democrat, however opportunist in reality, who makes a compelling case, supported by the unions, for government action to reduce unemployment and create high-wage jobs. But what about Kerry and the national Democrats?

The contrast is dramatic: the Kerry campaign, in fact, had almost nothing to say about the decline of the Appalachian coal industry, the death of the steel industry, or the loss of local factory jobs to Mexico or China. The wealthiest member of the U.S. Senate instead promised modest tax breaks for corporations that kept jobs at home. Even rhetorically, he failed to counter the Republicans' cultural populism and antielite attacks with rousing appeals to economic populism and a traditional blue-collar job ethos. Instead he offered endless renditions of his war record ("defending America" by assassinating poor peasants in the Mekong Delta) and film clips of himself windsurfing and ski-boarding at resorts ordinary West Virginians could never even dream of visiting.

Bush, on the other hand, had imposed a 30 percent temporary tariff on imported steel in 2001: a cynical Rove-inspired tactic(108) to capture blue-collar Democrats, but nonetheless a dramatic gesture that garnered applause in the industrial valleys. Indeed, from a West Virginia perspective, the Texas cowboy had the guts to stand up to European competitors, while the Boston Brahmin offered little more than aspirin and a pat on the back for terminal cancer. Bush was perceived (however incorrectly) as an economic nationalist while Kerry was tarred as an untrustworthy Europhile. Nor, as we shall see in a moment, did the Clinton era leave the Democrats with any record of defending industrial jobs to contrast with the performance of W. Bush.

Many voters in the heartland also continue to equate American military and industrial power. Better to manufacture swords than no swords or ploughshares at all. The Bush administration's orgy of defense and homeland security spending, like Reagan's "Second Cold War" defense boom in the early 1980s, is a Keynesian industrial policy—of a sort. Kerry, in contrast, had no industrial policy to offer, apart from an elitist faith in global markets and high technology. From the standpoint of the pro-jobs voter in West Virginia, then, the split vote for Bush and Manchin might reflect consistency, not contradiction, of economic self-interest.

Many liberal Democrats and so-called progressives, including Frank, are simply in denial over the national Democrats' abdication of the interests of core voters in declining industrial sectors and regions. Except at the very end of his book, where he makes some telling points about the Democratic Leadership Council, Frank generally portrays the Democratic Party as the obvious representative of working-class interests. But as the case of West Virginia shows, many traditional blue-collar Democrats no longer see a home in a national party dominated by the agenda of high-tech exporters, Hollywood moguls, and trial lawyers. To quote one West Virginia voter—"we didn't leave the Democrats, they left us."

4. The Clinton Legacy

Moreover, for a theory of false consciousness like Frank's to fully apply to the blue-collar electorate, Kansans (or West Virginians or Ohioans) must have the opportunity to make clear choices between "values" and "interests," between culture and class. But it is precisely the radical absence of such choices that defines current American politics.

As I have argued on several occasions, the great achievement (and strategic obsession) of the Clinton era was to realign the Democrats as the party of the "new economy," of the bicoastal knowledge industries, gaming/entertainment, and high-tech exporters. (The very concept of the "new economy," to be sure, was self-serving and the New Democrats played a large role in establishing its currency in popular consciousness and op-ed punditry.) The Clinton administration gave highest priority to the agendas of Hollywood, Silicon Valley, Las Vegas, and the side of Wall Street represented by Robert Rubin and Goldman Sachs. Accordingly, the communications and electronics sector increased its contributions (as reported to the Federal Election Commission) to the national Democrats from $10 million in 1990 to $71 million in 2000; the securities industry, from $7 million in 1990 to $41.5 million in 2000.(28)

Meanwhile the economic interests of much of the old Democratic base, especially manufacturing workers in the heartland, were sacrificed to the golden calf of free trade. Instead of an economic rescue package for the heartland as demanded by the industrial unions, Clinton rammed through the job-exporting North American Free Trade Agreement (NAFTA). Almost two million manufacturing jobs were lost between 1996 and 2001, with unionized plants disproportionately affected. Scores, if not hundreds, of historic CIO union locals were driven into extinction. Although the administration paid occasional lip service to defense of traditional industrial jobs, I doubt that anyone can name a single large American factory that Clinton White House policies saved from closure.

Moreover, as national income research has shown, economic inequality continued to increase dramatically during the Clinton years. One of the fundamental achievements of the New Deal —as we are constantly reminded by progressive advocates working within the Democratic Party—was the reduction of the income gap that had soared to such grotesque proportions during the Coolidge-Hoover climacteric of business hegemony. This gap, as traditionally measured by social scientists' Gini index, began to grow again with the Reagan Revolution and was the target of Democratic criticism in the elections of 1988 and 1992. Accordingly, the victory of Bill Clinton should have reversed or, at the very least, arrested the further growth of inequality. Instead the Gini index lurched sharply upward after his inauguration (and well before Republicans took control of the House): a stunning statistical symbol of the death of New Deal liberalism and the New Democrats' abandonment of their old social base.(120)

Kerry enthusiastically campaigned on this sorry legacy and, like Gore, he was heavily funded by the entertainment, software, gaming, securities, and venture capital industries, as well as by law firms and

pro-Israel groups. And, also like Gore, he campaigned without a compelling economic message or serious strategy for stemming the further loss of manufacturing jobs or reversing the Wal-Martization of
the heartland. Nor was there much evidence of solidarity with the
working class in Kerry's recent resume. Like other Democratic candidates in 2003 (Dennis Kucinich excepted) he had failed to fight
against the Bush administration's successful attempt to deny overtime
pay to several million workers by reclassifying them as "managers"—a
major rollback of the New Deal legacy.

The real Achilles' heel of the Democrats, in other words, was the
economy, not morality. The biggest wedge issue in the Appalachian
coal and steel valleys, as well as the textile towns of the southern Piedmont, was industrial decline (and its representation in images of national strength) not the threat of gay monogamy. This is not to deny
that Kulturkampf may have played an important role at the margin.
What Frank calls the "*latte* libel"—visceral blue-collar contempt for
the urban knowledge-industry elites—is, after all, grounded in real
historic defeat and class humiliation. Male workers of all races, without college education, have suffered dramatic erosion of their wage-
earning power and cultural status. With union halls shut down and the
independent press extinct, it is not surprising that many poor white
people search for answers in their churches or from demagogues like
Limbaugh and Dobbs on the radio. Or that they equate the loss of employment security with the decay of patriotism and family values.

It may be the case, for example, that in Ohio, with dramatic Democratic voter mobilizations in Cleveland and Columbus checked by
equally spectacular Republican turnouts in the suburbs, the margin of
Bush's victory principally came from the blue-collar Appalachian
counties in the southeast that had previously given their votes to that
devout and often saved Baptist, Bill Clinton. (Has anyone noticed, by
the way, the extraordinary preponderance of Baptists—Carter, Clinton, Gore, Gingrich, DeLay, Jesse Jackson, and so on—in recent American politics?)

On the other hand, the evidence from West Virginia, where Kerry won the poorest coal counties in the southern part of the state, is that abandoned Democrats are more likely to stop voting than to cross the road and become Republicans. In Mingo, Logan, Boone, and McDowell counties, which the United Mine Workers kept in the Kerry camp, the turnout was barely 30 percent, despite the assurances of the AFL-CIO that it "was the most important election in our lifetimes." (Overall, turnout for presidential elections in West Virginia plummeted from 78 percent in 1960 to just 46 percent in 2000.)

In contrast, 70 percent of voters in West Virginia's Potomac Highlands—increasingly a Republican exurb linked to greater D.C. sprawl—went to the polls to reelect George Bush: one of innumerable examples of Rove's strategy of beating the Democrats through generating higher percentage turnouts from the partisan base. The two parties, moreover, had almost opposite strategies: from the beginning, the Republicans focused on mobilizing their core constituencies, while Democrats were obsessed with swing voters. If Karl Rove knows his constituency down to the last country club membership or seat in the pew, the Democrats endlessly debate among themselves who their base really is.

5. The Evangelical Vote

Let's look at Bush's margin of victory from several alternative angles. Rove was reportedly frantic to bring to the polls the four million evangelicals whom he predicted would vote, but didn't, in 2000. (It is helpful to recall that Bush's supposedly invincible "brain" actually lost that popular election.) It is unclear, however, whether the Church Militant actually provided the key to victory in 2004. Although most exit poll data has been put under a cloud by poor sampling techniques, conservative Christians do not seem to have constituted a significantly larger proportion of the Bush vote than in 2000 despite the anti–gay marriage referenda that Rove orchestrated in key states. The absolute increase in evangelical voters, following the Republican decision to emphasize "motivation rather than persuasion," core supporters rather than independents, in their campaign effort, was counterbalanced by Democrat voter mobilizations.

Nor, as the media alleged after exit polls in Ohio, did "voting for values" increase last November. Quite the contrary: the number of voters who tell interviewers that they voted primarily on moral values has steadily declined: from 40 percent in 1996, to 35 percent in 2000, to 22 percent this year. The evangelical political base may not yet be fully mobilized, but the deep trends in American life suggest that it has reached its peak electoral influence. Unless Latino Protestant converts (mainly Pentecostals) fill the breach—which is unlikely—the Christian nation will soon begin to feel the backlash to the backlash. (The situation indeed is reminiscent of mainstream Protestantism's last hurrah in the 1920s, when the temporary victory of temperance heralded a false hegemony quickly offset by the explosive growth of an urban immigrant-origin population that came to political maturity in the great realigning elections of 1932 and 1936.)

But if evangelicals were not the critical swing factor, where and how, then, did Bush win his three-million-vote margin of victory? I assume that most people who follow their local op-ed page assume that Bush increased his vote in the Republican heartland of edge cities, exurbs, small towns, and rural counties. In fact, Bush's greatest proportional gains were in cities, especially big cities. His rural percentage was the same as in 2000, while Kerry took almost 10 percent more of the small-town vote than had Gore, a surprising achievement. But Bush made equally unexpected inroads in the Blue heartland: 7 percent increases in his vote in Rhode Island and New York, 6 percent in New Jersey, and 5 percent in Connecticut. He even improved his 2000 performance in Kerry's home of Massachusetts. Who were these new or converted Bush voters?

To begin with, they were Staten and Long Islanders, and other residents of New York City's commuter-shed in suburban New Jersey and Connecticut—together they contributed a half million additional votes to Bush. Their motivation? Religiously, according to the Pew Research Center, these new Bush voters were equally split between Catholics and Jews, on one hand, and Protestants, on the other. An estimated 56 percent of white Catholics voted Republican in November, but, interestingly, Bush's most significant gains were among less, rather than more observant, mass-goers.(119) The obvious implication, I think, is that the real wedge issues were national security and patriotism rather than abortion and gay-bashing; and it is hardly surprising that Bush picked up additional votes from white-collar commuters and skilled workers in the former shadow of the Twin Towers.

Bush's Latino vote also suggests that loyalty to the commander in chief in wartime was more important than the attacks on Kerry by some ultramontane prelates in Texas. Although some exit polls erroneously gave Bush a victory among Tejanos—when, in fact, Kerry won by a narrow margin of 2 percent—the president did make considerable gains. According to one analysis, his performance was most improved among men and among Latinos in the Northeast; if gay marriage and abortion were paramount issues for Latinos, then one would have expected a bigger Bush increase among Latinos than his mere one percent.

Of course, other explanations of the winning margin are possible. The "security mom" phenomenon may have been a real trend or a figment of pundits' imagination, but it is indisputable that Bush's margin of victory nearly equals his increased vote among women. In Ohio, especially, Kerry was hurt by his failure to retain or increase Gore's percentage of the female vote (50 percent versus 53 percent). With Gore's percentage of support from women, he also would have won, rather than narrowly lost, both New Mexico and Iowa. Democrats should fear few things more than further closing of the gender gap.

6. The Republican Base

More powerful statistical techniques will be eventually brought to bear on the analysis of Bush's winning margin, allowing us to better disentangle the "fear factor" and war vote from fundamentalist values. In the meantime, the 2004 election confirms the general trend of the entire modern Republican era, from the tax revolts of the late 1970s and election of Ronald Reagan: the Republican core constituencies are the fast-growing outer suburbs.

A watershed in American political history was the Republican sweep of the House of Representatives in 1994. As attested by their profiles in the *Almanac of American Politics*, all the new committee chairs and Republican leaders without exception, from Archer and Armey to Talent and Weldon, represented affluent "edge cities" and exurbs: Mesa, Waukesha, Plano, King of Prussia, Irving, Simi Valley, Naperville, West Valley City, Coral Springs, Roswell, and so on. None of the 1994 leaders were from traditional silk-stocking districts or rural constituencies: the old Republican heartlands. Bob Dole, in this sense, was the last of a breed. Kansas, indeed, is hardly an afterthought to Republican strategists, whose attention is instead riveted on that almost continuous corridor of conservative suburbs from the Beltway to San Diego, with outliers of the Republican Sunbelt in the fast-growing exurbs of Philadelphia, Milwaukee, and Chicago.

Certainly the results from Ohio, the key state to Bush's electoral college victory, corroborate how all-important the edge cities are to the maintenance of a Republican majority. Thanks to a tremendous effort by labor, Kerry harvested huge margins in Ohio's cities. His Cleveland margin (217,638) alone overcame Bush's sweep of traditionally Republican rural counties (208,975), yet he lost to unprecedented Republican mobilizations in the fast-growing, affluent edges of metropolitan Cincinnati (Butler and Warren counties) and Columbus (Delaware and Fairfield counties). (Similarly, Kerry's big majority in Milwaukee, meanwhile, was checked by historic GOP turnouts in the three suburban counties of Waukesha, Ozaukee, and Washington.) Nationally, the GOP is the dominant party in 97 of the 100 fastest-growing counties (mainly exurbs in Sunbelt states).

In a nation, however, where the majority of the electorate now votes in suburbs, the category "suburb" is no longer very useful to campaign strategists and electoral analysts. More important is the contrast between aging, inner-ring suburbs, bleeding jobs and fiscal resources, and outer suburbs—edge cities or "boomburbs," if you prefer—which are harvesting the same jobs and sales taxes. The major redistributive conflict in the United States is no longer between core cities and their suburbs, but between cities and their older suburbs, on one hand, and edge cities, on the other. *This is also the principal theater for the redefinition of Republican and Democratic politics.*

Rove's principal innovation in Republican strategy, reinforced by his savvy use of state-of-the-art micro-survey data, has been his consistent focus on building overwhelming Republican majorities in the high-growth metropolitan edges, where young, affluent white families—obsessed with education, crime, and family values—tend to live. Such communities are frequently political monocultures. Indeed, one of the most brilliant sections of *What's Wrong with Kansas?* is Frank's intimate portrait of a major Kansas City's exurb, Johnson County, where the most dramatic political conflict—a culture war within the culture war—is waged by the more plebian and extreme Republican *Cons* against the elite but socially permissive Republican *Mods*. In Frank's unremitting characterization, Johnson County is not a social landscape that leaves much hope for traditional liberalism.

But progressives should not write off the 'burbs. A more equivocal and complex situation exists in my Southern California backyard: the "Inland Empire" of western San Bernardino and Riverside counties. California was conceded to Kerry without a second thought by the media and its election results have drawn little analytic attention. In fact, the Republican Party continued to gain dramatic ground in inland high-growth counties from Colusa in the north to Riverside in the south. The two-county Inland Empire is particularly important since its Republican vote (604,000) will soon surpass that of Orange County (674,000), which provided the single largest Bush majority in the country last November. Expected to gain 2.5 million residents over the next fifteen years, the Inland Empire is already trumpeted by Republican strategists as the key to their party's future in California.(101)

But the Inland Empire is also the poor relation of such job- and tax-rich Republican outer suburbs as southern Orange and northern San Diego counties. Republicans in Rancho Cucamonga and Temecula are affluent but decidedly nonelite: more like the wrathful Johnson County *Cons* that Frank describes. They spend much of their lives gridlocked on the I-15 or 91 freeways, commuting to office or high-tech jobs in San Diego or Orange counties in order to pay mortgages on tract homes that cost $250,000 less than their coastal zone counterparts. Moreover, the Empire is a patchwork of white-collar suburbs and gritty blue-collar towns or lower-income apartment tracts like Fontana, Rialto, and Perris. And western San Bernardino (39 percent) and Riverside counties (36 percent) have large, rapidly growing Chicano populations.

There is nothing, in other words, that preordains the Inland Empire to be a Republican bastion for the next generation except for Democratic neglect. What should have been highly competitive terrain was ceded to the Republicans almost without a fight. In Riverside County, the Democratic Party relied on hired hands to sign up new voters; while the Republican Party mobilized ideologically committed volunteers. As a result, the Republicans signed up four times as many new voters between 2000 and election eve than did the Democrats. In San Bernardino County, once a Democratic bastion, the Republicans not only outspent the Dems 10 to 1, but they also mounted an impressive grassroots campaign, largely church based, that brought nearly two thousand precinct captains and volunteers to doors that Democrats ignored. "The county's Democratic Central Committee," reported a local newspaper," was so disorganized that its headquarters in the city of San Bernardino were closed and phones turned off."

Meanwhile Westside L.A. Democrats were raising millions of dollars for the national Kerry campaign, but nary a cent was sent to the Chicano and labor activists competing against the well-financed and populist Republican juggernaut seventy-five miles east. As a result, Bush increased his seven-thousand-vote margin of 2000 to more than fifty thousand votes last November. It made no difference, of course, to California's electoral college vote, but savvy Republicans were base-building for the future and investing in local leadership, not just canvassing for the president.

Except in big cities, where public-sector unions have revived Democratic electorates, the former party of Roosevelt seems to have lost any concept of grassroots politics over the long haul. Frank is absolutely right to contrast the "movement" character of suburban Republican politics with the top-down management of Democratic campaigns. The Democrats will make virtually any concession to suburban prejudices and selfish interests as they constantly shuffle rightward, but show little ability to organize around, or even identify, the issues and contradictions in suburban life that might support a more liberal, even progressive politics. But, then again, modern Democrats don't do "structural politics": that is to say, a politics that aims to control the space of discourse and set the agenda with the aims of maximally disorganizing the social base of the opponent while consolidating one's own. Since Eisenhower authorized the interstate highways or, at least, since Nixon shifted the bulk of federal urban grants to the suburbs, the Republican party has ceaselessly championed and rewarded urban sprawl. It is, after all, the Archimedean lever that ceaselessly transfers voters from blue to red columns.

7. Race Abides

Urban sprawl, of course, is also a euphemism for resegregation. A much commented-upon trend of the 1990s was the impressive growth of middle-class Black suburbs, especially around D.C. and Atlanta. There are also a few genuinely integrated outer suburbs, including parts of our Inland Empire, like Fontana and Moreno Valley, although they tend to be house-rich and job-poor. But, in general, outward growth and exurban flight are usually a quest to return to that Edenic state that existed before the Civil Rights revolution or the Latinization of big American cities. Frank may be correct that Kansans are reactionaries without being racists, and that local antiabortion protesters proudly claim the mantle of John Brown; but if so, this is a unique situation that undermines the ability to generalize from "What's the matter with Kansas" to "What's the matter with America." Elsewhere the crabgrass is prickly with racist barbs and anti-immigrant innuendo. Southern Californians saw this vividly during the recall of Gray Davis two years ago. For research reasons, I spent a month, from 3:00 to 6:00 p.m., tuned into California's most popular "rage jock," and sometime Rush Limbaugh replacement, Roger Hedgecock. This former felon and defrocked mayor of San Diego claims the glory of having brought recall passion to a boil and thus paved the way for the election of Arnold Schwarzenegger. He is the local epitome of backlash culture and, like his counterparts elsewhere, colonizes commute time when white guys in pickup trucks and Ford Explorers headed home to Escondido or Temecula are creeping along at 5 mph in infinite columns of fatigue and bad temper.

With a certain hypnotic monotony, Hedgecock hammered away, day after day, against the "alien invasion" that had gridlocked freeways, overwhelmed schools and social services, and turned Southern California into a "Spanish-speaking ant pile." Now, he thundered, Gray Davis and the Democrats wanted "to give bin Laden a driver's license." Meanwhile the long-suffering white producing classes were afflicted with the scourge of an odious license tax that only augured the day when homosexuals, illegal immigrants, and the Sierra Club would take their SUVs away. (If you think I am exaggerating, you simply haven't yet tuned into Roger or his local equivalent.)

As I suffered under Roger's lash every afternoon, I came to realize, however, that I was also attending the birth of a new discourse, one which blended nativism and traffic, the Brown peril and congestion. In 1978, the Reagan Revolution began with tax revolts; now the grievances are gridlock, single-family homes with parents perpetually on the road, and, in general, a claustrophobic sense in the Southwest of declining physical mobility. I don't know whether this sort of Republican "road rage" has any resonance outside of California, but it certainly played an important role in ensuring that a Hummer was parked outside the governor's mansion in Sacramento. It is also suggestive of how Frank's culture of anger ceaselessly adapts itself to the topography of suburban bigotry.

Is race still the key to the "emerging Republican majority" as Kevin Phillips claimed back in 1968? Probably—with the proviso that immigrant-bashing, largely directly toward the "Brown Peril," but encompassing Asians and Muslims as well, has reopened one of the oldest wounds in American history, with potentially deleterious effects in the long term for Republican candidates in rapidly Latinizing states. Meanwhile, Larry Bartels at Princeton's Wilson School has challenged Frank with data that suggests "low-income [whites] have become less Democratic in their partisan identifications, but at a slower rate than more affluent whites—and that trend is entirely confined to the South." Bartels also finds that "while social issue preferences have become more strongly related to presidential votes among middle- and high-income whites, there is no evidence of a corresponding trend among low-income whites."(10)

Although Frank's book retains value for its scalding portrait of conservative hypocrisy and Democratic incompetence, the true crisis of American politics has less to do with "backlash" than "dropout." Instead of too little class consciousness perhaps there is too much, as millions of workers refuse to vote for Democratic millionaires with nothing to offer but meaningless cant about free trade and globalization.

(UCLA, 2005)

Further data-crunching by political scientists has clarified the roles of the gender gap and the Latino vote in Bush's reelection. Karen Kaufmann, for example, has shown that the gender gap (so critical to national Democratic strategy since its appearance in 1968) actually increased, albeit very slightly, to Kerry's advantage in every region of the nation except the South. In Dixie, however, women stampeded to support Bush. "Southern women chose Bill Clinton over Bob Dole by a 17-point margin in

1996 and preferred Al Gore to George W. Bush by 9 percentage points in 2000. In 2004, however, Southern women favored *Bush* by a 2-point margin *over* Southern men." *Kaufmann's analysis of voter-survey data attributes this unusual reversal to the high salience of War on Terrorism and Iraq-related issues—still a curious finding unless one assumes that the South has disproportionately large numbers of military wives and moms who vote.*(78)

Meanwhile, other research has refuted claims that Bush won 44 percent of the Latino vote and even a majority of the Tejano vote in Texas: both assertions were the results of inexplicably poor sampling. On the other hand, the non-Cuban Latino Protestant vote (dynamized by rapidly growing Pentecostal churches) probably equaled or surpassed the Cuban-American electorate for the first time as a source of support for the Republicans. Indeed the only hope in the long run for the Republicans to retain political dominance in the rapidly Latinizing but core Bush states of Texas and Florida is an expansion of the GOP's Latino evangelical base. But as Thomas Edsall recently pointed out, the major casualty of the current anti-immigrant backlash in the Republican Party has been precisely this all-important alliance. He cites the example of Reverend Luis Cortes Jr., one of the most prominent Latino Protestants and head of the Philadelphia-based Esperanza community-development corporation, who aggressively supported Bush in 2004 but turned against the GOP in 2006 in disgust at its embrace of Minutemen and a 700-mile-long border fence.(46) *Karl Rove's hard work may be for naught unless Republicans can keep Latino evangelicals in the fold.*

NINE

THE DEMOCRATS AFTER NOVEMBER

Was the November 2006 midterm election an epic political massacre or just a routine midterm brawl? In the week after the Democratic victory, partisan spinmeisters offered opinions as contradictory as those of the protagonists in *Rashomon*, Kurosawa's famously relativistic account of rape and murder. On the liberal side, Bob Herbert rejoiced in his *New York Times* column that the "fear-induced anomaly" of the "George W. Bush era" had "all but breathed its last," while Paul Waldman (*Baltimore Sun*) announced "a big step in Nation's march to left," and George Lakoff (*CommonDreams.org*) celebrated a victory for "progressive values and factually accurate, values-based framing" (whatever that may mean). On the conservative side, the *National Review's* Lawrence Kudlow refused to concede even the obvious bloodstains on the steps of Congress: "Look at Blue Dog conservative Democratic victories and look at Northeast liberal GOP defeats. The changeover in the House may well be a conservative victory, not a liberal one." William Safire, although disgusted that the "loser Left" had finally won an election, dismissed the result as an "average midterm loss."

Victory and Its Woes

But Safire and ilk doth spin too much. Although the Democratic victory in 2006 was not quite the deluge that the Republicans led by Newt Gingrich, Dick Armey, and Tom DeLay unleashed in 1994 (see figure one), it was anything but an "average" result. Despite the comparatively low electoral salience of the economy (the opposition's classic midterm issue), the Democrats managed to exactly reverse the majority in the House (the worst massacre of Republicans since 1974) and reclaim the Senate by one seat. Indeed, the Senate gained its first self-declared "socialist," Bernie Sanders of Vermont, an independent who caucuses with the Democrats.

Democrats for the first time ever did not lose a single incumbent or open House seat. Independent voters (26 percent of the electorate) swung to the Democrats by an almost two-to-one ratio—"the biggest margin ever measured among independents since the first exit polls in 1976." With the strongest female leadership in American history, they outpolled Republicans among women 55 percent to 45 percent in House races; but more surprisingly, they also managed to reduce the GOP's famous lead among white men (a staggering 63 percent in the 1994 House contests) to 53 percent. According to veteran pollster Stanley Greenberg, one in five Bush voters moved into the blue column; but none so dramatically as the electoral market segment of "privileged men" (college educated and affluent) where the GOP lost 14 percent of its 2004 support. Although the slippage among the GOP hard core—evangelicals and white rural and exurban voters—was slight, the party of the moral majority declined 6 percent among devout Catholics, while angry Latinos, recoiling from the GOP grass roots' embrace of vigilantes and border walls, murdered Republicans in several otherwise close contests in the West.

In state races, the Democrats demonstrated even more traction. On election eve, the GOP boasted a majority of governorships (28 to 22) and a slight lead in control of state legislative chambers (49 to 47, with 2 tied). Contrasted to overwhelming Democratic dominance in state legislatures before 1994 (when Republicans controlled only eight states), this rough parity—according to John Hood, the president of a North Carolina conservative think tank—has been "one of the most significant and lasting products of the Republican revolution." But it is a legacy now lost as the Democrats have exactly reversed the partisan ratio of governors (leaving Republican executives in only three of the ten most populous states) while winning control of eight more state chambers (new total: 56 Democrat versus 41 Republican, with 1 tied). "What's worse for the GOP," Hood points out, is that the majority parties in state legislatures will control congressional redistricting in the wake of the rapidly approaching 2010 Census. "If Democrats retain their current edge, the U.S. House will get a lot more blue."

FIGURE ONE

1994 VERSUS 2006

	Republican Gains in 1994	Democratic Gains in 2006
House	54	31
Senate	8	6
Governorships	10	6
State legislatures	20	4
State reps.	472	320 (approx.)

Regionally, Republican candidates were decimated in the GOP's original heartland, New England (including notoriously conservative New Hampshire, where Democrats took over the legislature for the first time since the Civil War) and the Mid-Atlantic states, leading one prominent conservative to lament that "the Northeast is on its way to being lost forever to the GOP." Democrats also made surprising gains in the Midwest and the "red" interior West, especially in Colorado where high-tech money leveraged a growing Latino vote. Even in the South, the Democrats managed to arrest their long-term decline and claw back nineteen seats in state legislatures. (Despite the prevalent myth of a solidly Republican South, the Democrats still retain a 54 percent majority in Dixie state houses.)

In Kansas—Tom Frank's icon state of voter false consciousness—Democrat Nancy Boyda defeated incumbent Jim Ryun (the former

Olympic track star) in a congressional district that Bush had carried by 20 percentage points two years earlier. Popular Democratic Governor Kathleen Sibelius was easily reelected, while the other top state offices, the lieutenant and attorney generalships, were won by former Republicans running as Democrats—a startling reverse in the trend of political conversion. The state's foremost cultural conservative, the fanatically antiabortion attorney general Phill Kline, was pulverized, receiving barely one-third of the vote in the usually Republican exurbs of Kansas City (Johnson County). Nothing seemed particularly "the matter" with Kansas in the fall of 2006.

Such results convincingly refute the legend of invincibility that had been woven around Karl Rove's signature strategy of intensive base mobilization (usually stimulated by hysteria over some imperiled Christian value) and massive negative advertising (usually perpetuating some outright lie or slander against the opposition). According to Stanley Greenberg, "the Republican Party has ended up with the most negative image in memory, lower than in Watergate." But the Democratic pollster (writing in collaboration with Robert Borosage and James Carville) was adamant that Republican losses are not necessarily Democratic gains. "[T]he Democatic Party also ended up being viewed more negatively during this election than in 2004.... Democrats have only modest advantages—and are chosen by fewer than 50 percent on key attributes as being 'on your side,' 'future oriented' and 'for families.'"

Thomas Edsall agrees that "Democratic triumphs are fragile" and warns that they are "based far more on widespread dissatisfaction with the war in Iraq than on the fundamental partisan and ideological shift that was apparent in 1980 and 1994 Republican breakthroughs." Partisan registration remains closer to parity to (38 percent Democrat versus 37 percent Republican) than at any time since the late nineteenth century, and control of the House is arbitrated by swings of just a few percentage points: the reason the Republicans have been so keen to undertake controversial midterm redistrictings and gerrymanders to buttress their power.

FIGURE TWO

PERCENTAGE OF POPULAR VOTE IN HOUSE ELECTIONS

	Republican	*Democrat*
2000	48	48
2002	51	46
2004	50	47
2006	46	52

The victors, moreover, share no consensus about the direction of their party. In contrast to 1994 when the GOP was rapturously united around the program of its congressional "revolution," Democratic ideologues at the end of 2006 were fundamentally split. While progressives like Ezra Klein (*American Prospect*) fretted that Blue Dogs and DLCers were ready "to lock liberals out of the halls of power," Christopher Hayes (the *Nation*) applauded the "new Democratic populism," and Michael Tomasky (another *American Prospect* contributor) argued that the party was cleverly moving to the center and to the left simultaneously ("the party managed to sustain this left-center coalition and render the distinctions between the two groups less important.") Hillary Clinton and her chorus of sycophantic voices boasted of the miracle of the "vital, dynamic center," while other Democrats pessimistically agreed with Safire's acid prediction that the party was headed toward civil war.

In any event, the Democrats led by House Speaker Nancy Pelosi, House Majority Leader Steny Hoyer, and Senate Majority Leader Harry Reid have two years to consolidate their enhanced electoral support and effectively arm Hillary Clinton for a very nasty brawl with either John McCain or Rudy Giuliani in 2008. (Neither of the two mystery phenomena—Republican Mitt Romney and Democrat Barack Obama—are likely to survive the brutal scrutiny of the presidential primaries, although they may be recycled as vice-presidential timber.) The 110th Congress will give the Democrats extraordinary opportunities to repeal the reactionary agendas established in 1994 by the Republican Revolution and in 2001–02 by the War on Terrorism. But the Democrats will be torn between two categorical imperatives: on the one hand, to sink as many Republicans as possible with George Bush's ship of state; and, on the other hand, to reclaim the mystic "center" and the support of corporate lobbyists. If the recent past is any guide, a seriously populist and ideologically combative Democratic politics is totally incompatible with the Clintonite project of making the Democrats the representatives par excellence of the knowledge economy and corporate globalization.

More specifically, the new Democratic majority must test its ambiguous promises of crusading populism *and* inclusive centrism against the recalcitrant realities of the four mega-issues that will inevitably dominate the new Congress: (1) the Iraq fiasco and the War on Terrorism; (2) the legacy of Republican congressional corruption and corporate fraud; (3) urgent, unmet social needs (including the reconstruction of the Gulf Coast) in the context of the huge Bush deficits; and (4) the growing unrest over the social costs of economic globalization. In each case, the hopeful expectations of last November's voters for real changes in Washington are likely to be betrayed by the higher imperatives of electing Hillary and assuaging big business.

Smaller or Bigger War?

Unlike the 2004 presidential election and the controversy over the importance of "values voters," there was nothing equivocal about the key issue that mobilized a majority of voters in November 2006. With the housing-bubble economy still puttering along (although a real-estate-induced recession may not be far away), and with Mexican- and gay-bashing failing to ignite significant national backlashes, the defining issue was the looming defeat of the U.S. intervention in Iraq.

FIGURE THREE

GALLUP POLL (AUGUST 28–31)

(VOTERS WERE ASKED WHAT
THE PRESIDENT'S "TOP PRIORITIES" SHOULD BE)

DEMOCRATS	%	INDEPENDENTS	%	REPUBLICANS	%
1. War in Iraq	61	1. War in Iraq	52	1. War in Iraq	38
2. Economy	19	2. Economy	18	2. Fuel prices	20
3. Health care & fuel prices	18	3. Health care & fuel prices	14	3. Immigration	19
4. Energy crisis	10	4. Energy crisis	13	4. Terrorism	18
5. Disaster relief	10	5. Immigration	9	5. National security	12

Six out of ten voters told pollsters that they were upset at Bush's management of the war—the spiraling carnage in Baghdad and the paralysis in the White House—and had voted accordingly. Editorial page punditry, likewise, was united with exit-poll surveys in agreeing that Iraq was the Archimedean lever that had shifted independent voters so massively toward the Democrats. Conservative ideologues and business lobbyists, meanwhile, were appalled to see their domestic agendas upstaged by the Frankenstein monster of Iraq. Even that "wholly owned subsidiary of the Republican Party" (as columnist Rosa Brooks has called it), the military electorate, has begun to bolt the stable: A Military Times poll shows the percentage of soldiers identifying as Republicans declining from 60 percent in 2004 to 46 percent in late 2006. Only slightly more than one-third of GIs currently approve of Bush's handling of the war.

After twelve years of arrogant majority rule in Congress, the GOP has seemingly foundered on the contradictions of the new imperialism. Or has it? The irony of the antiwar vote, of course, was that it elected Democrats who are under no obligation to actually end the barbarous U.S. occupation. Writing shortly after the elections, Tom Hayden praised the citizen groups in Chicago and elsewhere who had fought to make the election a plebiscite on an increasingly unpopular war, but warned presciently that "neither party is prepared to accept that the war is a lost cause" and that the Iraq Study Group report would offer the Democratic leadership common ground with congressional Republicans "to eliminate 'immediate withdrawal,' as an option."

Despite majority public belief that Iraq is a "bad war" and the troops should come home, the current Democratic strategy is to snipe from the sidelines at Bush's ruinous policies while avoiding any decisive steps to actually end the occupation. Indeed, from the standpoint of cold political calculus, the Democrats have no more interest in helping Bush extract himself from the morass of Iraq than Bush has had in actually capturing or killing Osama bin Laden. Accordingly, as the *Los Angeles Times* recently reported, "Pelosi and the Democrats plan no dramatic steps to influence the course of the war." Democratic National Committee chair Howard Dean, who once claimed to be the very incarnation of the antiwar movement, now cautions that the most that the public can expect from the new majority is "some restraint on the president." Likewise Pelosi has renounced from the outset the Democrats' one actual power over White House war policy: "We will have oversight. We will not cut off funding."

The real Democratic opposition to the war (John Murtha's highly publicized defection aside) has come from the ranks of the Black Caucus, whose members (including John Lewis, Charles Rangel, and Barbara Lee) are also the chief instigators of the recently organized Out of Iraq caucus, chaired by Los Angeles's fiery Maxine Waters. The strong overlap between the antiwar caucus (which also includes ten or so Latino representatives led by New York's outspoken José Serrano) and the House membership most strongly committed to urban social programs is expressive of a fundamental political trend that the media has all but ignored: the widespread consciousness in communities of color that the interventions in Iraq and Afghanistan (costing more than $2 billion per week) are stealing critical resources from human needs in poorer inner cities and older suburbs, as well as putting immigrant communities under the shadow of disloyalty.

This new equation between urban needs, immigrant civil rights, and anti-imperialism could become a potent counter-agenda in American politics if it were reinforced by grassroots activism and consistent protest. But this is the rub. Although the Out of Iraq caucus has grown to seventy members in the wake of the November vote, its clout is considerably diminished by the absence of a national antiwar movement as well as by the failure of the major progressive trade unions such as SEIU, UNITE HERE, and the AFT to make withdrawal a political priority.

FIGURE FOUR

DEMOCRATS DIVIDED—2006
HOUSE MEMBERS AFFILIATED TO IDEOLOGICAL CAUCUSES
(SOME MEMBERSHIPS OVERLAP)

On the Left		On the Right	
Progressive Caucus	70	New Democrat Coalition	60
Black Caucus	43	Blue Dog Coalition	44
Out of Iraq Caucus	74	Democrats for Life	32

Indeed the electoral landscape in November was shaped by the central paradox of soaring antiwar sentiment without a visible antiwar movement. In contrast to 1968 and 1972—or even, for that matter, 1916 and 1938—voter opposition to foreign intervention was not buttressed by an organized peace movement capable of holding politicians' feet to the fire or linking opposition to the war to a deeper critique of foreign policy (in this case, the War on Terrorism). The broad, spontaneous antiwar movement of winter 2003—whose grassroots energy filled the void of Democratic opposition to Bush's invasion—was first absorbed by the Dean campaign in spring 2004 and then politically dissolved into the Kerry candidacy. The 2004 Democratic Convention, which should have been a forum for wide-ranging attacks on Republican foreign and domestic policies, was transformed into an obnoxious patriotic celebration of John Kerry as the Brahmin Rambo.

Although many activists hoped that an autonomous peace movement would reemerge from the ruins of the Kerry campaign, there have been only a few regional pockets of sustained protest. One of Howard Dean's principal assignments as national Democratic chair (and the major reason for his selection) has been to keep antiwar forces immobilized within a diffuse and hypocritical Anybody but Bush coalition. By making Bush and his political parents Cheney and Rumsfeld the paramount issues, Democratic sophistry has avoided a real debate on Iraq. Leading Democrats may bash Bush for the chaos in Baghdad, but none of them has offered a critique of American responsibility for the larger anarchy that is rapidly engulfing a vast arc of countries from Pakistan to Sudan. There has been no debate about the Bush administration's green light for the Israeli massacre of Lebanese civilians, or more recently, on the CIA's sinister role in instigating the Ethiopian invasion of Somalia. The Israeli right, meanwhile, knows that Hillary Clinton will be as intransigently supportive of its policies in Gaza and on the West Bank as any Texas fundamentalist eagerly awaiting Armageddon.

Indeed, the Democratic leadership—the Black Caucus and a few prominent progressives aside—has exploited domestic resentment against Bush policies in Iraq to *consolidate*, not debunk, the underlying Washington consensus about the War on Terrorism. Whereas a national antiwar movement would presumably have linked the apocalypse in Iraq with looming catastrophe in Afghanistan and a new regional war in the Horn of Africa, the Democratic platform, in contrast, reaffirmed commitment to the war against Islamists as part of a larger program of *expanding*, not reducing, global counterinsurgency. "Bringing the troops home now" was not a Democratic plank, but doubling the size of the Special Forces "to destroy terrorist networks" and increasing spending on homeland antiterrorism are centerpieces of the Democrats' "New Direction for America" (a collection of sound bites and slogans that offers a pale shadow to Gingrich's robust 1994 "Contract with America").

The Democratic leadership likewise has deliberately avoided a debate on the constitutional implications of the Patriot Act; not a single prominent Democrat has proposed the straightforward rollback of the totalitarian powers claimed by the presidency since 9/11. Indeed Hillary Clinton has signaled that she favors imprisonment without trial and even the use of torture in certain circumstances. Speaker Pelosi, meanwhile, has emphasized that the chief Democratic goals in the 110th Congress will be, first, to pick the uncontroversial, low-hanging fruit of mainstream reform (minimum wage, prescriptions, student loans, and so on), then move quickly to pass an "innovation agenda" for high-tech industries. Foreign policy debate in the House—thanks to the hawkish counterweight of more than 100 New Democrats and Blue Dogs—will not reach beyond the bipartisan assumptions of the Baker-Hamilton plan or whatever new, coercive strategy for Palestinian national self-liquidation is proposed by Condoleezza Rice.

What then has the antiwar vote actually won? At the end of the day, public disillusionment with the messianic politics of the neoconservatives has paved the way for a "realist" restoration under the aegis of the Baker-Hamilton plan that reconciles the foreign-policy establishments of Bush Sr. and Clinton. The bloodbath in Iraq has opened every sarcophagus on the Potomac, disgorging a palsied army of ancient secretaries of state and national security advisors (Scowcroft, Eagleburger, Brzezinski, and, of course, the chief mummy, Kissinger himself) eager to lecture Congress on "rational" approaches to imposing American will on the rest of the world. Hillary Clinton, of course, is the Queen of the Realists (except when it conflicts with Israeli interests), and the new Democratic majority in the House is unlikely to stray very far from the already manifest script of her 2008 campaign. In future debates with Rudy Giuliani or John McCain (who has recently appointed himself savior of "victory" in Iraq), Hillary is poised to be a hard-muscled G.I. Jane, parrying every macho gesture with even tougher stances on al-Qaeda, Iran, Palestine, and Cuba.

The silver lining, if it exists, is that the Democrats in Congress, with the Black Caucus and its allies lobbying for withdrawal, are more likely to be swayed by public anger as insurgency and civil war in Iraq continue to exhaust the resources of the occupation forces. In a desperate gambit to appease Sunnis and defend a zone of control in Baghdad, the Bush administration is currently weighing an all-out assault ("surge" is its military precondition) on the slum militias of Muqtada al-Sadr. A new war with the Sadr Army (hugely enlarged and better trained since its first battles with American troops in 2004) would open another Pandora's box, risking unsustainable American casualties and an explosive response from the entire Shiite world. (Inevitable U.S. air strikes on Sadr City would produce grim scenes reminiscent of the Israeli bombardment of southern Beirut.)

If Condoleezza Rice and Robert Gates sanction this ultimate escalation, they have a good chance of bringing some macho Democrats aboard (although they will almost certainly lose some leading Republicans). Senate leader Harry Reid has already demonstrated his epic confusion by endorsing and then quickly retracting support for the proposed "surge" of thirty-five thousand more U.S. troops into Baghdad. In the Senate, the hawkish Joe Lieberman, who was reelected as an independent after his defeat in the Democratic primary, will be a powerful swing vote in favor of escalation. Pelosi, at time of writing, is weighing resistance to new monies for the "surge," but will not tamper with funding for existing troop levels.

What stance Pelosi and Reid ultimately assume, and how hard they actually push for the "phased withdrawal" proposed in their six-plank November program, will be largely determined by the resurgence—or not—of the antiwar movement. Last November's voters certainly had fewer illusions than their candidates about the hopelessness of the situation (according to exit polls, "only about one in five voters say they think that either the president *or* the Democrats have a clear plan for Iraq") and public opinion may again find volcanic alternatives to an impotent Congress. Indeed, only mass protest, unfettered from the realpolitik of Howard Dean and MoveOn.org, can shift the balance of power in Congress toward a decisive debate on withdrawal.

The Limits of Inquiry

One of the most savory moments of the November vote was the election of Nick Lampson to Tom DeLay's old seat in the 22nd District of Texas. Lampson—a schoolteacher who was formerly the Democratic congressman from Galveston—had been one of the principal victims of DeLay's infamous 2003 redistricting of Texas: an unprecedented mid-decade gerrymander that was made possible by the massive and illegally laundered corporate donations that the House Majority Leader deployed to elect a Republican majority in the Texas Legislature the year before. Thanks to the courage of a local grand jury and Travis County D.A. Ronnie Earle, DeLay was indicted for perjury in September 2005 and soon afterward, under federal investigation for his close ties to corrupt lobbyist Jack Abramoff, he was forced to resign his majority leadership, then his congressional seat.

DeLay, of course, was the Robespierre of the 1994 "Republican Revolution," perhaps the most ruthless crusader for one-party government in U.S. history. As one of the cofounders of the so-called K Street Project, along with Rick Santorum and Grover Norquist, he was notorious for coercing huge campaign contributions from corporate lobbyists (as well as promises to hire only Republicans) in exchange for allowing them to directly write GOP legislation. As Majority Leader (or "Hammer," as he was known to Republicans as well as Democrats), he imposed unprecedented ideological discipline on the GOP (even defying a White House attempt to give a small tax break to low-income families) while slashing at every vestige of bipartisanship and collegial civility. In partnership with the infamous lobbyist Jack Abramoff, he was also the advocate of the sleaziest causes in the Capitol, ranging from support for indentured labor in the sweatshop paradise of the Northern Marianas (a U.S. territory without the protection of U.S. labor laws) to under-the-table favors for a giant Russian corporation that in turn kicked back money to DeLay-related causes.

After more than a decade of being roadkill in the wake of DeLay's sleaze-financed campaign juggernaut (with Karl Rove as hit-and-run driver), the Democrats now have the opportunity to begin to roll back the Republican Revolution—which is to say, to break up the corrupt flows of money and power personified by DeLay and the K Street Project. Congress, of course, has always been about "pay to play" and the lubrication of politics by lobbyists, but never before 1994 had the Republicans employed such stark coercion to impose themselves as the *obligatory* rather than simply the *natural* party of business. (In part, this was a reaction to Democratic successes in attracting support from bicoastal, new-economy sectors like entertainment, media, software, bio-tech, and gaming.)

The exhilarating promise of the November victory is that a cadre of veteran liberal Democrats—Charles Rangel (Ways and Means), Barney Frank (Financial Services), Henry Waxman (Government Reform), David Obey (Appropriations), Ike Skelton (Armed Forces), and John Rockefeller IV (Senate Intelligence Committee)—will use their hard-won committee chairships to mount sweeping inquisitions of the Himalayan corruption and collusion of the DeLay years. With subpoena power finally in the hands of the opposition, the interlocking special interests that dominate the Bush administration will face the comprehensive exposure and accounting that they managed to elude in the aftermath of the Enron scandal. Indeed, as the skeletons come tumbling out of Republican closet, and the public realizes how vast the extent of graft and fraud in the occupation of Iraq, the non-reconstruction of New Orleans, "homeland security" boondoggles like the phony Bioshield program, and the subsidization of the insurance, pharmaceutical, and oil industries—then voters will overwhelmingly endorse a new regime of government oversight, renewed environmental and health-safety regulation, and serious campaign finance reform.

This is the real opportunity to which the Democrats might rise in theory, but there is little chance that their leadership will actually allow congressional probes to follow money and corruption all the way upstream. Progressive hopes that Congress might return to the heroic days of Thurman Arnold's antitrust investigations of the late 1930s or the Watergate Committee's exposes of Republican lawbreaking in the 1970s are pipe dreams in the face of Pelosi's insistence that Democratic watchdogs be tightly reined in the interest of building "centrism." She has already extracted humiliating loyalty oaths from the two senior Black Democrats most likely to rock the bipartisan boat: forcing John Conyers (chair of the Judiciary Committee) to recant his advocacy of impeachment ("the country does not want or need any more paralyzed partisan government" he said recently) and making Charles Rangel (chair of Ways and Means), who has hammered Dick Cheney like no on else in Congress, sing a chorus or two of the company song ("I have to take a leadership view," he promised). Even more diabolically, she has put Henry Waxman ("White House Enemy No. 1") in charge of ensuring (in the words of analyst Brian Friel) that congressional oversight doesn't "open Democrats up to charges of obstructionism and extremism in the next campaign cycle."

In the absence of relentless pressure from labor and environmental groups, the Democrats are unlikely to discomfort powerful business interests that they would otherwise delight in wooing away from the Republicans. Certainly there will be some reckoning with Halliburton and contract fraud in Iraq, and perhaps the upcoming perjury trial of Scooter Libby (Cheney's indicted chief of staff) will be spiced with new revelations from Rockefeller and his Senate Intelligence Committee about the administration's lies and fabricated evidence on the road to Baghdad, but a widening circle of exposure will meet increasing resistance, not simply from Republicans fighting for their lives, but from Democrats trying to protect their renewed ties to the very corporate groups at the core of corruption and scandal. The opportunity to expose and reform will be counterbalanced at each step by the temptation to make deals and collect campaign contributions. As the *Economist* cynically but accurately put it, "the new house chieftains do not see themselves as revolutionaries. Their goal, after all, is not to enact a specific agenda, but to prepare the ground for the presidential election of 2008."

Because corporate lobbyists are scared of the subpoena power wielded by Rangel and Waxman (however constrained by Pelosi), they will happily seek refuge in Democratic campaign committees. The fusion between Corporate America and the Republican Party appears less permanent and unassailable than it did a year ago, and, as *BusinessWeek* predicted shortly after the election, "companies will be rushing to stock up on lobbyists with Democratic credentials." The Democratic leadership, for its part, is brazenly cruising for cash. The next election cycle will be the most expensive in history, and Hillary Clinton is unlikely to relish congressional hearings into the crimes of the pharmaceutical, oil, and military-construction industries that unleash massive corporate retaliation against her in 2008. From a strategic perspective, it makes far more sense for the Democrats to concentrate congressional expose on a handful of administration villains, while quietly rebuilding parity of representation on K Street, where many of the winged monkeys are reputedly rejoicing at their recent liberation from DeLay, the wicked witch of Texas.

As *BusinessWeek* reassured nervous readers, any tendency toward populist excess in the new Congress would be counteracted by the millionaires, corporate lawyers, and high-tech entrepreneurs in the ranks of Democracy itself, especially the fervently pro-business New Democrat Coalition (the House arm of the Democratic Leadership Council) chaired by Representative Ellen Tauscher of California. "In a narrowly divided Democratic House, Tauscher's band of about 40 economic moderates would wield extraordinary power to influence tax, trade, and budget policy." Moreover, CEOs worried about possible indictment or evil corporations fearful of losing their lucrative federal contracts could always appeal to K Street's new wonder, George Crawford, who as Nancy Pelosi's former chief of staff has positioned himself to be Washington's chief deal-maker. ("In recent months," reveals *BusinessWeek*, "he has added Exxon Mobil Corp. and Amgen Inc. to his client roster.")

Beyond the uncontroversial agenda of the "100 hours," few of the promised reforms that have attracted progressive voters to the Democrats are likely to make any headway against the coming hurricane of corporate lobbying and political fundraising organized by Crawford and other Democratic insiders. Energy policy, for example, has been one of the party's highest-profile issues, and Senator Barbara Boxer (new chair of the Environment and Public Works Committee) has rallied a broad coalition of environmentalists around tough emissions and fuel economy standards for automobiles. But as journalist Richard Simon recently reported in the *Los Angeles Times*, the Detroit automakers and Texas oilmen are surprisingly unworried. "We're confident that there are plenty of Democrats who know and understand us," a leader of the National Petrochemical and Refiners Association told him.

The "understanding Democrats" in the 110th Congress will include senators from energy-exporting states, such as Mary Landrieu (Louisiana) and Jeff Bingaman (New Mexico), as well as the powerful chair of the House Energy Committee, John Dingell (Michigan) who will fight to defend every last molecule of carbon dioxide emitted by a Ford Explorer or Chevy Suburban. Nancy Pelosi may take away some of the oil industry's more outrageous tax breaks, but Barbara Boxer will never take away rich Americans' SUVs or reduce their dependence on foreign oil. No matter how millions of people may be terrified by global warming's "inconvenient truth," there will always be Democrats to help filibuster any cap on greenhouse emissions or vote to preserve the oil industry's special entitlements.

Deficits and Dog Pounds

In contrast to most European parliamentary systems, the American party system is only partially "nationalized," and regional and local agendas preserve exceptional salience in the operation of Congress. The 2006 election is a spectacular case in point: whether or not the electorate actually shifted left, congressional clout—in one of the most dramatic geographical power shifts in memory—moved back to the Blue coasts. Texas, Florida, Virginia, and Georgia (whose suburbs were the strategic pivots of the 1994 Republican Revolution) are out, and California and New York (the pariahs of the age of Bush) are in. Or, to be more precise, Democrats representing the golden triangle of Wall Street, Hollywood, and Silicon Valley now rule Congress.

Although California and New York (together with Massachusetts and Washington) hegemonize the knowledge economy and the U.S. export of technologies, entertainment, and financial services, they have become cash cows for regionally redistributive Republican policies since 1994. California is perhaps the extreme case. For fifty years, from Lendlease until the fall of the Berlin Wall, California's aerospace and electronic industries had been irrigated by an aqueduct of defense dollars; since 1990 at the latest, fiscal subsidies have switched direction and California now exports its federal taxes to heavily Republican states. Whereas California once received $1.15 in federal expenditure for every dollar it paid in federal taxes, it now gets back only 79 cents. (The inequities are worse than depicted in figure three since California and New York also are the largest ports of entry for new immigrants and finance services that should be federal mandates.) Partly as a result of this shortfall, the world's premier science-based regional economy is supported by scandalously decayed physical, social, and educational (at least, K–12) infrastructures.

FIGURE FIVE (93)

HAVE VERSUS HAVE-NOTS

(RATIO OF FEDERAL SPENDING TO FEDERAL TAXES)

RED		BLUE	
Texas	1.00	California	0.79
Florida	0.98	New York	0.80
Virginia	1.59	Illinois	0.72
Georgia	0.96	Massachusetts	0.79
Arizona	1.23	Connecticut	0.67
Alabama	1.68	Minnesota	0.69
N. Carolina	1.08	Wisconsin	0.83
S. Carolina	1.36	Michigan	0.86
Kentucky	1.51	Oregon	0.99
Alaska	1.90	Washington	0.91

But the Democrats will have to fight themselves, and not just Republicans, if they want to reverse the relative decline of federal expenditure, especially in the aging cities of the Bluest states. While the new Congressional leadership, especially Pelosi and Clinton, have individually lobbied with great ferocity for their own districts' and states' needs, they have collectively tied the party's hands with a cargocultish commitment to deficit reduction and fiscal frugality. Although Iraq and political corruption were the most important issues among voters, that ancient Republican battle cry—"fiscal responsibility"—was the programmatic centerpiece of the Democrats' "New Direction for America."

Despite claims in the *Nation* and elsewhere that the Democrats are now channeling their "inner populist," the party remains completely in thrall to "Rubinomics"—the fervent emphasis on budgetary discipline rather than social spending that characterized the reign of former Goldman Sachs CEO Robert Rubin as Clinton's secretary of treasury. In practice, this translates not simply into a Democratic reluctance to undertake new spending, but also a refusal to debate the rollback of any of Bush's $1 trillion in tax cuts for the affluent. "Tax and spend, tax and spend, tax and spend," Senator Kent Conrad (chair of the Budget Committee) told the *New York Times*, "We're not going there." The president can give away the Treasury to the superrich and run up colossal debts as he invades the world, but the Democrats are now sworn to a path of anti-Keynesian rectitude that would have made Calvin Coolidge blush.

Indeed Congress's most "rabid budget-balancers" (this is the official description on their website) are the Blue Dogs, a caucus of conservative Democrats organized in 1995 in jealous emulation of Gingrich's Republicans. Hailing mainly from rapidly growing smaller cities and exurbs such as Merced, Tallahassee, and Hot Springs, the Blue Dogs cultivate a down-home guns-and-Bibles image in contrast to the cappuccino-drinking New Democrats (who tend to represent wealthier suburbs in Connecticut and California). Although they share the hawkish politics of the DLC New Dems, they are less friendly to hedge funds and free-trade agreements. The real fire in the belly of the Blue Dogs, however, is their demagogic opposition to state welfarism and, especially, federal aid to Black- and Latino-majority big cities. With forty-four members in their expanded "dog pound" and plentiful allies on the Republican side, the Blue Dogs vow to cap spending in the next Congress, while gathering votes for a constitutional amendment to require an annually balanced federal budget. One of their chief allies, South Carolina's John Spratt, will be chair of the House Budget Committee and, with Pelosi's blessing, the Party's "chief enforcer" of budgetary austerity.

Terrified of the perceived electoral and financial repercussions of attempting to reform the current tax system, and with Blue Dogs barking at their heels, the leadership prefers to let Republican deficits and tax cuts dictate Democratic policy. Karl Rove has quickly seen the opportunity to hoist the new majority on their own petard, and in the new year, had Bush invite the Democrats to join him in balancing the budget, "a goal that would tie the hands of the Democrats" leaving them "little or no room to maneuver their priorities through Congress."

New Orleans Versus Silicon Valley

The Democratic leadership's public preference for balanced budgets over human needs is thus partly a reflection of the balance of power within the party, where the Blue Dogs (either alone or in combination with the New Dems) now claim de facto veto power over new legislation. It was presumably this pressure from conservative white Democrats that led congressional election strategists under the command of Illinois representative Rahm Emanuel to deliberately delete any mention of New Orleans from 2006 campaign advertising.

The fate of New Orleans, of course, is one of the great moral watersheds in modern American history, but most Democrats deliberately refused to make federal responses to Hurricane Katrina, or the subsequent ethnic cleansing of the Gulf Coast, central issues in the campaign. Although President Bush himself had declared in his Jackson Square speech that "we have a duty to confront this poverty [revealed by Katrina] with bold action," the Democrats have shown no greater sense of "duty" or capacity for "bold action" than a notoriously hypocritical and incompetent White House.

Their priorities were exemplified by the six-plank national platform in November that stressed deficits and troop buildups but failed to mention either Katrina or poverty. Even the Black Caucus, with some individual exceptions, has been surprisingly listless in its response to an unending series of Bush administration provocations (including, most recently, the decisions to knock down four thousand units of little-damaged public housing in New Orleans and abruptly end housing aid to thousands of Katrina refugees outside the city). Although Harlem's Rangel has promised new congressional hearings on poverty in the light of the New Orleans catastrophe, he is unlikely to defy the leadership's deficit-reduction fetish. It will be easier to hand out more blame (richly deserved, of course) to Republican policies than to roll back tax cuts to pay for new social spending.

But Nancy, Harry, and Hillary do have one domestic crusade whose importance transcends other dogmas and constraints: the promotion of the "innovation agenda" that the Democrats hope will dramatically solidify their support among high-tech corporations and science-based firms across the country. If you wanted to find the missing urgency and passion that the Democrats should have focused on Katrina and urban poverty, it was evident last year in the rousing speeches that Pelosi and other leading Democrats delivered in tech hubs like Emeryville, Mountain View, Raleigh, and Redmond.

Unlike bringing the troops home from Iraq or rebuilding homes and lives in New Orleans, the innovation agenda is a "real" Democratic priority. Angry at the Republican failure to renew all-important R&D tax credits for Silicon Valley firms, tech industry leaders, including the CEOs of Cisco and Genentech, worked with Pelosi and her Bay Area Democratic colleagues to develop a list of key demands including new stock option accounting rules, permanent R&D credits, patent reforms, subsidies for alternative energy, a doubling of funding for the National Science Foundation, and "network neutrality" for the Internet—that the Democrats have promised to pass in 2007. (Democrats have also long supported the H1-B visa program that keeps Silicon Valley awash with cheap foreign engineers, most of whom do not have the right to join unions or organize.)

The Democrats' avid interest in patents and innovation was punctually rewarded with a 50 percent increase (over 2004) in campaign contributions from high-tech industries to the Democratic Congressional Campaign Committee. At the same time, according to the Center for Responsive Politics, the Republican share of Silicon Valley political money in 2000 "was 43 percent, now it's 4 percent." Since the first days of the Clinton administration, seducing the software and biotech sectors and their allied venture capitalists (along with deepening already profound ties to entertainment and media industries) has been the Democrats' equivalent of the Republicans' K Street Project.

Now with Al Gore sitting on the boards of Google and Apple, and Pelosi plotting virtual futures with Google founders Larry Page and Sergey Brin, the Millennium has arrived. Indeed with the ascent of Bay Area Democrats to such commanding positions in Congress, New Orleans may continue to molder in misery, but Silicon Valley and its outliers can now trade pork as equals with the oilmen and defense contractors still bunkered inside the White House.

Dark Populism

The Democrats, as Thomas Edsall frequently points out these days, represent two very different and largely incompatible population universes. Two out of five Democratic voters fit the stereotype of "well educated, well off, culturally liberal professionals," but the rest of the party's base are people who are "socially and economically disadvantaged" in the new Gilded Age: the Black and Latino working classes, white women in lower-end information-sector jobs, and white men in traditional but rapidly shrinking industrial occupations. The post–New Deal Party led by the Clintons is entirely mobilized to articulate and defend the interests of affluent knowledge workers and the globalized industries in which they work; the rest of the Democrats ride in the back of the bus on the cynical assumption that Blacks, immigrants, and Rust-belt whites have nowhere else to go and thus are an automatic Blue vote.

Since the rise and fall of Jesse Jackson's electrifying "Rainbow Coalition" campaign in 1984, there has been no serious challenge to the dominance of the New Democrats and their version of "Third Way" ideology, alloying economic neoliberalism and cultural tolerance. Yet the dream of a new populist, anti-Yuppie uprising, fueled by righteous blue-collar anger and rousing the party's long neglected majority, has continued to inspire progressives and veterans of the Rainbow as they have suffered under the arrogant yoke of DLC centrists and economic globalizers.

Then, a few days after his stunning upset of George Allen in Virginia, Democratic senator-elect James Webb published an op-ed piece in the *Wall Street Journal* under the provocative headline "Class Struggle." Webb, who was secretary of the Navy under Ronald Reagan, warned that an "ever-widening divide" of socioeconomic inequality was plunging the United States back into "a class-based system, the likes of which we have not seen since the nineteenth century." While their wages stagnated and their social security declined, working-class Americans were diverted by carefully orchestrated hysteria about "God, guns, gays, abortion, and the flag." "The politics of the Karl Rove era," warned the former leading Republican, "were designed to distract and divide the very people who would ordinarily be rebelling against the deterioration of their way of life."

Webb's column predictably shocked many *Journal* readers, but it delighted progressives, who recognized that he was quoting almost verbatim from *What's the Matter with Kansas?* and endorsing Tom Frank's call for the Democrats to reclaim the mantle of economic populism. Webb argued that the Democratic victory would ensure that "American workers [finally] have a chance to be heard" in their legitimate complaints about the social costs of free trade and job export. "And our government leaders," he intoned, "have no greater duty than to confront the growing unfairness in this age of globalization."

Bombast or the manifesto for the long awaited uprising? Writing in the *Nation* a few weeks later, Christopher Hayes argued that Webb's born-again concern for working-class victims of corporate globalization was part of a genuine populist trend within the Democratic Party whose standard-bearers also include congressional victor Heath Shuler in North Carolina and new Senator Sherrod Brown in Ohio. Certainly their appeals to economic patriotism (Shuler accused his Republican congressional opponent of "selling out American families") and strident denunciations of "internationalists" and "free traders" struck real sparks in Carolina and Virginia textile towns and the Appalachian counties of Ohio, where whole industries have died in the last decade. In 2004, John Kerry lost the mountains and Piedmont (including hard-core Democratic West Virginia) because he had almost nothing to say about the regional jobs crisis; this time around, the Democrats fielded first-class demagoguery in a local drawl.

But as Hayes himself eloquently emphasizes, "economic populism has a dark side," and he allows that other analysts "have raised the specter of the rise of a 'Lou Dobbs'-like wing of the party whose economic arguments are inextricably linked to a racialized nationalism, the kind of populism that's equally comfortable bashing corporations that outsource jobs and 'illegal aliens' who take away Americans' jobs here at home, and whose opposition to the Iraq War, like Pat Buchanan's, is rooted in an America-first isolationism." Although Hayes prefers to believe in the progressive trend of figures like Webb and Shuler, I think he is most accurate when he compares their politics to racist media demagogues like Dobbs and Buchanan.

A careful reading of Webb's "class struggle" article, for example, reveals precisely his belief that Mexican gardeners and investment bankers are coequal exploiters of the native working class, with a "vast underground labor pool from illegal immigration" waiting to drown American values and wages. A strange passage about the "unspoken insinuation" that "certain immigrant groups have the 'right genetics' and thus are natural entrants to the 'overclass'" can be decoded as a reference to the Yellow Peril fantasies that infuse Webb's public utterances. As secretary of the Navy he was one of the principal advocates of a continuing Cold War with China, which he later saw developing a "strategic axis with the Muslim world," and he broke with Bush policies in Iraq precisely because he feared that Rumsfeld was criminally "empowering" the real enemies—Iran and China.

Heath Shuler, the former star quarterback for the Washington Redskins, likewise turns many hard hats his way with passionate screeds against NAFTA and the export of heartland jobs. But like Webb, his populist message is poisoned by a nativism that has included television campaign ads depicting Shuler as a lone hero fighting against amnesty for illegal immigrants. Ezra Klein in the *American Prospect* recently argued that liberals should not worry unduly about the jingoism of Webb and Shuler, or about their reactionary positions on gays and abortion. In a Congress dominated by Democrats, Klein explains, "they'll have precious little opportunity to exercise their social conservatism. Their economic beliefs, however, will get more play in a Congress aching to, at long last, turn its attention to health care, jobs, inequality, corporate regulation, and all the other domestic issues Democrats so love to address."

Aside from Klein's heroic assumptions about Democrats' reforming intentions, he seriously underestimates the dangers posed by economic nationalism within Democratic ranks. Karl Rove and the White House, for their part, were dramatically blindsided over the last year by the explosion of anti-immigrant hysteria within the conservative grass roots; and the editors of the *American Prospect* may yet rue their underestimation of Democratic xenophobia. At least half of the thirty seats that the Democrats took from Republicans were won by candidates with conservative positions on immigration. Throughout the South and Midwest, moreover, Democrats attacked Republicans for being "soft on illegal immigrants," and one Democratic senate campaign committee's website even juxtaposed images of people scaling border fences with portraits of bin Laden and Kim Jong Il. The Blue Dogs, in particular, are avid supporters of a continental-scale border wall and the use of local police to enforce national immigration laws.

In the new Congress it will be interesting to see how far the Webbs and Shulers travel with their "proletarian" attacks on the free-trade principles held sacred by New Dems and Clintonians. (My hunch is that the hidden injuries of class will matter less to both politicians after they have had some heart-warming conversations with the wealthy high-tech types in the Research Triangle and Beltway science parks.) On the other hand, there is a very real chance that the anti-immigrant and sinophobic aspects of their erstwhile populism will be amplified in synergy with like-minded Republicans. The Democrats can take temporary delight from the self-destruction of the Republicans' "Latino strategy," but they are not immune to such devils within their own party. In the worst-case scenario, the long-hoped-for New Populism would simply become midwife to a bipartisan regroupment of bigots and cranks, while the Democratic leadership continues to take its cues from Goldman Sachs and Genentech.

(March–April 2007, *New Left Review*, all references can be found in the original publication.)

PART TWO

LEGIONS AT WAR

Watching barbarians die was a standard part of the fun.

—Peter Heather, *The Fall of the Roman Empire*

TEN

BUSH'S ULTIMATE THULE?

In the early summer of 1951, a group of Inuit hunters, guiding a French anthropologist on a daring expedition to Canada's Ellesmere Island, returned to their homes at Thule in the northwest of Greenland. When they had left the year before, Thule was one of the most remote communities on earth: twenty igloos and a trading post established in 1910 by Greenland's national hero Knud Rasmussen to provide a base for his famed ethnographic explorations.

As they crossed the still-frozen sea they were stunned by an extraordinary "mirage." "A city of hangars and tents, of sheet metal and aluminum, glittering in the sun amid smoke and dust, rose up in front of us on a plain that only yesterday had been deserted." In their absence, an American armada of 120 ships and twelve thousand men—the biggest amphibious operation since Okinawa—had taken possession of North Star Bay. Without any consultation with Thule's residents, the Pentagon was transforming their fox hunting grounds into a bomber base for the nuclear war that seemed imminent as U.S. and Chinese armies clashed head-on in Korea.

In 1953, in order to make room for a new Nike missile battery, the American commander gave the Thule people but four days to evacuate their homes. They were forcibly exiled to a new village—an "instant slum" in the opinion of some—125 miles away. Danish and American officials lied to the world that the move had been "voluntary."(97) Now, half a century later, their grandchildren, many of them members of the socialist Inuit Ataqatigiit Party (IA), have become arguably the biggest roadblock to Washington's "Star Wars" fantasy of global military omnipotence.

As in the early Cold War, Thule's top-of-the-world location, peeking over the pole at Central Asia and the Middle East, is again deemed one of the Pentagon's most important geopolitical assets. The Bush administration argues that the National Missile Defense (NDM) initiative urgently demands the upgrading of the huge BMEWS radar installations at Thule and Fylingdale in England. London's subservience, of course, was immediately forthcoming; while Copenhagen, although more discreet, also signaled its willingness to barter Thule, as in the past, in return for some small gratuities. But Nuuk, the tiny Home Rule capital of Kalaallit Nunaat (as its people call Greenland), has so far refused to be conscripted into "this insane project."

Indeed, in a historic election last December (2002), a majority of Greenlanders voted for an anti-NMD coalition of the social-democratic Siumut and radical IA parties, whose representatives are pledged to oppose any unilateral Danish deal over Thule and to accelerate progress toward complete independence. This shift to the left, in defiance of both Copenhagen and Washington, is a remarkable development, rooted in a bitter and little understood colonial experience.

Although the Danes established a theocratic colonialism in southwestern Greenland in the early eighteenth century, the east coast Inuit were not "discovered" until the 1880s and the Thule region remained self-governing (even with its own postage stamps) until the 1930s. In the same decade, general diplomatic recognition of the Danish claim to the whole island (long contested by Norway) coincided with reconnaissances of Greenland's air routes by German, British, and American military planners. (One German "explorer" of the period was an assassin of Rosa Luxemburg and Karl Liebknecht.)

In spring 1941, President Roosevelt, worried as much by a proposed Canadian landing as any German invasion, extended the Monroe Doctrine to Greenland, which soon became the largest span in the famous air bridge used to ferry B-17s and B-24s to England. A country that the Danes had kept as isolated as Tibet from the outside world was overwhelmed in a few months by thousands of GIs in seventeen bases along both southern coasts. With Denmark a German satellite, Greenland (together with Iceland) became an American military colony.

After the war, the Pentagon was keen to retain control over the "world's biggest aircraft carrier" and pressed the Truman administration to buy Greenland from Denmark. Eventually, Washington settled for the next best thing: a 1951 treaty that gave the U.S. Strategic Air Command (SAC) free reign to use Thule as a launching pad for Armageddon. In the fall of 1956, Thule-based B-47s made repeated deep incursions into Soviet airspace (Operation Home Run) that were designed to push Kremlin nerves to the limit. Later Curtis LeMay, the singularly sinister commander of SAC, wistfully recollected that "with a bit of luck we could have gotten World War Three started back then."

In 1961 SAC commanders almost ordered a nuclear strike after they lost contact with Thule due to a technical glitch that they misinterpreted as a Soviet sneak attack. Seven years later, a B-52B armored with four hydrogen bombs caught fire and crashed offshore of Thule. Although the Air Force insisted that it eventually recovered all the bombs, local salvage workers have always claimed that one bomb was never found. In 2001 the *Independent* (London) corroborated their account (missing bomb serial number 78252) and estimated that 12 kilograms of plutonium had escaped into the ecosystem. According to the Thule Workers Association, representing Greenlanders who worked on the salvage effort, that would explain high local incidences of cancer as well as bizarre phenomena like seals without hair and musk oxen with deformed hooves.

Although the B-52s were finally withdrawn from Thule during the war in Vietnam and the big U.S. bases at Narsarsuaq and Kangerlussuaq were closed down, the Pentagon never cleaned up its mess. Nor, for that matter, has the complicit colonial landlord, Denmark, ever protested the American waste. Yet, as Greenpeace has documented, there is massive toxicity and environmental blight in the archipelago of abandoned U.S. airbases and radar stations.

In the 1951 Treaty for the Protection of Greenland the quid pro quo for the Pentagon's militarization of the High Arctic was a strict prohibition of contact between Americans and Greenlanders. To ensure permanent Danish hegemony over the indigenous population, Greenland became part of the metropolis in 1953: a status, as in "French" Algeria, that aggravated rather than ameliorated civic inequalities. Over the next generation, Greenlanders—including the exiled hunters of Thule—were subjected to a coercive and paternalistic "modernization" that radically dislocated their culture. The Danish strategy was to concentrate the population of scores of outlying fishing villages and hunting camps into a few "efficient" centers around large canneries and administrative complexes.

Ruggedly independent Arctic hunters—now unemployed—were rehoused in multistory concrete tenements while their kids studied Danish and their wives worked as cleaners or on fish-processing lines. Skilled and professional work was generally reserved to a highly paid stratum of imported contract workers: the true beneficiaries of the soaring subsidies to Greenland that the Danish right loves to complain about. Copenhagen's policies acted in tandem with the political economy of the American bases—with their demand for service labor, their prodigious waste, and their celebration of consumerism—to catastrophically urbanize Inuit culture in a single generation.. One state-sanctioned result has been a plague of addiction. In contemporary Greenland, fifty six thousand people smoke 120 million cigarettes and drink 40 million cans of beer per year. Likewise, with only fifteen thousand residents, modern Nuuk manages to emulate South Central L.A., with angry graffiti on slab apartment walls, gang fights in the alleys, and hash dealers prowling in their tricked-out custom snowmobiles.

Greenlanders, highly conscious of their communitarian past and heroic way of life, have fought back vigorously against both American and Danish colonialisms. Home Rule in 1979 was both a concession to

Greenlandic nationalism and an attempt to neo-colonize Danish domination through the advancement of a new, Copenhagen-educated Inuit elite. The spanner in the works was the IA: a political formation created by an Inuit New Left inspired by Vietnam and the anticolonial revolutions of the 1970s. The IA (the party to which Smilla belongs in Peter Hoeg's famous novel, *Smilla's Sense of Snow*) is sometimes described as the Greenlandic counterpart to Denmark's centrist Socialist Peoples' Party, but its program is highly original: traditionalist, pan-Inuit, Green and Red at the same time. IA played a leading role in the creation of the Inuit Circumpolar Conference, an activist NGO that acts as a shadow government for 152,000 Inuit people in four countries and anticipates the IA's dream of a peoples' Arctic without atomic bombs, addiction, or pollution.

Last December it was widely expected that the IA would surpass social-democratic Siumut as Greenland's largest party. It narrowly failed to do so only because Siumut's leadership was captured by Hans Enoksen, an independence advocate who deposed longtime party leader and prime minister Jonathan Motzfeldt after the latter attended a NATO summit in Prague. But the new Siumut-IA coalition government headed by Enoksen self-destructed in January only weeks after its formation. Foreign papers caricatured the crisis as the result of a Siumut official's employment of a traditional "sorcerer" to exorcise government buildings of evil spirits. In fact, the IA walked out—as it had several years earlier—over growing corruption and favoritism in the government. Siumut promptly formed a new government with the neocolonial Atassut Party that shares Copenhagen's willingness to deal with Washington over Star Wars.

But the IA's break with Enoksen only strengthens its claim to be the only genuine voice of Greenlandic self-determination. Moreover it continues to fiercely oppose Washington's plans for the remilitarization of the Arctic. As Johan Olsen, one of the IA leaders, told European Parliament last year: "Greenland must not participate in any horse-trading deal with the USA with reference to furthering the American wish to upgrade the Thule radar.... It is our opinion that is necessary to declare the Arctic as a demilitarized, weapons-free zone."

(February 2002, *Socialist Review*; after a visit to East Greenland)

In 2004 the Home Rule government, desperately worried about cata-strophic climate change and the decline of the traditional hunting and fishing economies, acceded to the U.S. upgrade of Thule in exchange for a vague promise of economic aid and base jobs. Colin Powell stopped briefly in Nuuk to thank Greenlanders for again putting themselves on the front line of America's future cold wars and possible nuclear exchanges. So far, however, most of the new jobs at Thule have gone to expatriate Danes, leaving Greenlanders—the descendants of heroic hunters and explorers— to contemplate a future of melting ice caps, polar slums, and lost children.

ELEVEN

THE SCALPING PARTY

*I had become so thoroughly horrified with the hellish deeds
of my companions that dread feelings akin to the nightmare
took possession of me, making my days miserable and
my nights a series of fearful dreams.*

—Sam Chamberlain, *My Confession* (1850)

In his dark masterpiece, *Blood Meridian* (1985), novelist Cormac Mc-
Carthy tells the terrifying tale of a gang of gringo scalp-hunters who left
an apocalyptic trail of carnage from Chihuahua to Southern California
in the early 1850s. Commissioned by Mexican authorities to hunt ma-
rauding Apaches, the company of ex-filibusters and convicts under the
command of John Joel Glanton and his psychopathic lieutenant, "Judge
Holden," quickly became intoxicated with gore. Under the constant instigation of Holden (a bald giant who gave his companions arcane lec-
tures on geology when he wasn't sodomizing small children) the gang
exterminated local farmers and goatherds as well as hostile Indians, and
when there were no innocents left to rape and slaughter, they turned
upon themselves with shark-like fury.

Many readers have recoiled from the gruesome extremism of Mc-
Carthy's imagery: the roasted skulls of tortured captives, necklaces of
human ears, an unspeakable tree of dead infants, and so on. Others
have balked at his unpatriotic emphasis on the genocidal origins of the

American West, and the book's obvious allusion to "search and de-stroy" missions à la Vietnam. But *Blood Meridian*, like McCarthy's other border novels, is based on meticulous research. Glanton and Holden, the white savages, really existed, and one of the few survivors of their gang, the future Civil War hero and Massachusetts prison warden, Samuel Chamberlain, left an extraordinary memoir (*My Confession*) that McCarthy employs as narrative scaffolding.(29) Indeed, *Blood Meridian* should be read side by side with Chamberlain's chilling first-hand account of the satanic history of Manifest Destiny, which he illus-trated with eerie watercolors of massacres, burning churches, and buzzards devouring corpses.

But if Glanton and Holden are the ancestors that most Americans (particularly those who glorify the conquest of the Southwest) would prefer to forget, they are also the ghosts we can't avoid. Six weeks ago, a courageous hometown paper in Rust-belt Ohio—the Toledo *Blade*—tore the wraps off an officially suppressed story of Vietnam-era exter-mination that recapitulates *Blood Meridian* in ghastly and unbearable detail. The reincarnation of Glanton's scalping party was an elite 45-man unit of the 101st Airborne Division known as "Tiger Force." The *Blade*'s intricate reconstruction of its murderous march through the Central Highlands of Vietnam in summer and fall 1967 won the Pulitzer Prize and needs to be read in full, horrifying detail.(131)

Reporters Michael Sallah and Mitch Weiss interviewed more than one hundred American veterans and Vietnamese survivors. Tiger Force atrocities began with the torture and execution of prisoners in the field, then escalated to the routine slaughter of unarmed farmers, elderly people, even small children. As one former sergeant told the *Blade*, "it didn't matter if they were civilians. If they weren't supposed to be in an area, we shot them. If they didn't understand fear, I taught it to them."

Early on, Tiger Force began scalping its victims (the scalps were dangled from the ends of M-16s) and cutting off their ears as sou-venirs. One member—who would later behead an infant—wore the ears as a ghoulish necklace (just like Toadvine in *Blood Meridian*), while another mailed them home to his wife. Others kicked out the teeth of dead villagers for their gold fillings. A former Tiger Force sergeant told reporters that "he killed so many civilians he lost count." The *Blade* estimates that innocent casualties were in "the hundreds." Another veteran, a medic with the unit, recalled 150 unarmed civilians murdered in a single month.

Superior officers, especially Glanton-like battalion commander Gerald Morse (or "Ghost Rider" as he fancied himself), sponsored the carnage. Orders were given to "shoot everything that moves" and Morse established a body-count quota of 327 (the numerical designation of the battalion) that Tiger Force enthusiastically filled with dead peasants and teenage girls. Soldiers in other units who complained about these exterminations were ignored or warned to keep silent, while Tiger Force slackers were quickly transferred out.

As with Glanton's gang, or, for that matter, *Einsatzgruppen* in the western Ukraine in 1941, atrocity created its own insatiable momentum. Eventually nothing was unthinkable in the Song Ve Valley. "A 13-year-old girl's throat was slashed after she was sexually assaulted," and a young mother was shot to death after soldiers torched her hut. An unarmed teenager was shot in the back after a platoon sergeant ordered the youth to leave a village, and a baby was decapitated so that a soldier could remove a necklace.

Stories about the beheading of the baby spread so widely that the army was finally forced to launch a secret enquiry in 1971. The investigation lasted for almost five years and probed thirty alleged Tiger Force war crimes. Evidence was found to support the prosecution of at least eighteen members of the platoon. In the event, however, a half dozen of the most compromised veterans were allowed to resign from the army, avoiding military indictment, and in 1975 the Pentagon quietly buried the entire investigation.

The *Blade* says "it is not known how far up in the Ford administration the decision went," but it is worth recalling whom the leading actors were: the secretary of defense, then as now, was Donald Rumsfeld;

the director of the CIA was George Bush; and the White House chief of staff was Dick Cheney. Recently in the *New Yorker*, Seymour Hersh, who helped expose the My Lai massacre, decried the failure of the corporate media, especially the four major television networks, to report the *Blade*'s findings or launch their own investigations into the official cover-up. He also reminded us that the army concealed details of another large massacre of civilians at the village of My Khe 4, near My Lai, on the same day that atrocity was committed in 1968.(71)

The Tiger Force story, in fact, is the third major war crimes revelation in the last few years to encounter apathy in the media and/or indifference and contempt in Washington. In 1999, a team of investigative reporters from the Associated Press broke the story of a horrific massacre of more than four hundred unarmed Korean civilians by U.S. troops in July 1950. It occurred at a stone bridge near the village of No Gun Ri and the unit involved was Custer's old outfit, the 7th Cavalry regiment. As one veteran told the AP, "there was lieutenant screaming like a madman, fire on everything, kill 'em all…. Kids, there was kids out there, it didn't matter what it was, eight to eighty, blind, crippled or crazy, they shot them all." Another ex-soldier was haunted by the memory of a terrified child: "She came running toward us. You should have seen guys trying to kill that little girl with machine guns."(30)

A reluctant Pentagon enquiry in this Korean version of the Wounded Knee massacre acknowledged the civilian toll, but dismissed it as "an unfortunate tragedy inherent in war," despite overwhelming evidence of a deliberate U.S. policy of bombing and strafing refugee columns. (*The Bridge at No Gun Ri* [2001], by three Pulitzer Prize-winning AP journalists, currently languishes at near 200,000 on the Amazon.com sales index.)

Likewise there is little enduring outrage that a confessed war criminal, Bob Kerrey, reigns as president of New York City's prestigious and once liberal New School. In 2001, the former Navy SEAL and ex-U.S. senator from Nebraska was forced to concede, after years of lies, that the heroic engagement for which he received a Bronze Star in

1969 involved the massacre of a score of unarmed civilians, mainly women and children. "To describe it as an atrocity," he admitted, "is pretty close to being right." But the blue-collar ex-SEAL team member who revealed the truth about the killings at Thanh Phong under Kerrey's command was publicly excoriated as a drunk and traitor, while powerful Democrats—led by Senators Max Cleland and John Kerry—circled wagons to protect Kerrey from further investigation or possible prosecution. They argued that it was wrong to "blame the warrior instead of the war" and called for a "healing process."

Indeed, covering up American atrocities is a thoroughly bipartisan business. The Democrats, after all, are currently considering the bomber of Belgrade, General Wesley Clark, as their potential knight on a white horse. The Bush administration, meanwhile, blackmails the rest of the world with threats of aid cuts and trade sanctions unless they exempt U.S. troops from the jurisdiction of the new International Criminal Court.

The United States, of course, has good reason to claim immunity from the very Nuremburg principles it helped establish in 1946–47. American special forces troops, for example, were most probably complicit in the massacres of hundreds of Taliban prisoners by Northern Alliance warlords several years ago. Moreover, "collateral damage" to civilians is part and parcel of the new white man's burden of "democratizing" the Middle East and making the world safe for Bechtel and Halliburton. The Glantons thus still have their place in the scheme of empire, and the scalping parties that once howled in the wilderness of the Gila now range far and wide along the banks of the Euphrates and in the shadow of the Hindu Kush.

(December 2003, *Socialist Review*)

In the summer of 2006 researcher Nick Turse and Los Angeles Times *reporter Deborah Nelson published an account of a previously secret, nine thousand-page Pentagon investigation that responded to atrocity charges* raised by ex-GIs during the "Winter Soldier" hearings sponsored by Vietnam Veterans Against the War in Detroit in 1971. My Lai and the Winter Soldier incidents, it turns out, were just the tip of a vast iceberg of inhumanity. The Army investigators substantiated 320 separate war crimes involving "every Army division that operated in Vietnam." Another five hundred alleged atrocities were neither proven nor discounted.(150)

TWELVE

THE UNGRATEFUL VOLCANO

The Moors, though ignorant of justice, were impatient of oppression:
their vagrant life and boundless wilderness disappointed
the arms and eluded the chains of a conqueror...

—Gibbon

Does the Pentagon have a "bureau of history"? Is there a room somewhere in that vast labyrinth where monkish researchers toil over the ancient archives of power, exhuming the lessons of colonies won and lost, empires risen and fallen? I doubt it. The Pentagon's interest in history is probably the same as the Swiss passion for surfing or the Saudi Arabian enthusiasm for ice hockey. Rather oxymoronic.

Too bad. A great deal of carnage might have been avoided if Donald Rumsfeld—or, for that matter, Tony Blair—had bothered to read the letters of Gertrude Bell and the diaries of Winston Churchill. Gertie and Winnie knew the land between the rivers terribly well. After all, they were the ones who transformed three prosperous and ethnically distinct provinces of the Ottoman Empire into an unhappy British client state.

"Iraq? Been there and done it, old boy. Our turn was bloody tragedy; now you Yanks get the apocalyptic farce. Odd how history repeats itself on the banks of the Euphrates, isn't it? Cheerio."

Let us imagine what kind of memo these old imperials might have passed along to their cowboy descendants. A précis, as it were, of the previous occupation. It wouldn't really be a "cautionary tale"—after all, we are already far too far up river in the heart of darkness. Caution and humanity have already been stuffed into body bags. But the British precedent might indicate a general trajectory for imperial hubris. The Brits too started out expecting hugs and kisses, and ended up giving back bombs and genocide.

Miss Bell's Tea Party

What Woodrow Wilson would later denounce as the "whole disgusting scramble" for the Middle East began when the British invaded "Mesopotamia" in 1914. The War Office already knew that the twentieth century would be powered by petroleum. Officially, the British were only protecting their oil properties in neighboring Persia from untoward Turkish or German attentions. Unofficially, they were also prospecting for oil around Basra.

The conquest of Mesopotamia was supposed to be a triumphal procession in the face of desultory Turkish resistance. In the event, it was a singularly unhappy hike that involved a lot of heat, dust, thirst, and dying. The advance of Major-General Charles Townshend's army turned into an ignominious retreat and, then, utter catastrophe at Kut al-Amara in the spring of 1916 with the annihilation of more than twenty thousand English and Indian soldiers. London, stunned by a humiliation that rivaled Gallipoli, was forced to empty India of troops in order to mount a second, far larger expedition. In 1917 the Bengal Lancers finally fought their way into Baghdad and allowed Miss Bell to take her tea on the banks of the Tigris.

The general presumption was that now that the bad Turks were gone, the rest of the population would shower love upon the British. "It's a wonderful thing to feel the affection and confidence of a whole people around you," Bell enthused in the early months of the occupation. Officially the Oriental secretary (that is to say, the resident expert on the "Arab mind") in the British administration, the erudite and adventurous Miss Bell was Paul Wolfowitz avant la lettre: the optimistic ideologue of the happy occupation.(11)

Her blueprint was not dissimilar to the plan unveiled by the deputy secretary of defense in winter 2003. The occupation of Iraq, according to Bell, would be strictly pay as you go, with oil exploration—now doubled with the illegal British annexation in 1918 of the Mosul region—reimbursing the hard-pressed Exchequer, while Iraqis (although they weren't yet called that) policed themselves under British supervision. Liberated from the iron heel of Ottoman rule, the locals would be slowly tutored in democratic values, even if the new dispensation was, in fact, based on arrogant English sahibs ruling in partnership with a handful of Sunni notables while Kurdish sheiks were arrested, Shia clerics persecuted, and tribal oil lands confiscated.

But the population, in fact, drew unfavorable comparisons between Turkish rule, with its comfortable quotient of local self-government, and British rule with its drive for efficiency, especially in the collection of taxes. Despite growing restiveness, however, Miss Bell was still camped on a cloud. "On the whole," she wrote in 1918, "the country is being opened up, and on the whole the people like it.... Basra is under peace conditions, and we have had almost no trouble in Baghdad." Her boss and Paul Bremer's predecessor, Sir Arnold Wilson, was equally optimistic: "The average Arab, as opposed to the handful of amateur politicians of Baghdad, sees the future as one of fair dealing and material and moral progress under the aegis of GB."

The next year at Versailles, the broader Arab national cause, into whose service Bell and her colleague, Colonel T. E. Lawrence, had insinuated themselves early in the war, was being comprehensively betrayed by the Anglo-French division of the Middle East that gave Zionism its beachhead in Palestine and turned Syria over to France. Mesopotamia, meanwhile, was the object of a fierce intramural struggle inside the government of Lloyd George. On one side were the "Indianists" who wanted an old-fashioned colony with lots of permanent sinecures for unemployed British aristocrats, and "Arabists" like Bell who desperately want a throne to assuage the Hashemite dynasty just evicted by the Foreign Legion in Damascus. ("You will understand," one British official wrote to another, "that what is wanted is a king who will be content to reign but not govern.")

There was little concern about what the ordinary population thought about colonial satraps or foreign monarchs. The Kurds were especially impatient and in May 1919 rose up against the British and were crushed. Bell and others in Baghdad thought that was the end of the affair. In London they were more worried about the Americans and Standard Oil's demands for a piece of Mesopotamia.

The Churchill Doctrine

While all these machinations were taking place, some of the most brilliant minds in London were concentrated on how to reduce the soaring costs of the occupation. Winston Churchill, who was both secretary of state for war and for air, wrote to RAF head Sir Hugh Trenchard in February 1920 wondering if Britain couldn't economize by replacing troops with planes. He expressed interest in chemical weapons, like the mustard gas bombs that the RAF had used against the Bolsheviks. Sir Hugh was enthusiastic and in March responded with a detailed plan for air force control of Mesopotamia. It came just in time.

On May Day 1920, the Treaty of San Remo established Iraq as a British Mandate. Three weeks later, four British soldiers were killed at Tel Afar, near Mosul, after the arrest of a local sheik. An armored car squadron was dispatched to restore order but was ambushed and annihilated by local rebels. It was the beginning of a general uprising—such as the United States may yet face—by Miss Bell's "affectionate" subjects.

Later Churchill would cynically marvel in private over the occupation authorities' success in uniting the country against them. "It is an extraordinary thing that the British civil administration should have succeeded in such a short time in alienating the whole country to such

an extent that the Arabs have laid aside the blood feuds they have
nursed for centuries and that the Suni and Shiah tribes [sic] are working together. We have been advised locally that the best way to get our
supplies up the river would be to fly the Turkish flag..."(31)

The leadership of the rebellion was drawn both from the purged
cadre of the old regime (ex-Ottoman officers and officials) and from
the angry Shiite majority in the south. (Sound familiar?) By the middle of July fighting had spread throughout the lower Euphrates.
Brigadier Coningham lost thirty-five men storming the insurgent
citadel of Rumaitha only to find that rebels had moved on to seize the
town of Kifl. While marching on Kifl the Manchester Regiment was
surprised in its camp and almost massacred. Major General Leslie lost
180 killed and another 160 captured. There was near panic.

The Cabinet in London meanwhile was distracted by the guerrilla
war in Ireland as well as by the counterrevolution in Russia. In part,
after all the glowing reports from Baghdad by Miss Bell and other
"Arabists," there was disbelief that one hundred thirty thousand locals
were actually in arms against their liberator. But the crisis worsened in
August as the uprising reached the upper Euphrates and the outskirts
of Baghdad. Outbreaks in the Kurdish north soon followed. Rebels cut
off rail links to Persia and captured a number of key towns, including
Baquba and Shahraban, killing every English official they could lay
their hands on.

Churchill pressed the RAF to proceed with work on gas bombs
("especially mustard gas") but was finally forced to break the budget
by calling in Indian reserves. The tide began to turn against the insurgents. The British Army set a barbaric precedent by using poison gas
shells, while the RAF dropped bombs and, according to historian
David Omissi, "machine-gunned women and children as they fled
from their homes." The slaughter was often indiscriminate and was
complemented by the hanging of political prisoners in Baghdad.(114)

In September, T. E. Lawrence wrote an extraordinary letter to the
Sunday Times protesting the savagery of Britain's "friendly" occupa-

tion gone wrong. It might well be republished in the *New York Times* today. "Our government is worse than the old Turkish system. They kept 14,000 local conscripts embodied, and killed a yearly average of 200 Arabs in maintaining peace. We keep 90,000 men, with aeroplanes, armoured cars, gunboats, and armoured trains. We have killed about 10,000 Arabs in this rising this summer.... How long will we permit millions of pounds, thousands of Imperial troops, and tens of thousands of Arabs to be sacrificed on behalf of a colonial administration which can benefit nobody but its administrators?"(27, 114)

The Devil's Laboratory

Thanks to bombers, poison gas, and armored cars, the British finally regained control of the country in September 1920. Tough Indian Office types enforced a Carthaginian peace. Through Christmas, punitive expeditions ranged across the rebel zones burning villages, executing suspects, confiscating livestock, and enforcing punitive fines.

Churchill, soon to be promoted to colonial secretary, continued to advocate aerial terror as the cheapest and most effective way of ruling "ungrateful volcanoes" like Iraq and other Muslim colonies. In March 1921 the RAF put the finishing touches to an "air control" plan that envisioned eight squadrons of aircraft, including two of bombers, plus six RAF armored car companies, taking the place of most of the regular Army divisions. The essence of the strategy, explained Wing Commander Chamier, was that retaliation should never be half-hearted. The RAF must inspire terror. "All available aircraft must be collected; the attack with bombs and machine guns must be relentless and unremitting and carried on continuously by day and night, on houses, inhabitants, crops, and cattle."(31, 114)

Miss Bell attended, along with Arab notables, a thrilling RAF demonstration of the new incendiary weapons that it proposed to use on delinquent villages and recalcitrant tribes. "It was even more remarkable than the one we saw last at the Air Force show because it was more real. They had made an imaginary village about a quarter of a mile from where we sat on the Kiala dyke and the two first bombs dropped from 3,000 feet went straight into the middle of it and set it alight. It was wonderful and horrible. Then they dropped bombs all round it, as if to catch the fugitives and finally firebombs which even in the brightest sunlight made flares of bright flame in the desert. They burn through metal and water won't extinguish them. At the end the armoured cars went out to round up the fugitives with machine guns."(11)

Fiery death from the air, moreover, became punishment not only for armed rebellion, but even, and more commonly, for failure to pay taxes. As one of Churchill's biographers gently put it, in early June 1921 an "aerial action had been taken on the Lower Euphrates, not to suppress a riot, but to pressure on certain villages to pay their taxes." When Churchill queried the appropriateness of using bombers to collect taxes, Sir Percy Cox replied that he was merely implementing the Churchill doctrine and rhetorically asked if the secretary for war and air really wanted "to stifle the growing infant" of airpower. Churchill immediately avowed "I am a great believer in airpower and will help it forward in every way."(114)

Bombing and strafing, as a result, became fiscal and administrative, as well as military, policy. Iraq, so to speak, became the devil's laboratory for the Colonial Office's new experiment in using airpower to terrorize civilian populations. As Jonathan Glancey reminded readers of the *Guardian* last April: "terror bombing, night bombing, heavy bombers, delayed action bombs (particularly lethal against children) were all developed during raids on mud, stone, and reed villages during Britain's League of Nation's mandate."

From his new and higher perch in the Colonial Office in late 1921, Churchill observed with satisfaction that "aeroplanes are now really feared." He continued to lobby for use of poison gas in Iraq and elsewhere. When a Colonel Meinertzhagen, familiar with the horror of gas attacks on the Western Front, challenged the application of this "barbarous method of warfare" to Arab civilian populations, he was harshly rebuked by Churchill. "I am ready to authorize the construction of such bombs at once." On another occasion, the colonial secretary fumed: "I do not understand this sqeamishness about the use of gas. I am strongly in favour of using poison gas against uncivilized tribes."(31)

"Air control" remained official policy through the 1920s, under Labor as well as Tory governments. One of the worst atrocities occured in the late autumn and winter of 1923–24, when the Bani Huchaim tribal group in the Samawa area of Iraq was unable to pay its taxes. On the verge of starvation amid a severe water shortage, the Bani Huchaim pleaded destitution. As one historian emphasizes, "there was no suggestion that there had been any serious unruliness or disorder in the area." Nonetheless, they were given a 48-hour ultimatum and then set upon with bombers. The RAF officially recorded that 144 people, including women and children, were killed.

Although occasional opponents at home like Laborite George Landsbury denounced "this Hunnish and barbarous method of warfare against unarmed people," it was the foundation of the puppet throne upon which the British emplaced the foreign, Hashemite prince, Faisal, in 1921. His "election" by 96 percent of his new subjects—the triumph of Miss Bell's "Arabist" cause—was actually a rigged plebiscite patrolled by the RAF and orchestrated by the corrupt sheiks and notables. The real winner was the Iraq Petroleum Company and its shareholders in Chelsea and Pimlico. As one world-weary veteran of empire would observe in 1925: "If the writ of King Faisal runs effectively throughout his kingdom it is entirely due to British aeroplanes. If the aeroplanes were removed tomorrow, the whole structure would inevitably fail to pieces."(114)

The British, again instigated by Churchill, bombed Iraq again in the spring of 1941, two years after the death of Faisal (which some blamed on British agents) and following the seizure of power in Baghdad by the "Golden Square," a clandestine nationalist clique of Iraqi army and air force officers who supported the Islamist Prime Minister Rashid Ali el-Gailani. Faced with the possible cutoff of Iraqi oil at the very moment when General Erwin Rommel's newly arrived Afrika Korps was overrunning British positions in Libya, Churchill sent two armies into Iraq along with more than two hundred aircraft. In a short but vicious war, the RAF again pounded villages into rubble and, after annihilating the tiny Iraqi air force (as well as a driving a handful of German and Italian planes back to Vichy-governed Syria), massacred the helpless soldiers of the Golden Square. In the West, Churchill's 1941 attack on Baghdad became only an obscure, forgotten footnote to Allied military operations in the larger Mediterranean-Middle Eastern theater, but to ordinary Iraqis it has remained a bitter national memory.(122)

This history, probably unknown to most members of Congress, Democrat as well as Republican, who endorsed the U.S. attack on Iraq, remains, of course, a poisonous memory to all Iraqis. More broadly, ordinary people in the Muslim world remember that they were the original guinea pigs upon whom the European colonial powers, starting in Libya in 1911–12, perfected the terror bombing of civilian populations. The road to Guernica, Warsaw, Dresden, and Hiroshima began on the banks of the Tigris and the flanks of the Atlas. In addition to Iraq, the RAF inflicted the "Churchill doctrine" on civilian Egyptians, Palestinians, Somalis, Sudanese, Yemenis (Aden), and Afghanis in the 1920s. In the same decade, the Spanish and the French bombed and gassed the rebel villages of the Morrocan Rif. Who were the "terrorists" then?

(Originally published in Viggo Mortensen and Pilar Perez, eds., *Twilight of Empire: Responses to Occupation,* Perceval: Santa Monica, 2004)

THIRTEEN

WAR-MART

Imperial Washington, like Berlin in the late 1930s, has become intoxicated with over-reaching fantasies of total power. Thus, in addition to creating a new pro-American geopolitical order in the Middle East, we are now told by the Pentagon's deepest thinkers that the invasion of Iraq will also inaugurate "the most important 'revolution in military affairs' (or RMA) in two hundred years."

According to Admiral William Owen, a chief theorist of the revolution, the first Gulf War was "not a new kind of war, but the last of the old ones." Likewise, the air wars in Kosovo and Afghanistan were only pale previews of the postmodern blitzkrieg that will be unleashed against the Baathist regime. Instead of old-fashioned sequential battles, we are promised nonlinear "shock and awe." Although the news media will undoubtedly focus on the sci-fi gadgetry involved—thermobaric bombs, microwave weapons, unmanned aerial vehicles (UAVs), PackBot robots, Stryker fighting vehicles, and so on—the truly radical innovations (or so the war wonks claim) will be in the organization and, indeed, the very concept of the war. In the bizarre argot of the Pentagon's Office of Force Transformation (the nerve center of the revolution), a new kind of "warfighting ecosystem" known as "network centric warfare" (or NCW) is slouching toward Baghdad to be born. Promoted by military futurists as a "minimalist" form of warfare that spares lives by replacing attrition with precision, NCW may in fact be the inevitable road to nuclear war.

Military "revolutions" based on new technology, of course, have come and gone since air-power fanatics like Giulio Douhet, Billy Mitchell, and Hugh Trenchard first proclaimed the obsolescence of traditional armies and battleship navies in the early 1920s. This time, however, the superweapon isn't a long-distance bomber or nightmare H-bomb but the ordinary PC and its ability, via the Internet, to generate virtual organization in the "battlespace" as well as the marketplace.

Like all good revolutionaries, the Pentagon advocates of RMA/NCW are responding to the rot and crisis of an ancien regime. Although Gulf War I was publicly celebrated as a flawless victory of technology and alliance politics, the real story was vicious infighting among American commanders and potentially disastrous breakdowns in decision-making. Proponents of high-tech warfare, like the "smart bomb" attacks on Baghdad's infrastructure, clashed bitterly with heavy-metal traditionalists, while frustrated battlefield CEO Norman Schwarzkopf threw stupefying tantrums.

The battles continued back in the Pentagon where the revolutionaries—mostly geekish colonels bunkered in a series of black-box think tanks—found a powerful protector in Andrew Marshall, the venerable head of research and technology assessment. In 1993, Marshall—a guru to both Dick Cheney and leading Democrats—provided the incoming Clinton administration with a working paper that warned that Cold War weapons "platforms" like Nimitz-class aircraft carriers and heavy tank battle groups were becoming obsolete in the face of precision weapons and cruise missiles. Marshall instead proselytized for cheaper, quicker, smarter weapons that took full advantage of American leadership in information technology. He warned, however, that "by perfecting these precision weapons, America is forcing its enemies to rely on terrorist activities that are difficult to target." He cast doubt on the ability of the Pentagon's fossilized command hierarchies to adapt to the challenges of so-called "asymmetric warfare."

The revolutionaries went even further: preaching that the potentials of twenty-first century war-making technology were being

squandered within nineteenth century military bureaucracies. The
new military forces of production were straining to break out of their
archaic relations of production. They viciously compared the Pentagon to one of the "old economy" corporations—"hardwired, dumb,
and top-heavy"—that were being driven into extinction in the contemporary "new economy" marketplace.

Their alternative? Wal-Mart, the Arkansas-based retail leviathan. It
may seem odd, to say the least, to nominate a chain store that peddles
cornflakes, jeans, and motor oil as the model for a leaner, meaner Pentagon, but Marshall's think-tankers were only following in the foot-
steps of management theorists who had already beatified Wal-Mart as
the essence of a "self-synchronized distributed network with real-time
transactional awareness." Translated, this means that the stores' cash
registers automatically transmit sales data to Wal-Mart's suppliers
and that inventory is managed through "horizontal" networks rather
than through a traditional head office hierarchy.

"We're trying to do the equivalent in the military," wrote the authors
of *Network Centric Warfare: Developing and Leveraging Information Superiority*, the 1998 manifesto of the RMA/NCW camp that footnotes
Wal-Mart annual reports in its bibliography.(2) In "battlespace," mobile military actors (ranging from computer hackers to stealth bomber
pilots) would be the counterparts of Wal-Mart's intelligent sales points.
Instead of depending on hard-copy orders and ponderous chains of
commands, they would establish "virtual collaborations" (regardless of
service branch) to concentrate overpowering violence on precisely de-
lineated targets. Command structures would be "flattened" to a handful
of generals, assisted by computerized decision-making aides, in egalitarian dialogue with their "shooters."

The iconic image, of course, is the Special Forces operative in Pathan
drag using his laptop to summon air strikes on a Taliban position that
another op is highlighting with his laser designator. To NCW gurus,
however, this is still fairly primitive Gunga Din stuff. They would prefer
to "swarm" the enemy terrain with locust-like myriads of miniaturized

robot sensors and tiny flying videocams whose information would be fused together in a single panoptic picture shared by ordinary grunts in their fighting vehicles as well as by four-star generals in their Qatar or Florida command posts.

Inversely, as American "battlespace awareness" is exponentially increased by networked sensors, it becomes ever more important to blind opponents by precision air strikes on their equivalent (but outdated) "command and control" infrastructures. This necessarily means a ruthless takeout of civilian telecommunications, power grids, and highway nodes: all the better, in the Pentagon view, to allow American psych-op units to propagandize, or, if necessary, terrorize the population.

Critics of RMA/NCW have compared it to a millennial cult, analogous to Bible-thumping fundamentalism or, for that matter, to al-Qaeda. Indeed, reading ecstatic descriptions of how "Metcalfe's Law" guarantees increases of "network power proportional to the square of the number of nodes," one wonders what the wonks are smoking in their Pentagon basement offices. (Marshall, incidentally, advocates using behavior-modifying drugs to create Terminator-like "bioengineered soldiers.") Their most outrageous claim is that Clausewitz's famous "fog of war"—the chaos and contingency of the battlefield—can be dispelled by enough sensors, networks and smart weapons. Thus Vice-Admiral Arthur Cebrowski, the Pentagon director for "force transformation," hallucinates that "in only a few years, if the technological capabilities of America's enemies remain only what they are today, the US military could effectively achieve total battlespace knowledge."

Donald Rumsfeld, like Dick Cheney (but unlike Colin Powell), is a notorious addict of RNA/NCW fantasies—already enshrined as official doctrine by the Clinton administration in 1998. By opening the floodgates to a huge military budget (almost equal to the rest of the world's military spending combined), 9/11 allowed Rumsfeld to go ahead with the revolution while buying off the reactionaries with funding for their baroque weapons systems, including three competing versions of a new tactical fighter. The cost of the compromise—which most Democrats have also endorsed—will be paid for by slashing federal spending on education, health care, and local government.

A second Iraq war, in the eyes of the RNA/NCW zealots, is the inevitable theater for demonstrating to the rest of the world that America's military superiority is now unprecedented and inimitable. Haunted by the 1993 catastrophe in Mogadishu, when poorly armed Somali militia defeated the Pentagon's most elite troops, the war wonks have to show that networked technology can now prevail in labyrinthine street warfare.

To this end, they are counting on the combination of battlefield omniscience, smart bombs, and new weapons like microwave pulses and nausea gases to drive Baghdadis out of their homes and bunkers. The use of "nonlethal" weapons against the civilian populations, especially in light of the horror of what happened during the Moscow hostage crisis last October, is a war crime waiting to happen.

But what if the RNA/NCW's Second Coming of Warfare doesn't arrive as punctually promised? What happens if the Iraqis or future enemies find ways to foil the swarming sensors, the night-visioned Special Forces, the little stair-climbing robots, the missile-armed drones? Indeed, what if some North Korean cyberwar squad (or, for that matter, a fifteen-year-old hacker in Des Moines) manages to crash the Pentagon's "system of systems" behind its battlespace panopticon? If the American war-fighting networks begin to unravel (as partially occurred in February 1991), the new paradigm—with its "just in time" logistics and its small "battlefield footprint"—leaves little backup in terms of traditional military reserves. This is one reason why the Rumsfeld Pentagon takes every opportunity to rattle its nuclear saber.

Just as precision munitions have resurrected all the mad omnipotent visions of yesterday's strategic bombers, RNA/NCW is giving new life to monstrous fantasies of functionally integrating tactical nukes into the electronic battlespace. The United States, it should never be forgotten, fought the Cold War with the permanent threat of "first use" of nuclear weapons against a Soviet conventional attack. Now the threshold has been lowered to Iraqi gas attacks, North Korean missile launches, or, even, retaliation for future terrorist attacks on American city. For all the geekspeak about networks and ecosystems, and millennarian boasting about minimal, robotic warfare, the United States is becoming a terror state pure and simple: a twenty-first century Assyria with laptops and modems.

(March 2003, *Socialist Review*)

FOURTEEN

THE PENTAGON AS GLOBAL SLUMLORD

The young Marine is exultant. "It's a sniper's dream," he tells a *Los Angeles Times* reporter on the outskirts of Fallujah. "You can go anywhere and there are so many ways to fire at the enemy without him knowing where you are.... Sometimes a guy will go down, and I'll let him scream a bit to destroy the morale of his buddies. Then I'll use a second shot.... To take a bad guy out," he explains, "is an incomparable adrenaline rush." He brags of having "24 confirmed kills" in the initial phase of the brutal U.S. onslaught against the rebel city of three hundred thousand people.(117)

Faced with intransigent popular resistance that recalls the heroic Vietcong defense of Hue in 1968, the Marines have again unleashed indiscriminate terror. According to independent journalists and local medical workers, they have slaughtered at least two hundred women and children in the first two weeks of fighting. The battle of Fallujah, together with parallel conflicts unfolding in Shiite towns and Baghdad slums, are high-stakes tests, not just of U.S. policy in Iraq, but of Washington's ability to dominate what Pentagon planners consider the "key battlespace of the future": the Third World city.

The Mogadishu debacle of 1993, when neighborhood militias inflicted 60 percent casualties on elite army rangers, forced U.S. strategists to rethink what is known in Pentagonese as MOUT, or Militarized Operations on Urbanized Terrain. Ultimately a National Defense Panel review in December 1997 castigated the army as unprepared for protracted combat in the impassable mazelike streets of poor cities. As a result, the four armed services launched crash programs to master street fighting under realistic Third World conditions. "The future of warfare," the journal of the Army War College declared, "lies in the streets, sewers, high-rise buildings, and sprawl of houses that form the broken cities of the world."(118)

Israeli advisers were quietly brought in to teach marines, rangers, and navy SEALs the state-of-the-art tactics— especially the sophisticated coordination of sniper and demolition teams with heavy armor and overwhelming airpower—so ruthlessly used by Israeli defense forces in Gaza and the West Bank. Artificial cityscapes were built to simulate combat conditions in the densely populated neighborhoods of cities like Baghdad or Port-au-Prince. The Marine Corps Warfighting Laboratory also staged realistic war games ("Urban Warrior") in Oakland and Chicago, while the Army's Special Operations Command "invaded" Pittsburgh.

Today many of the Marines inside Fallujah are graduates of these Urban Warrior exercises as well as mock combat at "Yodaville" (the urban training facility at Yuma, Arizona) while the army units encircling Sadr City and Najaf are alumni of the new $34 million MOUT simulator at Fort Polk, Louisiana. This tactical "Israelization" of U.S. combat doctrine has been accompanied by a "Sharonization" of the Pentagon's worldview. Military theorists envision the evolving capacity of high-tech warfare to contain, if not destroy, chronic "terrorist" insurgencies rooted in the desperation of growing megaslums.

To help develop a geopolitical framework for urban war-fighting, military planners turned in the 1990s to the RAND corporation, Dr. Strangelove's old alma mater. RAND, a nonprofit think tank established by the air force in 1948, was notorious for war-gaming nuclear Armageddon in the 1950s and helping plan the war in Vietnam in the 1960s. These days RAND does cities—big time. Its researchers ponder urban crime statistics, inner-city public health, and the privatization of public education. They also run the Army's Arroyo Center, which has published a small library of recent studies on the context and mechanics of urban warfare.

One of the most important RAND projects, initiated in the early 1990s, has been a major study of "how demographic changes will affect future conflict." The bottom line, RAND finds, is that the urbanization of world poverty has produced "the urbanization of insurgency" (the title, in fact, of their report). "Insurgents are following their followers into the cities," RAND warns, "setting up 'liberated zones' in urban shantytowns.... Neither US doctrine, nor training, nor equipment is designed for urban counterinsurgency." As a result, the slum has become the weakest link in the American Empire. The RAND researchers reflect on the example of El Salvador, where the local military, despite massive U.S. support, was unable to stop FMLN guerrillas from opening an urban front. Indeed, "Had the Farabundo Marti National Liberation Front rebels effectively operated within the cities earlier in the insurgency, it is questionable how much the United States could have done to help maintain even the stalemate between the government and the insurgents."(143)

More recently, a leading Air Force theorist has made similar points in the *Aerospace Power Journal*. "Rapid urbanisation in developing countries," writes Captain Troy Thomas, "results in a battlespace environment that is decreasingly knowable since it is increasingly unplanned." Thomas contrasts modern "hierarchical" urban cores, whose centralized infrastructures are easily crippled by either air strikes (Belgrade) or terrorist attacks (Manhattan), with the sprawling slum peripheries of the Third World, organized by "informal, decentralized subsystems," where "no blueprints exist, and points of leverage in the system are not readily discernable."(148)

Using the "sea of urban squalor" that surrounds Karachi as an example, Thomas portrays the staggering challenge of "asymmetric combat" within "non-nodal, non-hierarchical" urban terrains against "clan-based" militias propelled by "desperation and anger." He cites the sprawling slums of Lagos and Kinshasa as other potential nightmare battlefields. However, Captain Thomas (whose article is provocatively entitled "Slumlords: Aerospace Power in Urban Fights"), like RAND, is brazenly confident that the Pentagon's massive new investments in MOUT technology and training will surmount all the fractal complexities of slum warfare. One of the RAND cookbooks (*Aerospace Operations in Urban Environments*) even provides a helpful table to calculate the acceptable threshold of "collateral damage" (a.k.a. dead babies) under different operational and political constraints.

The occupation of Iraq, of course, has been portrayed by Bush ideologues as a "laboratory for democracy" in the Middle East. To MOUT geeks, on the other hand, it is a laboratory of different kind, where marine snipers and air force pilots test out new killing techniques in an emergent world war against the urban poor.

(May 2004, *Socialist Review*)

FIFTEEN

THE URBANIZATION OF EMPIRE

As [the barbarians] had been deprived by the ministers of the emperor
of the common benefits of nature and the fair intercourse of social life,
they retaliated the injustices on the subjects of the empire.

—Gibbon

The great colonial empires of the nineteenth and early twentieth centuries were brutal engines for the extraction of rents, crops, and miner-
als from tropical countrysides. Colonial cities and entrepots, although
often vast, sprawling, and dynamic, were demographically rather in-
significant. The urban populations of the British, French, Belgian, and
Dutch Empires at their Edwardian zenith probably didn't exceed 3 to 5
percent of colonized humanity. The same ratios probably prevailed in
the decayed Spanish and Portuguese Empires, as well as in the late conquests of nouveaux riche powers like Germany, Italy, Japan, and the
United States. Although there were some important exceptions—for
example, Ireland, Cuba, Algeria, Palestine, and South Africa (after
1910)—even in these cases, city-dwellers were rarely more than one-
sixth of the population.

Nor were colonial cities the principal hearths of native resistance. It
might have been expected that the ports and administrative centers,
with their extreme inequalities, their concentrations of indigenous intellectuals, and their embryonic labor movements, would have been

the principal incubators of revolutionary nationalism. In many cases, indeed, the urban milieu was the decisive progenitor of nationalist and anticolonial politics, but the colonial city was only episodically, and usually very briefly, the actual theater of violent revolt.

It is striking, in fact, how few repressive resources, especially European troops, were needed to control large colonial cities like Cairo, Havana, Bombay, Manila, and Dublin. In part this was a reflection of the conservative influence of comprador middle classes, whose nationalism, if it existed, usually took cautious, incremental, and nonviolent forms. But many of the urban poor were also integrated—as soldiers, servants, prostitutes, and petty traders—into the parasitic ecology of the colonial metropolis. In Dublin in 1916, for instance, the slum poor (many of whose sons were at the Western Front fighting for the crown) jeered the survivors of the Easter Rebellion as they were led away to British prisons.

The sustainable zones of anticolonial resistance were in the countrysides, particularly where export agriculture conflicted most sharply with the survival of small farmers and traditional rural communes. In his impressive comparative analysis of rural protest across the world, Jeffery Paige singled out both sharecropping and settler-based estates as agricultural systems that produced chronic violence and episodic uprisings. "Conflict developed between foreign owners of the new agricultural organizations and their wage laborers, between the new agrarian upper class and the old pre-industrial landlords it replaced, and between landlords converted into commercial entreprenueurs and their former tenants now bound by ties of wages and rent. The strength of colonial and imperial political controls long prevented the political expression of these conflicts, but with the decline of colonial power in the postwar era, the commercial export sectors of the underdeveloped world have become centers of revolutionary social movements."(116)

Moreover, the recurrent pattern of modern national liberation movements—as far back even as the North American and Irish revolutions of the late-eighteenth century—has been the flight of urban revolutionary vanguards to rural redoubts with durably anchored traditions of revolt. Thus the Cuban nationalists both in the 1860s and 1950s abandoned the cities for the rebel sierras of eastern Cuba; urban Arab nationalists took refuge in the Rif or the villages of Upper Egypt; Sinn Fein fled Dublin and Cork for the Wicklow and Galty hills; Gandhi turned to the great soul of the Indian countryside; Emilio Aguinaldo retreated from Manila to the rugged mountainsides of Luzon; and the young Communist parties of China, Vietnam, and Indonesia all made their long marches from the cities to remote rural fortresses.

For the pre-1940 empires, therefore, imperial control was largely a problem of rural counterinsurgency. The classic Victorian response, of course, was the punitive expedition that sought not only to reduce rebellion in the hinterland but also to devastate its subsistence base: thus the Seventh Cavalry exterminating the Plains bison, German troops decimating the herds of the Herero, French marines destroying the rice stores of Tonkin, and so on. But the work of imperial armies was usually incomplete, leaving behind embers of insurgency that might again be fanned into open rebellion.

During the second Cuban war of liberation in the 1890s, the Spanish General Valeriano Weyler offered a more radical solution. Weyler was Spain's greatest expert on rural counterinsurgency, having fought insurgents in Santo Domingo and Cuba in the 1860s, as well as Carlists in Navarre in the 1870s. Faced once again with an intransigently anti-Spanish countryside, he attempted to separate *insurrectos* from their social base by forcibly herding peasants and rural workers into fetid "reconcentration" camps. The "empty" countryside then became a shoot-on-sight killing field without discrimination as to target. As the *reconcentrados* began to die in huge numbers (almost two hundred thousand) from disease and poor sanitation,(24) Weyler's strategy was denounced as "barbarism" in the American press and soon became one of the formal pretexts for President McKinley's declaration of war against Spain in 1898. But the American army was soon instituting its own deadly concentration camps and free-fire zones against Filipino nationalists in southern Luzon and the Visayas, while the British were doing the same thing in the Transvaal, and the Germans, in Southwest Africa. The ruthless principles underlying Edwardian colonial warfare were famously codified by Colonel C. E. Callwell, a veteran of both the Second Afghan and Boer wars, in the 1904 edition of his *Small Wars: Their Principles and Practice*—a text that currently enjoys a cult revival among American officers in Iraq and Afghanistan.

But as the Boer War demonstrated, population concentration and punitive expeditions were still an incomplete strategy for coercing sullen and rebellious countrysides. The next step was aerial bombardment of peasant or nomadic insurgents. The first experiments had been undertaken by the Italians in their conquest of Libya on the eve of World War I, but the master colonial bombers were the British. In 1919–20, faced with the soaring costs of occupying Mesopotamia, Air Minister (and soon, Colonial Minister) Winston Churchill became the chief apostle of using "cheap" airpower, supplemented by flying columns of armored cars, against the rural centers of revolt. As we have seen in an earlier discussion of Iraq's "Ungrateful Volcano," the Churchillian doctrine of air control was as much about creating mass terror as hitting specific targets. During the next decade, the RAF would bomb and strafe rural insurgents in Mesopotamia, Somalia, Afghanistan, and Aden, as well as urban demonstrators in Egypt.(114)

The American war in Indochina was the historical climax and comprehensive recapitulation of these canonical strategies of punitive expeditions (or "search-and-destroy missions"), population concentration (renamed "strategic hamlets"), and free-fire no-go areas (now applied to areas of more than one million population). Most of all, aerial terror was unleashed with unprecedented ferocity, ultimately consuming more than the total tonnage of bombing in all previous wars, with the goal or result of destroying entire rural ecosystems, social structures, and populations.

The Informal Proletariat

The New Imperialism of the early twenty-first century, however one defines it, still contains zones of conflict in the classic pattern. The Tenth Mountain Division in southern Afghanistan heedlessly follows in the footprints of Russian commandos and the Bengal Lancers, while in Mindanao, a large contingent of U.S. Special Forces fights the great-grandchildren of the same rebels who ambushed "Black Jack" Pershing's patrols a century earlier. U.S. participation, in official and clandestine guises, in the dirty war in Colombia, meanwhile, is part of a continuous history of intervention going back to Nicaragua and Haiti in the 1920s.

But the Third World—the main arena of neo-imperial discourse about "failed states" and postmodern white men's burdens—is increasingly a universe of urban slums and peri-urban shantytowns. Mao's paradigmatic countryside no longer so much surrounds the city as implodes into it. Far more rapidly than anticipated by the famous Club of Rome report in the early 1970s, humanity has passed an epochal threshold: inhabitants of some fifty thousand cities now outnumber those of two-million-plus villages.

Indeed, according to UN demographers, the world's rural population has now reached a maximum plateau of three billion people and will never significantly increase. Cities, on the other hand, are growing by sixty million per year, and 90 percent of the increase in world population over the next generation will be accommodated by the urban areas of less-developed regions. By 2030, in other words, two billion more people will struggle for survival in cities, especially in the teeming metropolitan complexes of Africa and Asia.

As UN researchers pointed out in their watershed 2003 report, *The Challenge of Slums*, this urban population explosion will be almost completely delinked or "disincorporated" from industrial growth and the supply of formal jobs.(151) Although studies of the so-called urban informal economy have shown myriad secret liaisons with outsourced multinational production systems, the larger fact is that hundreds of millions of new urbanites must further subdivide the peripheral economic niches of personal service, casual labor, street vending, rag picking, begging, and crime. This outcast proletariat—perhaps 1.5 billion people today, 2.5 billion by 2030—is the fastest growing and most novel social class on the planet. By and large, the urban informal working class is not a labor reserve army in the nineteenth-century sense: a backlog of strike-breakers during booms, to be expelled during busts, and then reabsorbed in the next expansion. On the contrary, this is a mass of humanity structurally and biologically redundant to global accumulation and the corporate matrix.

It is ontologically both similar and dissimilar to the historical agency described in the *Communist Manifesto*. Like the traditional industrial working classes, it has "radical chains" in the sense of having little vested interest in the reproduction of private property. But it is not a socialized collectivity of labor and lacks significant power to disrupt or seize control of the means of production, much less to reorganize modern industrial life upon the basis of its own class culture. It does possess, however, yet unmeasured powers of subverting urban order and disrupting vital global flows of people and information.

The ranks of the informal proletariat are ceaselessly expanded and the urban crisis deepened, the authors of *Challenge of Slums* emphasize, by international economic regulation. Debt regimes strip-mine the public finances of developing countries and throttle new investment in housing an infrastructure. Externally imposed structural adjustment programs decimate public employment, destroy import-substitution industries, and displace tens of millions of rural producers unable to compete against the heavily subsidized agrocapitalism of the rich countries. Even China's market miracle has produced a floating urban population of one hundred million disenfranchised, despised, and superexploited rural migrants.

Privatization of public utilities and social property, meanwhile, is just a euphemism for plunder and piracy on a scale not seen since the

Nazi conquest of Europe. As the UN points out, the creation of a score of billionaires in the ex-Comecon blocs has been paid for by a rise in deep poverty, from under three million in 1988 to almost one hundred seventy million today. It is tempting to characterize this "triumph of market democracy" as the greatest peacetime social regression in history, except that this title more fully belongs to sub-Saharan Africa in the postliberation era. The exploitation of Nigeria's enormous oil wealth, for instance, has gone hand in hand with an almost exponential increase of poverty from 28 percent in 1980 to 66 percent in 1996. Indeed the urban corridor that runs from Abidjan to Ibadan is predicted to become the greatest slum belt on Earth, with more than fifty million impoverished inhabitants.

The UN report draws somber but straightforward lessons: "The collapse of formal urban employment in the developing world and the rise of the informal sector is seen as a direct function of liberalization.... Urban poverty has been increasing in most countries subject to structural adjustment programs, most of which are deliberately anti-urban in nature."(151) In UN-Habitat's view, the state's capacity to create formal jobs and housing has been sacrificed to the golden calf of monetary stability. Under the current neoliberal regime of globalization—indeed, under almost any foreseeable form of post-Keynesian capitalism—the new urban poor are unincorporatible: *a surplus humanity*.

The corollary to this urbanization of world poverty, of course, is the extraordinary proliferation of slums on the outskirts of Third World cities. By the UN's conservative definitions, the global slum population is now almost equal to the population of the world in 1844 when the young Friedrich Engels first ventured into the mean streets of Manchester. By 2030 the world will look roughly as follows:

(1) Of 8 billion humans, 5 billion will live in cities.

(2) 1 billion urbanites—owners, managers, technicians, and skilled information-sector workers—will provide the principal demand for branded international production.

(3) 1.5 to 2 billion workers—ranging from Mexican-American nurses' aides in Los Angeles to teenagers in Ho Chi Minh City sweatshops—will provide the metropolitan labor power for the global economy, including the increasing demand for elder-care in rapidly aging rich societies.

(4) 2 to 3 billion informal workers—at least 2 billion of whom will live in classic slums or shantytowns—will somehow exist outside the formal relations of production, in Dickensian squalor or worse, ravaged by emergent diseases and subject to the various mega-disasters following in the wake of global warming and the exhaustion of urban water supplies. Social marginality will increasingly correspond to age as well as race, and this new "wretched of the earth" will be the youngest cohort of humanity.

The Twilight Struggle

The new urban poor, however, will not go gently into this dark night. Their resistance, indeed, becomes the principal condition for the survival of the unity of the human race against the implicit triage of the new global order. It is a resistance, however, whose ideological and political expressions have as yet no global unification or historical polestar: nothing remotely equivalent, say, to the Communist International or the Tricontinental movement. The urban informal working classes, although they share the same iron rations of neglect and marginalization, constitute a startling spectrum of differential identity, belief, and activism.

First, the poorest of the poor tend to be linguistic, ethnic, or religious minorities. Thus South Asia's biggest slum, Dharavi in Bombay, is a Tamil-speaking enclave in a sea of Marathi and Hindi speakers. Second, the informal working class, without membership in large-scale collectivities of labor, lacks a centripetal organizing principle as well as strategic social power. Third, slum populations tend to be sociologically anomic because of the atomizing impacts of addiction and violence: Los

Angeles, Medellín, and Soweto offer sobering examples. (Criminal networks, however, can sometimes generate impressively organized paragovernments of the poor, as in the traditional case of the Camorra in Naples or, more recently, the favela gangs in Rio de Janeiro.)

But even the poorest slum communities can also preserve and transmit ancient rural and urban solidarities, including extinct cultures of factory and mine labor. Thus the *colonias populares* of Mexico City, as Carlos Monsiváis has shown in his brilliant book, *Entrada Libre*, defy any linear correlation between poverty and informality, on one hand, and collapsed civil society, on the other. In the face of megadisasters—an earthquake and pipeline explosion, for example—the *colonias* have demonstrated formidable capacities for self-organization in the face of inefficient or corrupted state interventions.(107) Likewise, the Chavista movement in the precarious hillside settlements of Caracas mobilizes rich historical traditions, as do the popular movements in El Alto, La Paz's Cinderella sister, where the revolutionary culture of former miners has been transmuted into urban resistance.

However, the highest quotients of civil organization among the new urban poor are probably found in the Muslim world. The complex educational and philanthropic networks of Islamic civil society provide a moral regulation of slum life that has no real equivalent in other cultures. One result is a dramatic reduction of levels of criminality or spontaneous violence: Cairo is the paradigmatic example. On the other hand, the same institutions can sustain immensely difficult and protracted resistance to otherwise overpowering occupations.

Thus wave after wave of high-tech Israeli repression seem to break futilely on the rock of Gaza (not to mention Hezbollah in South Lebanon), while in Iraq, the U.S. occupiers fear most the eruption of the Shia volcano of east Baghdad (Sadr City). Everywhere, the Muslim slums are reservoirs of highly disciplined desperation. Not surprisingly, the recent suicide bombers in Turkey came from Istanbul's sprawling slum of Bagcilar, as well as from the grim provincial city of Bingöl, where 60 percent of the population is jobless. Car bombs, land mines, and other improvised explosive devices (IEDs in Pentagonese)—especially when the attackers are willing to sacrifice themselves to ensure that the target is achieved—have proven extraordinarily difficult for armies trained in either classical heavy warfare or Vietnam-era rural counterinsurgency to defeat in dense urban settings where airpower is often impotent and population concentration rebounds to the benefit of the insurgents.

But in the last instance—and this is my principal claim—this is not a "war of civilizations" but an oblique clash between the American imperium and the labor power that it has expelled from the formal world economy. The future contours of this new "twilight struggle" (as the Cold War was once called) are difficult to foresee. Trends may persist or wholly original developments, including unexpected ideological hybrids, may emerge.

Who, for example, could have predicted in 1900 the convergence just twenty-five years later between urban Marxism and the rural rebellion in Asia? The current vogue of Pentecostalism and Islamism in the new slums of Latin America, Africa, and Asia may be permanent hegemonies or, then again, the urban poor's version of the peasant millenarian movements and anticolonial Ghost Dances of the 1890s. What is clear is that the contemporary mega-slum poses unique problems of imperial order and social control that conventional geopolitics has barely begun to register. If the point of the war on terrorism is to pursue the enemy into his sociological and cultural labyrinth, then the poor peripheries of developing cities will be the permanent battlefields of the twenty-first century.

(Winter 2004, *Social Text* 81)

PART THREE

THE UNEASE IN GAUL

Ibi totum licet (There, anything goes).

—a Roman writer's description
of fifth-century Gaul

SIXTEEN

HEAVY METAL FREEWAY

War is the moral equivalent of traffic—or is it the other way around? Forgive me if my categories are slightly scrambled, but I live in Southern California which, to misquote Woody Guthrie, is "a paradise to live in or see, but only if you got an SUV." My daily commute, a grim ninety miles each way, increasingly resembles the famed tank battle of El Alamein. What a writer back in the 1920s called "Southern California's juggernaut of pleasure" is now war without mercy as 18 million people in 14 million vehicles struggle with the worst traffic congestion in the country. Each morning I saddle up my own personal armored vehicle—a sinister-looking V8, 4-wheel-drive Toyota Tundra pickup—and plow into one of the middle lanes of Interstate 5. For the next hour and half, I fight my fellow citizens—no quarter given or requested—for freeway lebensraum.

Panzer divisions of "sports utility vehicles"—imagine the old-fashioned family station wagon on steroids and meth—now dominate the freeways. Pole position on a Southern California freeway has always been a harrowing place, but it is especially terrifying now that heavy metal rules. The basic strategy of rush-hour road war is to terrorize the car in front of you. This is especially easy when you are driving some huge hunk of combat steel like a Chevy Suburban or Ford Explorer while the poor sod ahead of you is puttering along in his pathetic Corolla or Ford Escort.

Ideally you should take him by surprise. The standard practice is to stealthily pull up a few microns behind his rear bumper. It is bad form (or worse, a New York custom) to honk. It is better to wait until he suddenly notices your towering menace in his mirror. His panicked lane change is then sweetly savored social deference. Most of the time, however, one SUV simply piles up behind another. Class privilege cancels itself out, and there is no alternative but to wait until someone's nerves crack and he or she moves out of the way. As in war and other blood sports, coolness under stress is the supreme virtue. Who cannot but admire the brave Westside housewife, so calmly sipping a cappuccino and chatting on her cellular, as her massive Dodge bears down suicidally on the snarled traffic ahead?

It is true that recovering heart patients, poor immigrants in jalopies, frightened moms with babes on board, and followers of Mahatma Gandhi usually cling to the slower right lanes of the freeway. But it is a foolish sanctuary since they are either directly in the path of merging SUVs entering the freeway at warp speed or sandwiched between 70-foot-long semis that can crush them like aluminum cans. Inevitably, the hegemony of SUVs in traffic dictates defensive rearmament and a logic of mutual deterrence. Although, as a tree-hugging radical, I would theoretically prefer to drive an eco-friendly electric car, or, better, bike to work under the warm California sky, I see no realistic choice but to protect myself with a gangsterish pickup.

We need to remind our children, however, that traffic, even in Southern California, was not always this red in tooth and claw. There was a time, roughly between tail fins and SUVs, and in the aftermath of the 1973 energy crisis, when plucky, fuel-efficient little compacts, made by ingenious Japanese elves, temporarily dominated the freeways. This was internal combustion's Middle Earth. Why did it disappear so abruptly in the 1990s?

The answer, I am sure, is because there was such a perfect pathological fit between the SUV and middle-class anxiety in the early 1990s. It is surely not accidental that Detroit's new generation of family tanks appeared at the moment when "carjackings" and freeway shootings dominated prime-time news. Or when good burghers by the hundreds of thousands were retreating into gated suburbs guarded by armies of private security guards. The SUV was similarly perceived to be a steel cocoon of middle-class security in the freeway badlands. These huge hunks of Japanese and Korean steel also quickly became the muscular symbols of the new, I-will-invade-your-country-and-kill-your-momma Republicanism. The 9/11 attacks added flagpoles as auto accessories, giving Suburbans and Explorers bedecked with Old Glory the patriotic panache of the Seventh Cavalry charging into a Sioux village.

Finally, SUVs are luxury temporary housing for enduring commute hell. Southern California traffic remains the worst in the United States (although Seattle and Washington, D.C., are not far behind) with drivers from its outer suburbs sacrificing the equivalent of two extra work weeks per year (seventy-five hours) to the demon god of gridlock. The estimated annual economic cost to commuters is almost 9 billion dollars or $1,668 per person in the Los Angeles region. Traffic, moreover, is increasing much faster than population and new freeways are clogged within four years of construction. A recent study has shown that Los Angeles is the most difficult metropolitan area to escape from through travel on weekends: scientific confirmation for the angry claustrophobia that is replacing the region's once vaunted culture of physical mobility and long weekend drives. In a recent, authoritative survey of Southern California public opinion, traffic ranked far ahead of jobs, crime, education, and housing as the region's foremost problem.

Local talk radio and right-wing blogs are clogged toilets of nativist hysteria blaming gridlock on illegal immigrants. But the real motor of congestion is sprawl and land inflation, not demography. In their ceaseless quest for affordable housing far away from epicenters of urban violence, several million families have moved out to the edge of the desert or beyond. Since jobs, by and large, have not followed them, the price tag of the Southern California dream is now a three-hour round-trip each day between interior homes and coastal jobs. At the same time, California's transportation infrastructure—once the freeway wonder of the world—now lags hopelessly behind the standards of the rest of the advanced industrial world. Since the tax revolts of the late 1970s, the state's roadways have become as potholed and unreliable as its collapsing inner-city schools and decrepit power grids. Despite twenty years of apocalyptic warnings, the gap continues to widen between the state's concentrated wealth and coastal home values, on one hand, and its expenditures on physical and social infrastructure, on the other.

The failure of local political systems to stem violence, control sprawl, or invest in efficient mass transit ensures that the vast parking lot of the Southern California freeway system will become even more nightmarishly congested over the next generation. The current seven hours per day of rush-hour immobility will eventually become twenty hours, and average freeway speeds will decline to horse-and-buggy velocities. Indeed, regional planners worry that the predicted 30 percent increase in traffic will literally strangle the world's twelfth largest economy to death. Before future mass transit can ride to the rescue, Southern California stands to lose myriads of middle-class jobs and middle-class residents to metropolitan areas with less gridlock, shorter commutes, and higher qualities of life.

In the meantime, SUVs provide magical, if temporary, compensations of power and comfort. In the dreary democracy of gridlock, they seemed to confer a noblesse oblige, or, at least, an arrogant ability to hog the left-hand lanes. (Their owners, however, tend to ignore the fact that their size and high center of gravity, which makes them so intimidating to smaller cars, also make them lethally unstable and prone to fiery rollovers.)

The irresistible trend, then, is toward an SUV-led militarization of the freeways in synchronization with a more general militarization and immobilization of urban space. The most blatant symbol of this is the current mass marketing of a literal war wagon, the army's Humvee, as state-of-the-art family transport. The scarcely modified civilian version, the Hummer, is the emergent Tyrannosaurus Rex of the freeways, and chief enthusiast and salesman is actor Arnold Schwarzenegger, whose own customized Hummers (he owns four) have long been tourist attractions in Santa Monica. A rising star in the Republican Party, Schwarznegger is also rated as a leading contender for governor of California. It is a prospect dreaded by environmental activists. With the Terminator himself in power and millions of barrels of "liberated" Iraqi oil on the market, the Age of the SUV may never end.

(2003, *Il Manifesto*)

Shortly after his election in November 2003, Schwarzenegger rewarded SUV drivers and dealers (some of his most important campaign contributors) by repealing recently enacted car license fees. The resulting $4 billion budget shortfall in the state budget was compensated with cuts in vital services for the poor. In the wake of soaring gas prices, I sold my gangster truck and bought a smaller (but scarcely greener) SUV; but after being pushed around by the yuppie megafauna on I-5, I have decided to return to heavy armor as soon as possible (preferably with custom-mounted twin 50-caliber machine guns). Yield right of way or die.

SEVENTEEN

CRY CALIFORNIA

Every candidate in California's dark recall-election comedy should be obliged to answer the question: "Whither Duroville?" "Duroville" is the California visitors never see and that pundits ignore when they debate the future of the world's sixth largest economy. Officially this ramshackle desert community of four thousand people in the Coachella Valley doesn't even exist. It is a shantytown—reminiscent of the Okie camps in *Grapes of Wrath*—erected by otherwise homeless farmworkers on land owned by Harvey Duro, a member of the Cahuilla Indian nation.

The Coachella Valley is the prototype of a future—Beverly Hills meets Tijuana—that California conservatives seem to dream of creating everywhere. The western side of the Valley, from Palm Springs to La Quinta, is an air-conditioned paradise of gated communities built around artificial lakes and eighteen-hole golf courses. The typical resident is a sixty-five-year-old retired white male in a golf cart. He is a zealous voter who disapproves of taxes, affirmative action, and social services for the immigrants who wait on him.

The east side of the Valley, from Indio to Mecca, is where the resort maids, busboys, pool cleaners, and farmworkers live. There is an artificial mountain built out of five hundred thousand tons of sludge (solid sewage) trucked in from Los Angeles, but nary a blade of grass. In Duroville the largest body of water is the sewage lagoon and the local playground is a dioxin-contaminated landfill. The typical resident is eighteen years old, speaks Spanish or Mixtec, and works all day in the blast-furnace desert heat. She/he, most likely, is not yet a citizen and therefore ineligible to vote.

Squalor, exploitation, and disenfranchisement are not just anomalies of California's agricultural valleys and "factories in the field." There are urban Durovilles as well, like the sprawling tenement district just a few blocks west of downtown Los Angeles. On the gilded coast north of San Diego, an estimated ten thousand immigrant day laborers and service workers sleep rough in the wild canyons behind $800,000 tract homes. Throughout the state, hundreds of thousands of immigrant workers live in illegal garage conversions, derelict trailers, even chicken coops.

Economic inequality in California has soared in the last generation, particularly in the southern half of the state. In the Los Angeles area, for example, the top 20 percent of the workforce earns *twenty-five times* more on average than the bottom 20 percent. Similarly, a third of Los Angeles residents lack medical insurance and must depend on a handful of overcrowded county hospitals whose doctors have recently given chilling testimony about the rising number of needless deaths from shortages of staff and beds. Nearly one million poor Angelenos, moreover, experience episodic hunger with the percentage increasing, especially among pregnant women, in the 2001–05 period. Indeed, the nutrition crisis is so severe that the Los Angeles Regional Foodbank distributes about 45 million pounds of food per year without coming close to meeting the demand.

This Third World California, which Duroville poignantly symbolizes, is no accidental creation. The famous tax revolt of the late 1970s was racial politics coded as fiscal populism. As the Latino population soared, white voters, egged on by right-wing demagogues, withdrew support from the public sector. California became a bad-school state in lockstep with becoming a low-wage state. Overcrowded classrooms and dangerous playgrounds are part of a vicious circle with sweatshop jobs and slum housing.

The California labor movement, reinvigorated by a new generation of organizing, has fought to halt this creeping "Mississippization" with living wage ordinances, increased school spending, and the closure of tax breaks for the rich. There have been some victories (mainly in funding education) but progressive politics fights uphill against two huge structural obstacles. First is the legacy of Proposition 13 itself, which requires supermajorities to raise most taxes. Second, and more daunting, is the glacial pace of the enfranchisement of new immigrants. Although Anglos are now a minority of the population, they still constitute 70 percent of the electorate. Even in 2040, according to the projections of the Public Policy Institute of California, whites (only 35 percent of the population) will still cast 53 percent of the votes. If current trends continue, this geriatric white minority will also consume a majority of public entitlements and tax resources.

The conservative worldview, of course, inverts these realities. Led by former governor Pete Wilson, Republicans argue that the state has become a dumping ground for shiftless and uncultured beggars from the South. Mexico, as depicted in a notorious Wilson campaign ad ("They're coming!"), is invading Anglo California and imposing huge burdens of taxes, crime, and pollution upon its honest burghers. The true wretched of the earth are long-suffering, overtaxed white guys in their golf carts.

Reason dies screaming in the face of such nonsense, but it is peddled twenty-four hours a day by the pit-bull talk-show hosts who dominate California AM radio and, increasingly, commercial television. White rage is also the steroid that Republican strategists hope will pump up Arnold Schwarzenegger for heavy lifting in the recall of Gray Davis. Liberal commentators have attacked the hulking muscle man and movie star for his singular lack of articulate positions on decisive issues. But the criticism is unfair.

The Terminator, in fact, has a long history of ideological commitments that, for tactical reasons, his campaign minders want to downplay. Most striking has been his extensive involvement in the nativist crusades to deny health care and education to undocumented immigrants, and to make English the exclusive official language. The poor boy from the Alpine boondocks, who admits that he worked illegally in his first years in America, was a key endorser of anti-immigrant Proposition 187 in 1994 and, even more sinisterly, a longtime board member of U.S. English, a national organization with notorious ties to men in white hoods.

But it would be a mistake, in any case, to think that Arnie is the actual star of his latest and most lavish film. As all the punters in Sacramento have pointed out, the real title should be: "Return from the Grave: Wilson Part Three." The ex-governor is the specter haunting the recall. His veteran staff (including George Gorton, who recently ran Boris Yeltsin's reelection) controls all the important strings moving Schwarzennegger's vital parts, while Wilson himself drives a sales campaign that has successfully recruited most of the billionaires in the state. As a result, the inner circle of Schwarzennegger's "populist" crusade looks like a Bohemia Grove toga party: Donald Bren, George Schultz, David Murdoch, Warren Buffett, and so on—down to huge contingents of land developers and SUV dealers. Wilson, of course, is anathema to Latinos, Blacks, and the labor movement. Supposedly California was done with his racist divisiveness when voters in 1998 rejected his protégé, Attorney General Dan Lungren, and then, last year, when they voted down another wealthy Wilson clone. So who forgot the silver stake?

Now that the rats are on dry ground, it has been easy for many Democrats to dismiss embattled incumbent Gray Davis as a singularly unfortunate choice: a charisma-less robot with an open palm who let the state be pillaged by Enron during the phony energy crisis three years ago. But again in fairness, Davis exemplifies precisely those qualities—pro-corporate, politically centrist, and hard law-and-order—which the Democratic Leadership Council has for so long recommended as the salvation of the Democratic Party. Nor is his disintegration unique: just look at the other "moderate" Democrats dead in the starting blocks of the presidential primary.

This is why the labor wing of the California Democrats should have embraced the opportunity of the recall to push forward one of their own. Davis has been generally detested by union activists. Yet the state federation of labor, and almost no one else, remained pathetically loyal to His Grayness and allowed his cunning and unprincipled lieutenant governor, Cruz Bustamante, to run off with the party endorsement.

Bustamante may be preferable to Pete Wilson hiding inside the Trojan horse called Schwarzenegger, but the difference is probably less than most Democratic voters imagine. Some years ago, Bustamante got into a pissing contest with (then governor) Wilson. They were talking about amending state law to allow the execution of minors. When Wilson suggest death sentences for criminals as young as fourteen, Bustamante responded that he might "with a tear in my eye, cast a vote to execute 'hardened criminals' as young as 13."

The major alternative to the child killers is California's Green Party. In last year's gubernatorial election, Green candidate Peter Camejo won 5 percent of the vote and emboldened thousands of progressives to envision life after the Democrats. Camejo, a veteran of Berkeley in the 60s, retains a fire in his belly, and chased around the state playing Michael Moore to Gray Davis's "Roger." He's one of the first Greens to make some impact in unions and among Latinos.

Unfortunately much of the media attention that otherwise might have accrued to the Greens has been hijacked by Arianna Huffington, running as an independent. A professional television guest and columnist, formerly married to one of the state's richest Republicans, she's undertaken an unusual journey in the desert of American politics: moving from the far right to the moderate left. Huffington, for example, has been an eloquent and effective critic of the Bush War on Terrorism. But unlike Camejo, selected by a poll of the Green membership, she is strictly freelancing with the aid of Hollywood money and her privileged access to media. Her populist credibility, moreover, has been diminished by the revelation that, although she owns a $7 million mansion, she has paid virtually no income tax in recent years.

The most likely effect of her candidacy, despite promises to coordinate with Camejo, will be to reduce rather than enhance the left-of-the-Democrats vote.

Regardless of the outcome in November, the recall battle has already clarified some of the new terrain of California politics. Republicans, on their side, have gained tremendous confidence in their ability to thwart any future legislative effort toward tax reform or economic justice. Liberal Democrats, on the other, have had their faces rubbed in the moral rot of their party. In Duroville, meanwhile, they look across their sewer lake at the fat life of a rapidly receding California dream.

(September 2003, *Socialist Review*)

EIGHTEEN

THINK BIG: RECALL THE SYSTEM

So where are the bold visions and radical dreams for which California was once world famous? If the political marketplace really works the way that neoliberal theorists have always claimed, then the recall against Gray Davis should be a movable feast of competing ideas. With 135 candidates screaming for our attention, we should be overwhelmed with diverse programs and substantive debate. Instead, the recall is almost as boring, and certainly as mean-spirited, as last year's regular election. So many candidates, yet so few genuinely new ideas; so little to inspire our millions of alienated nonvoters to make the trip to the registrar's office or the polling booth.

Political vacuity, indeed, has acquired a new gold standard with the Schwarzennegger campaign. Here is the would-be leader of 35 million people who is so intellectually fragile that his handlers refuse to let him go out and play with the other candidates. We wait for Pete Wilson to wean him. His conservative competitor, Paul McClintock, to be sure, has plenty of refreshingly outspoken opinions, but they principally date from the McKinley era. He's the ghost of Republicans past.

Lieutenant Governor Cruz Bustamante, the centrist Democrat contender, meanwhile has barbaric positions on the death penalty, an opportunist stance on farm labor, and appears to be a wholly owned subsidiary of the gaming industry. He would change the hairline of the Davis camp but leave intact its addiction/compulsion to permanent fundraising. On Bustamante's left flank is a professional charmer and tax avoider whose long-term commitment to any ideal other than · self-publicity has yet to be proven. Arianna Huffington has some enticing slogans ("schools not prisons"), but most labor Democrats are justifiably skeptical of populist pronouncements coming from a $7 million log cabin in Santa Monica.

Meanwhile the dozens of minor candidates, who should have been a wonderful carnival of cranky outside ideas, are instead largely a lonely hearts club. They are cruising for dates (or venture capital or fans for their latest porn film), not enriching our political universe with unorthodox thinking and underpublicized causes. Only the Green Party, in my opinion, presents elements of a truly alternative vision. Thousands of hours of grassroots debate have been invested in hammering out thoughtful positions on solar energy, old growth forests, livable wages, gay rights, health care, and education.

But the Green program tends to be a coalition of causes, not an integrated vision. The campaign of Peter Camejo, as a result, exudes sincerity but lacks a moral center, a crusading theme. Indeed the left in general has failed to define a priority as compelling as conservative visions of a parasitic public sector or an alien invasion. Yet the "issue of issues" screams at us from the sidelines of the election: the scandal of child poverty in California.

Surely the most fundamental moral measure of any social system is the status of its children and the quality of their childhoods. Yet an incredible 43 percent (4.36 million) California kids live near or below the federal poverty line. This is almost double the percentage in 1960 and well above the current national rate. California now ranks first in billionaires but thirty-seventh in a national survey of the quality of children's lives (American Community Survey). Hard-core child poverty is especially endemic in the San Joaquin Valley (36 percent in Fresno County; 40 percent in Tulare County) and in Los Angeles County (35 percent). These are Dickensian as much as Steinbeckian realities.

Contemporary poverty, moreover, defies conservative stereotypes of welfare mothers or indigent immigrants. Four-fifths of poor children live in working families. Their parents aren't deadbeats or parasites, but, for the most part, paragons of toil. They are the postmodern peons who constitute the backbone of California agriculture, construction, domestic service, tourism, and light manufacturing. If the economic textbooks were right, the phantasmagoric dot-com boom and wealth explosion of the late 1990s should have significantly lifted their boats and given their children new hope. It didn't. Instead hard-core child poverty increased by 430,000. The invisible hand, indeed, seems no more capable of alleviating working poverty in contemporary California than it was in ending mass unemployment during the Depression. Market forces alone only lock the gates around the low-wage prison.

The dictionary definition of "radical" is "to go to the root." A truly radical vision of the state's future, therefore, would recall the system that reproduces and perpetuates this chronic poverty . It would guarantee poor children equal and substantive participation in a renewed Californian dream. It would promise to rebuild a once glorious but now failed public education system that now fails to graduate more than 40 percent of Black and Latino kids from high school. Here, then, is a real crusade to rally Greens and the labor wing of the Democratic Party. End the poverty that clouds our common future and threatens our future prosperity. Make children's rights, not corporate privileges and luxury lifestyles, the polestar of Sacramento.

Does this have an oddly familiar ring? Once upon a time, we had visionaries (to paraphrase our state motto) "big enough to match our mountains." One of them was the muckracking writer and popular novelist Upton Sinclair. Seventy years ago he launched End Poverty in California (EPIC). Uppie told voters that mass poverty in a land as rich as California was an unconscionable sin. He proposed to take the unemployed off county relief and put them back to work producing their own subsistence using idled means of production and raw materials. In August 1934 he detonated a political earthquake by sweeping the Democratic primary with a million crossover votes from Southern California Republicans.

Modern California politics was born in the ensuing gubernatorial battle between Sinclair and Hoover Republican Frank Merriam. A utopian political movement, with enormous grassroots passion, squared off against the state's largest corporations and landowners. Big business said EPIC was a Trojan horse for the confiscation of wealth and Soviet-style communism. Sinclair replied that is was merely the political application of the Sermon on the Mount.

The world's pioneer political consultants, Clem Whitaker and Leone Baxter, organized the smear campaign against Sinclair and EPIC. They recruited Hollywood moguls like Louis B. Mayer to fabricate phony newsreels of a "bum invasion" of California and used the Republican-controlled press, especially the *Los Angeles Times*, to print false stories about the puritanical Sinclair as the seducer of girls. In the end, Whitaker and Baxter defeated Sinclair. But EPIC was hardly a dead end. The moral energy that it generated continued to galvanize progressive politics in California for more than two decades.

On the other side, Whitaker and Baxter became the Barnum and Bailey of the modern California political circus. The reign of political consultants and politics-as-public-relations began in 1934 and has never stopped. Its major tendency has been to drive idealism, programmatic principle, and radical thinking out of electoral politics. Whitaker and Baxter even codified for insiders the cynical principles upon which the political media age was founded. "The average American doesn't want to be educated; he doesn't want to improve his mind... [he] likes to be entertained. He likes the movies.... So if you can't fight, PUT ON A SHOW!" And so, the show goes on and on. (And what could be more entertaining than one millionaire candidate after another promising to drive the money changers out of the temple.) The current recall election is an epitome of this system, not its nemesis.

Yet the embers of EPIC and other lost crusades have survived to kindle a few political imaginations. Recently, state senators Richard Alarcon and Gloria Romero created a Senate Select Committee on Ending Poverty in California in direct homage to Sinclair. The young

Democrats from the Latino neighborhoods of Los Angeles have made the committee into a bully pulpit to advocate a new statewide war on poverty. Yet few leading Democrats or Greens have paid attention to their extraordinary hearings or responded to the concept of a new EPIC movement built around the needs of California's working poor. The Democratic centrists (Nixonian Republicans in substance) prefer to stick with law and order, while too many Greens—marooned in self-righteous lifestyles and unable to prioritize their struggles—lack a strategic understanding of working-class issues.

California is ripe for burning, yet only the right wing seems to know how to start fires. Alarcon and Romero, whatever their flaws on other issues, genuinely seem to understand this, and by evoking the precedent of EPIC, they have highlighted their own party's lack of fundamental moral passion. Pity the state that has lost its utopias and buried all its prophets.

(September 2003, *San Francisco Chronicle*)

NINETEEN

THE DAY OF THE LOCUST

The mobs howled again in California, rattling windows on the Potomac. Are the hordes marching eastward, as they did after the famous tax revolt of the late 1970s, or is this just another West Coast full-moon episode with little national consequence? The larger meaning of Schwarzenegger's triumph of the will, of course, depends on how you interpret the grievances that provided the recall's extraordinary emotional fuel. But I must warn you that analyzing this election is an adventure in a realm of stupefying paradox and contradiction. All the same, it may tell us a great deal about the emerging landscape of American politics.

The hard-core ideologues of zero government and McKinley-era capitalism are trumpeting the recall of Democratic governor Gray Davis as a new populist revolution in the spirit of Howard Jarvis's Proposition 13 in 1978. They echo local Republican claims that a venal Democrat in league with big unions and the welfare classes was turning off the lights of free enterprise and driving the hardworking middle classes to Arizona with huge, unfair tax increases. Davis, in a word, was the Antichrist, wrecking California's golden dream on behalf of his selfish constituencies of schoolteachers, illegal immigrants, and casino-rich Indians. The Terminator, they assure us, has literally saved California from the yawning abyss of "tax, tax, tax; spend, spend, spend."

From the outside, this seems rather ridiculous. Davis, to begin with, is an autistic centrist in the Democratic Leadership Council mode who has governed California for the last five years as a good Republican. In fiscal policy, as well as in prisons, education, and the lubrication of corporate interests, there has been no significant departure from the paradigm of his predecessor (and Schwarzenegger guru), Republican Pete Wilson. Indeed, Davis has been such a raving executioner and fanatic prison-builder that crime and punishment has all but disappeared as a Republican wedge issue. Californians' onerous tax burden, meanwhile, is simply a Republican lie, endlessly repeated: the state actually ranks behind GOP utopia, Arizona, and even skinflint Utah in combined state and local taxes per capita.

Moreover, if California's middle classes have any cause to feel raped and pillaged in recent years, clearly the culprits are Arnold's éminence grise, Pete Wilson, who deregulated the utilities and the Bushite power cartels like Enron who looted California's consumers during the phony energy crisis of 2000–01. And it is the Bush administration that has told bankrupt state and municipal governments everywhere to "drop dead" while it shovels billions into the black hole it has created in Iraq. The fiscal crisis, in other words, should be an issue owned by the Democrats.

Strange, then, that almost two-thirds of the voters in the megastate that supposedly belongs lock, stock, and barrel to the Democrats either endorsed the stealth return of Pete Wilson—the mind whirring within Arnie's brawn—or voted for a right-wing quack, Tom McClintock. These are the kinds of election returns you expect to see from GOP bedrock states like Idaho or Wyoming, not from the vaunted Left Coast. When you peer at the dynamics of recall rage up close, moreover, the whole phenomenon becomes stranger still.

Here in San Diego, where I live and where the recall originated, the Schwarzenegger blitzkrieg seemed to suck anger out of the clear blue sky. This, after all, isn't Youngstown or even Stockton or San Bernardino. Republican voters, as far as I know, are not being evicted en masse from their McMansions or forced to steal milk for their starving babies. Far from it, the value of the median family home soared almost $100,000 last year and the area is once again awash with Pentagon dollars. The freeways are clogged with Hummers and other mega-SUVs, while those with luxury lifestyles, carefully tended by armies of brown-skinned laborers, bask in the afterglow of Bush's tax cuts.

Enlistment in Arnie's army of "hell no, we're not going to take it anymore" tax protesters bore little demonstrable relationship to actual economic pain. Indeed exit polls show that, in San Diego as well as statewide, support for Schwarzenegger increased with income and topped out at the country-club and gated-community level. Yet, for weeks, suburban San Diego has been contorted into visceral, self-righteous rage over the supposedly satanic regime in Sacramento.

So are California's fat cats merely impersonating populist anger? With so little correlation between actual economic hardship (greatest, of course, in pro-Democrat Latino and Black inner-city neighborhoods and rural valleys), what explains this astonishing mobilization of voter emotion, particularly in affluent white suburbs? In my microcosm, part of the answer could be found at the lower end of the AM dial. At KOGO 600, "San Diego's Radio Mayor," Roger Hedgecock, presides over what, even before the official campaign began, was boastfully labeling itself "Recall Radio." A former mayor convicted of conspiracy and perjury in the 1980s, Hedgecock, who occasionally fills in for Rush Limbaugh on national hate radio, takes credit for the "heavy lifting" that put Arnold Schwarzenegger in the governor's mansion in Sacramento. Republicans acknowledge that he has been the recall's most influential voice in Southern California.

From 3:00 to 6:00 p.m., "Roger," as he is universally called by his more than three hundred thousand regular listeners, rules over afternoon freeway gridlock in a vast radio market that extends as far north as Santa Barbara. Southern California, of course, has the worst traffic congestion in the country and the ever lengthening commutes are a continuous, grinding source of free-floating anger. Hedgecock deftly plays off this afternoon, stuck-in-traffic frustration. He is the angry tribune of white guys in their 4x4 Dodge pickups and Ford Expeditions.

For almost two decades, his major obsession has been the Brown Peril, the supposed "Mexican invasion" of California. He was a key instigator of anti-immigrant Proposition 187 in 1994 as well as local semi-vigilante protests against border-crossers. On the eve of the recall, he continually warned his listeners that the Mexican threat was now of apocalyptic proportions, given Gray Davis's signing of a bill to allow undocumented immigrants to obtain driver's licenses.

"This is the end of American democracy, the end of fair elections," he fulminated. "Vast numbers of operatives," he warned, were enlisting newly ID'd immigrants to cast hundreds of thousands of illegal ballots to keep Davis in power. San Diego, moreover, was facing an "invasion" of trade unionists from alien Los Angeles who would "tear down pro-recall signs" and generally terrorize neighborhoods. Roger urged locals to defend their homes and resist the hoards of illegals and L.A. labor thugs "in the spirit of 1776."

In several weeks of listening to Roger's screeds, punctuated by hallelujahs and amens from the choir on their cellular phones, the only issue that came remotely close to the same decibel level as illegal immigration was a hike in the registration tax on cars. Hedgecock ignored the fact that the automatic escalation of the car tax (2 percent of its value) had originated in Wilson-era legislation. Instead, he linked it squarely (and absurdly) to illegal immigrants "whose cost to the state of California is almost exactly the budget deficit." "That's how bad things are, ladies and gentlemen," he intoned constantly. Car taxes and wetbacks were his incessant rave.

The mainstream media has done a poor job of documenting the organization of the recall at the grassroots level where AM voices like Roger's, or his counterparts Bill Handel's in Los Angeles and Eric Hogue's in Sacramento, roused thousands of mini-Terminators. As a result, there has been an overly respectful legitimation of "economic populism" in the recall dynamic and only a faint registration of the central role of traditional racist demagoguery and the revival of the Brown Peril rhetoric. To adapt a rap phrase, "It's all about fear of a brown planet."

Yet, I don't want to suggest that this is a simple repeat of Pete Wilson's anti-immigrant Proposition 187 in the context of a recession and a nationwide crisis of state financing. Arnold Schwarzenegger does add something genuinely novel to the mix. He is not just another actor in politics but an extraordinary lightning rod, both in his movie persona and in real life, for dark, sexualized fantasies about omnipotence.

Pleasure in the humiliation of others—Schwarzenegger's lifelong compulsion—is the textbook definition of sadism. It is also the daily ration of right-wing hate radio. As governor he becomes the summation of all smaller sadisms, like those of Roger Hedgecock, that in turn manipulate the "reptile within" of millions of outwardly affluent but inwardly tormented commuter-consumers. In their majesty, the predominantly white voters of California's inland empires and gated suburbs have anointed a clinically Hitlerite personality as their personal savior.

The last word about all this should, of course, belong to Nathanael West. In his classic novel *The Day of the Locust* (1939), he clearly foresaw that fandom was an incipient version of fascism. On the edge of Hollywood's neon plains, he envisioned the unassuageable hungers of California's petty bourgeoisie. "They were savage and bitter, especially the middle-aged and the old…. Their boredom becomes more and more terrible. They realize they've been tricked and burn with resentment…. Nothing can ever be violent enough to make taut their slack minds and bodies."

(October 2003, *Sacramento Bee*)

TWENTY

STRIKING SOUTHERN CALIFORNIA

The most common sight in Southern California these days isn't a movie shoot or a beach party. It is a militant picket line. From Malibu to the Mexican border, seventy thousand supermarket workers—two-thirds of them women—have been on strike or locked out since October 11. More than 850 individual stores are involved. It is the biggest private-sector union dispute on the West Coast since the Hollywood general strike of 1946. Moreover, no strike in modern history—even recent shutdowns of bus transport and schools—has so comprehensively affected the general public. Almost everyone of the region's 20 million residents has had to wrestle with the personal moral decision of whether or not to cross a picket line.

The issues are stark. The strikers, represented by the United Food and Commercial Workers (UFCW) union, are resisting a brutal attempt by California's three largest supermarket chains to dismantle their contractual health benefits and roll back the wages of new hires. The terrain is local but the issues—above all, health care—are national. As labor historian Nelson Lichtenstein told the *Los Angeles Times:* "The national labor movement certainly sees this as a decisive event which will set the course for social policy in the U.S. for many years to come."

The United States, of course, is exceptional among rich industrialized nations for the absence of any universal entitlement to health care. Union membership, rather than citizenship, has traditionally provided access to subsidized medical treatment. But with union density shrunken to under 9 percent of the private-sector labor force, and with medical costs skyrocketing, a huge and growing share of most family budgets must be diverted to the purchase of HMO membership. A large minority of working families, however, cannot afford to join a private HMO and must turn to public hospitals instead.

Los Angeles County, the nation's sweatshop capital, is a shocking case in point. An incredible 4 million residents are uninsured and lack the most elementary medical or dental care. In life-threatening situations, they crowd the emergency rooms of an underfunded and collapsing county hospital system. Angry physicians have recently testified that patients are routinely dying for lack of attention or access to proper medical technology.

The retail sector, meanwhile, is the "third world" of the U.S. economy and contains the highest percentages of low-wage, contingent, and uninsured workers. Unionized supermarket workers are the dramatic exception and their wage-benefit package has been a powerful beacon to the unorganized. This is not to say that UFCW members are fat cats or aristocrats of labor. Most struggle to get by on average wages of $12 to $14 an hour. But their comprehensive benefits provide a family health security that most non-union workers can only dream about.

However, the major current trend in U.S. industrial relations is for large corporations to jettison their health care obligations. Their model is that modern colossus of greed and super-exploitation: Wal-Mart. Indeed the supermarkets' public explanation for demanding givebacks from UFCW is Wal-Mart's imminent invasion of California. The non-union retail giant, one union official explains, is "the third party now that comes to every bargaining situation." The three grocery chains claim that without major concessions from the union they will be unable to compete with the forty new "Supercenters" that Wal-Mart is planning to open in 2004–05. They point out that Wal-Mart employees often earn half the wage of unionized workers and must pay the greater share of their own health coverage (a reason why a majority don't have any).(92)

Wal-Mart, of course, has replaced General Motors as the world's largest corporation. The Bentonville, Arkansas–based chain has made the Walton clan the richest family in America (current net worth in excess of $100 billion) by combining "just in time" technology with the most savage features of Victorian capitalism and colonialism. Notorious for paying poverty wages and cheating overtime from its one million American employees, Wal-Mart is even more sinister overseas where it ceaselessly pressures its thousands of suppliers in Bangladesh, China, and Central America to reduce labor costs and abrogate workers' rights. Indeed it is the biggest indirect employer of sweated and child labor on earth. "Wal-Martization," therefore, has become synonymous with the race to the bottom, the total gutting of historic worker rights and social citizenship. It also the most convenient excuse for other retail corporations, like the supermarket chains, to launch preemptive offensives against their employees.

These issues are well understood by all unions and the UFCW has garnered impressive solidarity from teachers, machinists, janitors and hospital workers. On one occasion three thousand longshoremen marched from the Los Angeles docks to demonstrate at a nearby market. And, in a dramatic break with its usually selfish traditions, the powerful Teamsters' Union recently refused to haul food and produce from market distribution centers. The most remarkable and unexpected development, however, has been the sustained solidarity of the general public. Hundreds of thousands, if not millions, of Southern Californians have changed their shopping habits, often commuting long distances, to avoid crossing picket lines. There is an invigorating whiff of the 1930s in the air.

Yet, despite a huge drop in holiday sales and profits, the three supermarket chains, united in an illegal "mutual aid" pact, have refused to withdraw their principal demand for a cap on health-care contributions. They're fighting a war to the finish. Thus the strike will most likely grind on through the new year. It may be odd to think of a labor dispute in sunny California as a watershed for American trade unionism, but everyone is grimly aware that the UFCW must win this strike at all costs if it is ever to have a chance of organizing Wal-Mart's sweatshop empire.

(December 2003, *Socialist Review*)

Despite terrific public support and the dogged endurance of its rank and file, the badly misled UFCW threw in the towel after nineteen weeks and conceded virtually all of the employers' demands at the beginning of March 2004. Although candidate John Kerry made a brief appearance on the picket line during the last week of the strike, little of the vast muscle of the Democratic Party in Los Angeles or so-called Hollywood liberalism was mobilized on behalf of the embattled supermarket workers. Likewise the UFCW refused to extend the strike to Chicago and other cities where contracts had also expired: sending the disastrous message to grocery giants that they could easily pick off the union one city or region at a time. As a result of the UFCW's surrender, the wages and health benefits of new hires will be dramatically cut, paving the way for the chains to compete with Wal-Mart by pauperizing their employees. The "middle class" in Los Angeles will ultimately be smaller as a result.

TWENTY-ONE

MEL'S NAZI MATINEE

The most evil film ever made was probably *Jud Süss*, commissioned by Nazi propaganda minister Joseph Goebbels in 1940 to fan hatred of the Jews on the eve of the Final Solution. A thousand years of European anti-Semitism were condensed in the image of the cowering rapist Süss, with his dirty beard, hook nose, and whining voice. The audience was instigated to rejoice in the lynching of this subhuman monster at the film's end.

To anyone who has ever seen *Jud Süss* (as I did in college), the most startling thing about Mel Gibson's *The Passion of the Christ*—even more than its perversely eroticized cruelty—is its extraordinary fidelity to the anti-Semitic conventions of Hitlerian cinema. Indeed, the high priest Caiaphas and his colleagues are such exact, blatant replicas of Süss that I suspect they must be direct borrowings. (Gibson's penchant for a fascist aesthetic had been earlier noted by the writer Jonathan Foreman, who claimed in the *Guardian* in July 2000 that "if the Nazis had won the war in Europe, and their propaganda ministry had decided to make a film about the American revolution, *The Patriot* is the sort of movie you could expect to see.")(55)

Moreover, *Passion* is one of the most manipulative films ever made and, after two hours watching Jewish mobs howling in delight at Christ's suffering, it is no wonder that many devout American viewers, like their German predecessors, have left theaters muttering, "I hate the Jews." The Romans, on the other hand, are shown as noble imperialists. In contrast to the vile Caiaphas, Pontius Pilate is depicted by Gibson as a sympathetic, even saintly figure, tragically trapped between orders from Rome (no more uprisings) and the implacable machinations of the high priests.

As in *Süss*, moreover, there is a relentless contrast of somatic stereotypes: Mediterranean types—the two Marys, Pilate and his wife, and so on—are rendered with softened features and sensitive spirits, while the Semites—Caiaphas, sybaritic King Herod, and so on—are depicted as coarse and repulsively sensual. (In a contemporary American context, such heavy-handed visual anti-Semitism, of course, instantly summons up anti-Arab connotations as well.)

Gibson's insistence on using original languages—Aramaic and Latin—has impressed naive viewers that *Passion* represents some new benchmark in historical accuracy. In fact, history (the little actually recorded of these events, apart from the posthumous theology of the gospels) is bizarrely inverted. Jesus, of course, is an utterly enigmatic figure. The only "facts" in his life—as attested by both Roman and Jewish historians—is that he existed and was executed by the Romans. Pilate, on the other hand, has left a slightly larger record. Unlike Gibson's kindly fiction, the historical Pilate was an ordinary imperial procurator in a third-class province who kept his legions busy with brutal executions of Jewish and Samaritan rebels. Palestine, then as today, lived under an iron heel, and the *Passion*'s confusion of oppressor and oppressed is morally obnoxious.

Some American critics, however, have tried to defend *Passion* by pointing out that Gibson's real bête noire is the Vatican, not the Jews. Indeed Gibson explicitly made the film to promote the religious vision of the rabid Catholic traditionalist splinter group in which he grew up. (*Passion*'s tormented Jesus, Seattle actor James Caviezel, is also a fundamentalist Catholic who regularly stuns interviewers with his accounts of personal visitations from the Virgin.) But the "tradition" that he so zealously defends (and which he inherited from his Holocaust-denying father) is precisely the anti-Semitic Catholic fascism of former Spanish dictator General Francisco Franco and Pope Pius XII. And, like Franco ideologues and their Croatian fascist counterparts of that era, Gibson has the same morbid, vengeful obsession with pain, mutilation, bodily corruption, and the ever-present temptations of Satan (who constantly prowls the perimeter of his film).

In short, *Passion* is the medieval vision of a pogromist, amplified by Hollywood special effects and the cachet of celebrity. It is protected by a formidable wall of enthusiastic endorsements from the American religious right (including some conservative Jews like Rabbi Daniel Lapin, Michael Medved, and David Horowitz) as well as by the tolerance of ordinary Gibson fans who just can't believe that their goofy, handsome hero is really such a grotesque reactionary.

(February 2004, *Tomdispatch.com*)

All the king's publicists and all the king's talent agents will not likely put Mel Gibson back together again. Since he snarled "fucking Jews" at a Jewish deputy during his drunk-driving arrest in Malibu in August 2006, it has become easier to defend the flatness of the Earth or the existence of the Easter Bunny than to exculpate the actor from his bigotry. In light of Gibson's rabid assertion that "the Jews are responsible for all the wars in the world," it is interesting to revisit the self-righteous claims by his conservative Jewish allies that poor Mel was unfairly "crucified" by liberal critics of Passion *(so said Michael Medved in* American Enterprise *magazine, January 2004). In truth, these Likud supporters have revealed that they are prepared to go to almost any length, including contorted apologies for blatant anti-Semitism, in order to appease Israel's allies on the Christian Right. It is sobering to think that until very recently, this same alliance of forces was promoting Gibson as a potential Republican candidate for high office. But then again, Californians already have one former, self-avowed admirer of Adolf Hitler, Arnold Schwarzenegger, as their governor.*

TWENTY-TWO

INSIDE THE SUNSHINE GULAG

Khem Singh was little more than a shriveled skeleton when he died of starvation in early February (2004) while on hunger strike in California's notorious Corcoran State Prison. The 72-year-old Sikh priest, who spoke almost no English, had been given a draconian 23-year sentence in 2001 for "inappropriately touching a young girl." Although he had been on hunger strike for weeks, and had shrunken to less than eighty pounds, prison staff failed to monitor Singh's decline or move him into intensive care. Guards told a reporter that they "didn't notice that the prisoner was wasting away."

It was the second such grisly "surprise" in a two-week period at Corcoran—a sprawling, notorious penal complex in the heart of California's Central Valley. On February 1, another inmate, hooked up to a faulty kidney dialysis machine, was allowed to slowly bleed to death in his cell. Although other prisoners testified that fifty-eight-year-old Ronald Herrera howled for help all night long, nearby guards, engrossed in television, refused to respond. In the morning, a new guard shift noticed a large pool of what appeared to be "raspberry Kool-Aid" seeping from Herrera's cell. Inside, his corpse was slumped on the floor, grotesquely pallid and drained of blood.

The deaths of Singh and Herrera, coming on the heels of the mysterious hanging of two teenage inmates a month earlier at another institution, have provided a bizarre backdrop to an unprecedented legislative investigation of inhuman conditions within California prisons. The ongoing hearings, chaired by state Senator Gloria Romero—a progressive Democrat from Los Angeles—have produced sensational testimony about corruption, conspiracy, and murder by guards and administrators in a corrections system that incarcerates more inmates (170,000) than the prisons of the United Kingdom and West Germany combined.

The hearings are the result of a long campaign by human-rights activists that began in the mid-1990s after revelations that guards at Corcoran—organized into a gang called the "Sharks"—were staging deadly gladiatorial combats between inmates for "amusement and blood sport." Inmates from opposing prison gangs were routinely set against each other in a closed exercise yard, and then, if they failed to kill each other, sometimes deliberately executed by guards firing rifles from overlooking towers.

Indeed guards throughout the California system killed thirty-nine inmates fighting with other inmates during the 1990s: a higher total than all the rest of America's prisons combined. According to testimony to the California Senate, guards and administrators covered up these atrocities with an institutional code of silence. Perjury has been alleged against guards at Pelican Bay prison—the infamous "supermax" institution on the Redwood Coast—who reputedly organized inmates to attack, even murder other inmates; as well as in the case of the "Green Wall," a gang of guards at Salinas Valley State Prison, who tortured and beat scores of prisoners. Likewise, the administration at Folsom Prison is accused of covering up a bloody riot (twenty-four inmates seriously injured) that appears to have been deliberately engineered by guards.

Why has it taken a decade for the Legislature to investigate a prison system run by gangs of sadistic guards who routinely abuse and murder inmates? California's gulag annually devours $7 billion of state revenue in order to generate inhumanity on a scale normally associated only with the most evil, totalitarian societies. In truth, state government in Sacramento has been massively corrupted by the powerful lobbyists for prison guards and contractors. Defrocked governor Gray Davis (a Democrat), for example, received $3.4 million in campaign contributions from the guards' union alone. In return, Sacramento built a dozen new prisons and raised guards' salaries (currently $74,000 per year) to twice the level of the next highest-paying state.

Now a special investigator appointed by a federal judge is urging the prosecution of ex-prison chief Edward Almeida—long the darling of both Democrats and Republicans—and his chief deputy. The Senate commission is also likely to recommend a purge of lying wardens and rogue guards. California's new muscle governor, Arnold Schwarzenegger, has likewise sworn to tame the arrogance of the prison guards' lobby. The recipient of handsome campaign donations from giant rent-a-cop (and break-a-strike) corporations like Florida-based Wackenhut, he has indicated an interest in privatizing parts of the sunshine gulag. Incarceration is a high-profit international industry and California is a potential convict mother lode for private corrections firms.

From inmates' point of view, of course, it matters little whether their guards are public employees or private mercenaries. Equally, the punishment of a handful of lying wardens—however richly deserved—will do nothing to reform the grim daily life in California's overcrowded and hyperviolent prisons. The root problem remains a bipartisan political consensus in favor of ruthless "three-strikes" laws, a catastrophic "war on drugs," and long sentences without the slightest opportunity for inmate education or job training. California, moreover, remains the only state that routinely segregates prisoners by race and tolerates virtually incessant interethnic and racial warfare within its county jails and prisons. Until the racial bias and class basis of super-incarceration are attacked head-on, California's prisons will remain graveyards of human rights.

(March 2004, *Socialist Review*)

Two-and-a-half years later, 172,000 prisoners were sleeping in triple-decker bunks or in cots in hallways and mess halls in thirty-three state prisons. California comfortably retains its national leadership in worst prison overcrowding, highest rate of inmate recidivism, and most prison violence. The only good news, thanks to their powerful union, is that six thousand prison guards now report annual earnings of more than $100,000 per year (one lieutenant made $252,000 in 2005 with over-time)—making them the highest paid corrections officers in the world.

In October 2006 Schwarzenegger declared a "state of emergency" in order to claim authority to transfer ten thousand or more prisoners out of state without their consent. Although under severe pressure from federal courts, the governor is less concerned with the inhuman conditions than with rewarding the private corrections corporations who run most of the designated recipient prisons in Arizona, Oklahoma, and Tennessee. He previously reopened two privately run low-security prisons in California that the guards' union had long opposed, but his best opportunity to reward the private prison sector (like SUV dealers, major Arnie campaign donors) is to ship—or rather, sell—them out of state.

The return of ex-governor (and more recently, mayor of Oakland) Jerry Brown to Sacramento as attorney general is unlikely to moderate any of the savagery of what passes for justice and corrections in California. Indeed it was Governor Brown in 1979 (at a time when the prison population was only 21,000) who abandoned inmate rehabilitation as a social goal and adopted tougher sentencing. Indeed Jerry and Arnie will likely make a swell team: two utterly incoherent but vast ambitions joined together in a self-serving duet of cruelty.

TWENTY-THREE

RIOTOUS REAL ESTATE

Last February the sirens howled in Hollywood as the LAPD rushed reinforcements to the 5600 block of La Mirada Avenue. While a police captain barked orders through a bullhorn, an angry crowd of three thousand people shouted back expletives. A passerby might have mistaken the confrontation for a major movie shoot, or perhaps the beginning of the next great L.A. riot. In fact, as LAPD Captain Michael Downing later told the press: "You had some very desperate people who had a mob mentality. It was as if people were trying to get the last piece of bread."

The bread-riot allusion was apt, although the crowd was in fact clamoring for the last crumbs of affordable housing in a city where rents and mortgages have been soaring through the stratosphere. At stake were fifty-six unfinished apartments being built by a nonprofit agency. The developers had expected a turnout of, at most, several hundred. When thousands of desperate applicants showed up instead, the scene quickly turned ugly and the police intervened.

A few weekends after this tense confrontation in Hollywood, another anxious mob—this time composed of more affluent home-seekers—queued up for hours for an opportunity to make outrageous bids on a single, run-down house with a cracked foundation in a nearby suburb renowned for its good schools. "The teeming crowd," wrote *Los Angeles Times* columnist Steve Lopez, "was no surprise given the latest evidence that California's public schools are dropout factories."

Los Angeles' underfunded, overcrowded, and violent schools, according to a recent report by Harvard researchers, currently fail to graduate the majority of their Black and Latino students, as well as one-third of whites.(32) Another study, by UCLA researchers, found a cluster of public high schools where failure rates were literally catastrophic: "less than one-third of ninth-graders graduated on time."(70) Parents, as a result, are willing to make extraordinary sacrifices to move their children to suburbs with functioning public education. This gives the old adage that "location is everything" in real estate a new twist: Housing in Southern California is universally advertised and graded by the prestige of local school districts.

The Southern California housing crisis, of course, has a sunnier side as well. In the last five years median home values have increased 118 percent in Los Angeles and an extraordinary 137 percent in neighboring San Diego. According to a 2005 report by the California Building Industry Association, California homeowners as a whole have reaped a *$1 trillion* increase in equity since 2000; with a median equity gain to the owners of single-family homes of an astonishing $230,386.(110) (The prestigious UCLA Anderson [Business School] Forecast in March 2005 made the even more dramatic claim of a *$1.7 trillion* increase: "the equivalent of about 35 percent of the total personal income in the state since 2001.") The family ranch, as a result, has become a private ATM machine, providing owners with magical, unearned cash flows for purchasing new sports utility vehicles, making down payments on vacation homes, and financing increasingly expensive college educations for their kids.

The great American housing bubble, like its obese counterparts in the UK, Ireland, the Netherlands, Spain, and Australia, is a classical zero-sum game. Without generating an atom of new wealth, land inflation ruthlessly redistributes wealth from asset-seekers to asset-holders, reinforcing divisions within as well as between social classes. A young schoolteacher in San Diego who rents an apartment, for example, now faces an annual housing cost ($24,000 for a two-bedroom in a central area) equivalent to two-thirds of her income. Conversely, an older school bus driver who owns a modest home in the same neighborhood may have "earned" almost as much from housing inflation as from his unionized job.

The current housing bubble is the bastard offspring of the stockmarket bubble of the mid-1990s. Housing prices, especially on the West Coast and in the East's Bos-Wash corridor, began to rocket in the second half of 1995 as dot-com profits were ploughed into real estate. The boom has been sustained by sensationally low mortgage rates, thanks principally to the willingness of China to buy vast amounts of U.S. Treasury bonds despite their low or negative yields. Beijing has been willing to subsidize American mortgage borrowers as the price for keeping the door open to Chinese exports.

Similarly, the hottest home markets—Southern California, Las Vegas, New York, Miami, and Washington, D.C.—have attracted voracious ant columns of pure speculators, buying and selling homes in the gamble that prices will continue to rise. The most successful speculator, of course, has been George W. Bush. Rising home values have propped up a stagnant economy and blunted criticisms of otherwise disastrous economic policies. According to surveys by the Wharton Business School, second mortgages and home refinancings have generated several trillion dollars in additional consumer spending since Bush stole the 2000 election. Accordingly, if "values" were the basis for Bush's reelection in November 2004, they were property values not moral principles or religious prejudices.

The Democrats for their part have failed to address seriously the crisis of millions of families now locked out of homeownership. In California, for example, incomes lag so far behind land inflation and housing costs that in the last decade the California population has increased by nearly 10 million yet only one million new homes have been built and sold. Statewide, the proportion of Californians able to finance mortgages on entry-level homes fell from 44 percent in 2003 to 24 percent two years later. In bubble cities like San Diego, Santa

Ana, and San Jose less than 15 percent earn enough to participate in the housing market without exceptional sacrifice. In these areas of superinflated equity, moreover, low-income families are increasingly forced to share single-family homes or seek shelter in illegal garage conversions—a growing plague in many parts of Los Angeles County.

In the face of these perverse trends, the Kerry campaign, as with health-care costs and the export of jobs, was simply running on empty. It offered no compelling alternative to the status quo. But the Republicans have more serious things to worry about than Democrats. As the real-estate bubble reaches its peak, George Bush may discover that he has been surfing a tsunami and that a towering cliff looms ahead.

What will life be like in California or other bubble states after the home-equity ATM shuts down? In California's case, *where an astonishing 2 percent of working-age adults in the state are licensed agents or brokers*, the reliance on the real-estate industry is now as great as the former addiction to dot-com stocks and capital gains taxes. Half of the jobs (approximately 250,000) created in California over the last few years are real-estate dependent and thus subject to extinction if the bubble bursts or even deflates. "Even a simple slowdown in the accumulation of equity in the state," a spokesman for the Anderson Forecast told the *Los Angeles Times*, "could harshly depress spending habits, job creation, and economic expansion."

The national economy may be equally vulnerable to property deflation, with a mild jolt sufficient to end the current American boom, and perhaps throw all the dollar-pegged economies into recession. Several eminent Wall Street economists, like Stephen Roach of Morgan Stanley, have long warned of the dangerous negative-feedback loop between the foreign-subsidized housing bubble and the huge U.S. trade and budget deficits. "The funding of America," he has written, "is an accident waiting to happen."

At the end of the day, American military hegemony is no longer underwritten by an equivalent global economic supremacy (as in the

1950s and 1960s), and the housing bubble, like the dot-com boom before it, has temporarily masked a mess of economic contradictions. If land inflation slows down or reverses itself in bubble states like California, the second term of George W. Bush may hold some first-class Shakespearean surprises.

(April 19, 2005, *Los Angeles Times*)

The true damage that land inflation has inflicted on California was revealed in December 2006 in a study by the State Department of Finance and the Public Policy Institute of California. Despite reasonably healthy growth in employment, the state was suffering the first net population flight since the recession and riots in the early 1990s. The larger part of the exodus (441,000 from 2000 to 2005) continued to be relatively affluent Anglos, cashing in their equities for trophy homes in Utah, beach pads in Hawaii, and retirement condos in Baja California. But researchers also found that working-class Latinos were being pushed out of California by unaffordable housing: 320,000 more leaving than arriving from other states. Even as home prices begin to fall in the most science-fiction-like markets (Beverly Hills and Malibu, for example), it will offer scant relief to low-income renters, particularly in inner-city neighborhoods beginning to undergo rapid gentrification in Los Angeles, San Diego, and San Jose. The expected recession in the sales of trophy properties, moreover, will have an exaggerated impact on state revenues, which are unduly dependent upon capital gains taxes, and thus upon social services and education. As California's "Karl Marx," the political economist and social prophet Henry George, foresaw more than 125 years ago, the future of democracy and equality in the state depends upon the social control of land inflation.

TWENTY-FOUR

THE GREAT WALL OF CAPITAL

When delirious crowds tore down the Berlin Wall in 1989 many hallu-
cinated that a millennium of borderless freedom was at hand. The
people themselves had abolished a dark age of electrified death-
fences, frontiers strewn with antipersonnel mines, and cities guillotined by walls. Globalization was supposed to inaugurate an era of
unprecedented physical and virtual-electronic mobility.

Instead neoliberal capitalism has stimulated the greatest wave of wall
building and border fortification in history. The physical reality looks
more like the late-Roman or Sung Empires than the Victorian Liberal
golden age of Cobden and Gladstone. This Great Wall of Capital, which
separates a few dozen rich countries from the Earth's poor majority,
completely dwarfs the old Iron Curtain. This is not just a figurative addition of national borders but, increasingly, a single interlocking system
of fortification, surveillance, armed patrol, and incarceration.

It girds half the Earth, cordons off at least twelve thousand kilometers of terrestrial borderline, and is comparably more deadly to desperate trespassers. Unlike China's Great Wall, the new wall is only
partially visible from space. Although it includes traditional ramparts
(the Mexican border of the United States) and barbed wire fenced
minefields (between Greece and Turkey), much of globalized immigration enforcement today takes place at sea or in the air, and borders
are now digital as well as geographical.

Take, for example, Fortress Europe, where an integrated data system (upgrading the Strasbourg-based Schengen network) with the sinister acronym of PROSECUR will become the foundation for a common system of border patrol, enforced by the newly authorized European Border Guards Corps. The EU has already spent hundreds of millions of euros beefing up the so-called Electronic Curtain along its expanded eastern borders and fine-tuned the Surveillance System for the Straits that is supposed to keep Africa on its side of Gibraltar. Tony Blair, moreover, recently asked his fellow EU leaders to extend white Europe's border defenses into the heart of the Third World. He proposed "protection zones" in key conflict areas of Africa and Asia where potential refugees could be quarantined in deadly squalor for years.

Blair's model, of course, is Australia, where right-wing prime minister John Howard has declared open war on wretched Kurdish, Afghan, and Timorese refugees. After last year's wave of riots and hunger strikes by immigrants indefinitely detained in desert hellholes like Woomera in south Australia, Howard used the navy to intercept ships in international waters and intern refugees in even more nightmarish camps on Nauru or malarial Manus Island off Papua New Guinea. Blair, according to the Guardian, has similarly scouted the use of the Royal Navy to interdict refugee smugglers in the Mediterranean, and the RAF to deport immigrants back to their homelands.

If border enforcement has now moved offshore, it has also come into everyone's front yard. Residents in the U.S. Southwest have long endured the long traffic jams at "second border" checkpoints far away from the actual lines. Now stop-and-search operations are becoming common in the interior of the EU. As a result, even notional boundaries between border enforcement and domestic policing, or between immigration policy and the War on Terrorism, are rapidly disappearing. "Noborder" activists in Europe have long warned that the Orwellian data systems used to track down non-EU aliens will be turned against local antiglobalization movements as well.

In the U.S., likewise, trade unions and Latino groups regard with fear and loathing Republican proposals to train up to one million local police and sheriffs as immigration enforcers. Indeed, Congress has already authorized pilot programs in Alabama and Florida, while local governments in California, Pennsylvania, and the South yield to pressures from Minutemen and other organized nativists to criminalize day laborers soliciting work in front of hardware stores and even to prohibit landlords from renting to tenants without proof of citizenship.

Meanwhile the Justice Department, the Pentagon, and the Department of Homeland Security are fostering a technological revolution in border surveillance. The National Security Entry-Exit Registration System, launched with great fanfare by Attorney General John Ashcroft in June 2002, uses biometrics to identify and track foreign visitors. New digital scanning systems at airports, harbors, and land borders will use the same biometrics to monitor and gather data on foreign individuals. Meanwhile, the San Diego-Tijuana region has become the field laboratory for the federally sponsored Border Research and Technology Center (headquartered in a downtown San Diego skyscraper),which is constantly working to improve the Border Patrol's high-tech intrusion detection systems—networks of hidden seismic, magnetic, and infrared sensors as well as video surveillance cameras that are now uplinked to satellites to allow remote viewing from a central command post.

The Pentagon, after a long absence, became reinvolved in border enforcement in 1989 with the establishment of Joint Task Force 6 at Fort Bliss, Texas. JTF6 (which officially "synchronizes and integrates Department of Defense resources") as originally limited to missions against major *narcotraficantes* smuggling large quantities of cocaine across the southern border. Now, as the cartels supposed have "expanded their operations to include or become intertwined with criminal syndicates engaged in human trafficking," the task-force mission has been enlarged by Congress to include surveillance and interdiction of illegal immigration. The Pentagon relishes this enlarged role because "there's no better place in America to get the kind of training that will prepare a unit for deployment to Afghanistan or Iraq."

Everywhere, as borders are remilitarized, and immigrants and refugees are shunted into more desperate routes, the human toll grows inexorably. According to human rights groups, nearly four thousand immigrants and refugees have died at the gates of Europe since 1993—drowned at sea, blown up in minefields, or suffocated in freight containers. Thousands more have perished in the Sahara en route to Morocco or Tunisia. Meanwhile, the American Friends Service Committee, which monitors the carnage along the U.S.-Mexico border, estimates that a similar number have died over the last decade in the furnace-hot deserts of the Southwest. In the context of so much inhumanity, the White House's recent proposal to offer temporary guest-worker status to undocumented immigrants and others might seem a gesture of compassion in contrast to the heartlessness of Europe or the near fascism of Australia.

In fact, as immigrant rights groups have pointed out, it is an initiative that combines sublime cynicism with ruthless political calculation. The Bush proposal, which resembles the infamous Bracero program of the early 1950s, would legalize a subcaste of low-wage labor without providing a mechanism for the estimated 5 to 7 million undocumented workers already in the U.S. to achieve permanent residence or citizenship. Toilers without votes or permanent domicile, of course, is a Republican utopia. The Bush plan would provide Wal-Mart and McDonald's with a stable, almost infinite supply of indentured labor.

It would also throw a lifeline to neoliberalism south of the border. The decade-old North American Free Trade Agreement, even former supporters now admit, has proven a cruel hoax—destroying as many jobs as it has created. Indeed the Mexican economy has shed jobs four years in a row. The White House neo-Bracero proposal offers President Vicente Fox and his successors a crucial economic safety valve. Finally—and this is the truly sinister serendipity—the offer of temporary legality would be irresistible bait to draw undocumented workers into the open where the Department of Homeland Security can identify, tag, and monitor them. Far from opening a crack in the Great Wall, it heals a breach, and ensures an even more systematic and intrusive policing of human inequality.

(February 2004, *Socialist Review*)

TWENTY-FIVE

VIGILANTE MAN

The local people whipped themselves into a mould of cruelty.
Then they formed units, squads, and armed them—
armed them with clubs, with gas, with guns.
We own the country. We can't let these Okies get out of hand.

—John Steinbeck, *The Grapes of Wrath*

The vigilantes are back. In the 1850s they lynched Irishmen; in the 1870s they terrorized the Chinese; in the 1910s they murdered striking Wobblies; in the 1920s they organized "Bash a Jap" campaigns; and in the 1930s they welcomed Dust Bowl refugees with tear gas and buckshot. Vigilantes have been to the American West what the Ku Klux Klan has been to the South: vicious and cowardly bigotry organized as a self-righteous mob. Almost every decade some dismal group of self-proclaimed patriots mobilizes to repel a new invasion or subversive threat.

Their wrath has almost always been directed against the poorest, most powerless, and hardworking segments of the population: recent migrants from Donegal, Guangdong, Oklahoma, or now Oaxaca. And their rant, as broadcast daily on dozens of AM hate-radio programs across California and the Southwest, is still the same as described by Steinbeck: "Men who had never been hungry saw the eyes of the hungry.... They said, 'These goddamned Okies are dirty and ignorant.

They're degenerate, sexual maniacs. These goddamed Okies are thieves. They'll steal anything. They've got no sense of property rights.'"

The most publicized of today's vigilantes are the so-called Minutemen, who began their armed patrol of the Arizona-Mexico border—appropriately—on April Fool's Day. The Tombstone, Arizona–based group is the latest incarnation of the anti-immigrant patrols that have plagued the borderlands for more than a decade. Vowing to defend national sovereignty against the Brown Peril, a series of shadowy paramilitary groups, led by racist ranchers and self-declared "Aryan warriors"—and egged on by right-wing radio jocks—have harassed, illegally detained, beaten, and murdered immigrants crossing through the desert cauldrons of Arizona and California.

The Minuteman Project is both theater of the absurd and a canny attempt to move vigilantism into the mainstream of conservative politics. Its principal organizers—a retired accountant and a former kindergarten teacher, both from Southern California—mesmerized the press with their promise of one thousand heavily armed super-patriots confronting the Mexican hordes along the international border in Cochise County.

In any event, they turned out 150 sorry-ass gun freaks and sociopaths who spent a few days in lawn chairs cleaning their rifles, jabbering to the press, and peering through binoculars at the cactus-covered mountains where several hundred immigrants perish each year from heatstroke and thirst. Armageddon on the border was never very likely, if only because undocumented immigrants read or hear the news like everyone else. Confronted with the Minutemen and the hundreds of extra border patrol sent to keep them out of trouble, campesinos simply waited patiently on the Sonora side for the vigilantes to get sunburned and go home.

Yet it would be a mistake to underestimate the impact of this incident on Republican politics. For the first time, the Bush administration is feeling seriously embattled—not by Democrats (they would never be so impolite), but by incipient rebellions on its own flanks.

The unpopularity of Bush's attempted privatization of Social Security has provided so-called moderate Republicans (think Colin Powell and John McCain) with a wedge issue to contest the presidential succession in 2008. More importantly, the activist grass roots of the party, especially in the West and the South, are aflame with anger about the president's proposed guest-worker treaty with Mexico, as well as his larger strategy of wooing Latino voters.

The anti-Latino backlash, which that evil sorcerer, former California governor Pete Wilson, helped summon to life in the early 1990s, has failed to quietly die away as Karl Rove and other Republican strategists might have wished. Over the last decade, instead, the campaigns against immigrant social rights and the use of Spanish in schools, which originated in California, have been exported to Arizona, Colorado, and southern states with growing Latin American populations. Like earlier antiabortion protests (which culminated in right-wing terrorism), the vigilante movement offers a dramatic tactic for capturing press attention, galvanizing opposition to immigration, and shifting the balance of power within the national Republican Party.

Their principal allies have been the demagogues and mini-Himmlers on talk radio, such as KFI-AM's Bill Handel—the most popular English-language radio host in the Los Angeles region—who spews bigotry every day on his morning commute time slot. "Los Angeles is going into the toilet," he raves, "because illegal aliens have poured over the border, this town has gone to hell in a handbasket over the past twenty years." Similar rants (what Handel proudly calls a "wall of hate") can be heard on car radios from Long Island to San Jose, wherever suburban commuters are stranded in traffic and, thus, a captive audience for nativists and admirers of the vigilantes.

To the discomfort of the White House, moreover, the Minutemen have found an ardent (if inconsistent) admirer in California governor Arnold Schwarzenegger: "I think they've done a terrific job. They've cut down the crossing of illegal immigrants a huge percentage. So it just shows that it works when you go and make an effort and when you work hard. It's a doable thing." Later, after furious Latino leaders accused him of "scapegoating and immigrant bashing," Schwarzenegger defiantly re-iterated that he would welcome the help of the Minutemen on the California border. (As he so often does, the governor followed this with the non sequitur reassurance that he was a "champion of immigrants.")

If the governor sounds like he is channeling his "inner Nazi," it is be-cause he is desperate. His hulking celebrity is no longer a novelty, and Schwarzenegger is dogged everywhere he goes these days by the angry nurses, schoolteachers, and firefighters whose budgets he has slashed. In recent months his rating in opinion polls has fallen by twenty points and the ghost of Gray Davis now shadows his future. So Arnie has gone back to the same dismal swamp of hate radio and angry white guys in pickup trucks where he won the governorship in 2003. The issue then was driver's licenses for illegal immigrants (how would we know that bin Laden himself wasn't tooling down the Hollywood freeway?). Now it's the right of citizens to "help the border patrol," to render Western justice themselves to the alien invaders. With a Vigilante Man in the governor's mansion in Sacramento, the next Minuteman provocation ("tens of thousands of volunteers blockading the Mexican border this fall") may be tragedy, not farce.

(May 2005, *Socialist Review*)

"Are we all destined to be Minutemen?" a California journalist recently asked. He had just visited www.texasborderwatch.com, the website spon-sored by Texas Governor Rick Perry that invites Internet users to monitor the webcams that stream live views of that state's border with Mexico. If one of Perry's virtual vigilantes spies a suspicious person or activity, she can simply click a button to notify Texas police or the Border Patrol. Ac-cording to the governor's press office, "Texas will use $5 million to begin placing hundreds of surveillance cameras along criminal hot spots and common routes used to enter this country. Perry said the cameras will cover vast stretches of farm and ranchland located directly on the border

where criminal activity is known to occur." The site is extraordinarily popular and in the first week of operation had 2.1 million hits. Thus no need to sit in a lawn chair in the hot sun with a shotgun on your lap, when you help patrol the border from your bedroom, office, or swimming pool. Indeed the mind boggles at the future applications of this idea: a partici-patory-democratic version of Orwell's nightmare with one part of the public enthusiastically recruited to spy on immigrants, prisoners, kids, or simply their neighbors. SDS meets 1984. Turn over Jeremy Bentham.

TWENTY-SIX

BORDER INVASION

The visitor crossing from Tijuana to San Diego these days is immediately slapped in the face by a huge billboard screaming, "Stop the Border Invasion!" Sponsored by rabidly anti-immigrant Grassfire.com—conservative allies of the vigilante Minutemen—the same truculent slogan reportedly insults the public at other border crossings in Arizona and Texas. (The San Diego sign's location, however, is especially obscene since it is located near the site of a former McDonald's restaurant where twenty-one customers, mostly Mexican, were mowed down by racist mass-murderer James Huberty in July 1984.)

The Minutemen and their splinter groups, once caricatured in the press as gun-toting clowns, are now haughty celebrities of grassroots conservatism, dominating AM hate radio as well as the even more hysterical ether of the right-wing blogosphere. In heartland as well as border states, Republican candidates vie desperately for their endorsement. With the electorate alienated by the carnage in both Baghdad and New Orleans, the Brown Peril suddenly has become the Republican deus ex machina for retaining control of Congress in the November elections.

Faltering GOP hegemony, too long sustained by the scraps of 9/11 and the imaginary weapons of Saddam Hussein, now has a new urgency in its appeal to the suburbs. Not since Kofi Annan conspired to send his black helicopters to terrorize Wyoming has such a clear and present danger threatened the Republic as the sinister armies of would-be busboys and gardeners gathered at the Rio Grande.

To listen to some of these demagogues, one would assume that the Twin Towers had been blown up by followers of the Virgin of Guadalupe or that Spanish had recently been decreed the official language of Connecticut. Having failed to scourge the world of evil by invasions of Afghanistan and Iraq, Republicans, supported by some Democrats, now propose that we invade ourselves: sending the marines and Green Berets, along with the National Guard, into the hostile deserts of California and New Mexico where national sovereignty is supposedly under siege.

Nativism, today as in the past, is bigotry as surreal caricature, reality stood on its head. The ultimate irony, however, is that there really is something that might be called a "border invasion," but the Minutemen's billboards are on the wrong side of the freeway. What few people, outside of Mexico at least, have bothered to notice is that while all the nannies, cooks, and maids have been heading North to tend the luxury lifestyles of irate Republicans, the Gringo hordes have been rushing South to enjoy glorious budget retirements and affordable second homes under the Mexican sun.

Yes, in former California Governor Pete Wilson's immortal words, "they just keep coming." Over the last decade, the U.S. State Department estimates that the number of Americans resident in Mexico has soared from two hundred thousand to one million (or one-quarter of all U.S. expatriates), while the Mexico Association of Real Estate Professionals reports that gringos now own 1.5 million homes in Mexico. A dramatic recent increase in remittances from the United States to Mexico ($9 billion to $14.5 billion in just two years), initially interpreted as representing a huge spike in illegal workers, turns out to be mainly money sent by Americans to themselves in order to finance Mexican homes and retirements.

Although some are naturalized U.S. citizens returning to towns and villages of their birth after lifetimes of toil *al otro lado*, the director general of FONATUR, the official agency for tourism development, recently characterized the typical investors in Mexican real estate as

American "baby boomers who have paid off in good part their initial mortgage and are coming into inheritance money."

Indeed, according to the *Wall Street Journal*, "the land rush is occurring at the beginning of a demographic tidal wave. With more than 70 million American baby boomers expected to retire in the next two decades…some experts predict a vast migration to warmer—and cheaper—climates. Often such buyers purchase a property 10 to 15 years before retirement, use it as a vacation home, and then eventually move there for most of the year. Developers increasingly are taking advantage of the trend, building gated communities, condominiums, and golf courses."(3) As a result, according to a *Los Angeles Times* report, the number of American homeowners in Mexico "is expected to jump to 12 million within 20 years as more baby boomers retire south of the border."(75)

The extraordinary rise in U.S. Sunbelt property values, moreover, gives gringos immense economic leverage. Shrewd baby boomers are not simply feathering nests for eventual retirement, but also increasingly speculating in Mexican resort property, driving up property values to the detriment of locals whose children are consequently driven into slums or forced to emigrate. As in Galway, Corsica, or, for that matter, Montana, the global second-home boom is making life in beautiful natural settings unaffordable for their traditional residents.

Many expatriates prefer such well-established havens for *Norteamericanos* as San Miguel de Allende or Puerto Vallarta, while others are experimenting with more exotic settings such as the Riviera Maya or Tulum in Quintana Roo. Here the *Norteamericanos* make themselves at home in more ways than one. An English-language paper in Puerto Vallarta, for instance, recently applauded the imminent arrival of a new shopping mall that would include Hooters, Burger King, Subway, Chili's, and Starbucks. Only Dunkin' Donuts (*con salsa*?), the paper complained, was still missing.

But the gringo invasion is largest (and brings the most significant geopolitical consequences) in Baja California, the thousand-mile long desert appendage to the gridlocked state-nation governed by Arnold Schwarzenegger. Baja real-estate websites, indeed, ooze almost as much hyperbole as those devoted to stalking the phantom menace of illegal immigrants. As a *Los Angeles Times* writer recently pointed out, the attraction of Baja is almost irresistible: "you can buy an oceanfront home in Baja for about one-third of what it would cost 30 minutes north of the border."

In essence, Alta California is beginning to overflow into Baja, an epochal process that, if unchecked, will produce intolerable social marginalization and ecological devastation in Mexico's last true frontier region. All the contradictions of postindustrial California— runaway land inflation in the coastal zone, sprawling suburban development in interior valleys and deserts, freeway congestion and lack of mass transit, astronomical growth of motorized recreation, and so on—dictate the invasion of the gorgeous "empty" peninsula to the south. To use a term from a bad but not irrelevant past, Baja is Anglo California's lebensraum.

Indeed the first two stages of informal annexation have already occurred. Under the banner of NAFTA, Southern California has exported hundreds of its sweatshops and toxic industries to the maquiladora zones of Tijuana and Mexicali. The Pacific Maritime Association, representing the West Coast's major shipping companies, has joined forces with Korean and Japanese corporations to explore the construction of a vast new container port at Punta Colonel, 150 miles south of Tijuana, that would undercut the power of longshore unionism in San Pedro and San Francisco.

Secondly, tens of thousands of gringo retirees and winter residents are now clustered at both ends of the peninsula. Along the northwest coast, from Tijuana to Ensenada, a recent conference blurb from UCLA boasts that "there are presently over 57 real-estate developments…with over 11,000 homes/condos with an inventory value of over $3 billion…all of them geared for the U.S. market," including a Donald Trump project.

Meanwhile, at the tropical end of Baja, yet another "Gold Coast" has emerged in the twenty-mile strip between Cabo San Lucas and San Jose de Cabo. In the 1960s, the region was home to less than one thousand fishermen; now Los Cabos is part of that global archipelago of real-estate hot spots where continuous double-digit increases in property values suck in speculative capital from all over the world. Although top-end villas in such exclusive enclaves as fabled Pedregal sell for $10 million or more, ordinary gringos can participate in the glamorous Los Cabos land casino through the purchase and resale of fractional time-shares in condominiums and beach homes.

Although western Canadian and Arizona speculators have left their oversized footprints all over Baja's southern cape, Los Cabos—at least judging from the registration of private planes at the local airport—has become a resort suburb especially of Orange County, the home of the most vehement Minutemen chapters. (For many wealthy Southern Californians, presumably, there is no perceived contradiction between fuming over the "alien invasion" with one's conservative friends at the Newport Marina, then flying down to Cabos the next day for some sea-kayaking or celebrity golf.)

The next step in the late colonization of Baja is the controversial "Escalera Nautica": a $2 billion "ladder" of twenty-seven marinas and coastal resorts being developed by FONATUR that will open up pristine sections of both coasts to the yacht club set as well as spurring more auto tourism. FONATUR's goal is to attract an additional one million tourists and fifty thousand private boats by 2014, with a "land bridge" midway between Ensenada and Cabo that will allow vessels to be towed between the Pacific and the Gulf of California without having to make the complete voyage around the peninsula. In addition to environmental concerns about the fate of gray whales in Scammon's and San Ignacio lagoons, the project is also opposed by fishermen in the Gulf who fear the "gentrification" of their waters. The celebrated environmentalist and poet, Homero Aridjis, has complained that "it could open the door to chaotic development beyond the control of a government that can't even control the sale of gum."(84)

The "Truman Show," meanwhile, has arrived in the picturesque little city of Loreto on the Gulf side of the peninsula. FONATUR has joined forces with an Arizona company and "New Urbanist" architects from Florida to develop the Villages of Loreto Bay: six thousand homes for expatriates in a colonial-revival motif, an instant San Miguel de Allende on the Sea of Cortez. The $3 billion Loreto project boasts that it will be the last word in green design, exploiting solar power and restricting automobile usage. Yet at the same time it will balloon Loreto's population from the current fifteen thousand to more than one hundred thousand in a decade, with the same kind of social and environmental consequences that can be seen in the slum peripheries of Cancun and other mega-resorts.

One of the irresistible attractions of Baja, of course, is that it has preserved a primordial wildness that has disappeared elsewhere in the West. Local residents, including a very eloquent indigenous environmental movement, cherish this incomparable landscape as they do the survival of an egalitarian ethos in the peninsula's small towns and fishing villages. Thanks to the silent invasion of the baby boomers from the North, however, much of the natural history and frontier culture of Baja could be swept away in the next generation. One of the world's most magnificent wild coastlines could be turned into generic tourist sprawl, waiting for Dunkin' Donuts to open. Locals, accordingly, have every reason to fear that today's mega-resorts and mock-colonial suburbs, like FONATUR's entire tourism-centered strategy of regional development, are simply the latest Trojan horses of Manifest Destiny.

(October 2006, *San Francisco Chronicle* and *Dallas News*)

TWENTY-SEVEN

ARNIE REPROGRAMMED

The Terminator has become as elusive and difficult to defeat as his archfoe, the infinitely malleable and almost indestructible cyborg, T-1000. One moment he is a zealous Conservative heading a crusade of the righteous against deficits and Democrats; the next, he is the reincarnation of Pat Brown, leading the Democrats back to the promised land of more freeways and schools. Shoot down the budget-cutting Republican, and the big-spending Democrat springs to life with a glint in his eye and smile on his lips. Run the bully over with a truck like the teachers and nurses did in November 2005, and he will immediately reassemble himself as education and health care's best friend. Some Democrats, to be sure, protest the unfairness and hypocrisy of Arnold Schwarzenegger's "flip-flops," but the Governator (or is he actually the Cat in the Hat?) simply somersaults over their heads, laughing madly as he changes his spots from red to blue to suit opinion polls.

For those who live outside California or have recently barricaded themselves in their homes, let me briefly recall the history of Arnie's extreme makeover. Following his pulverization of California's sleazy lieutenant governor Cruz Bustamante in a special election in October 2003, the populist hero Schwarzenegger arrived in Sacramento accompanied by his personal trainer (former Republican governor) Pete Wilson and a gaggle of corporate lobbyists and Hollywood groupies. After the usual inaugural homilies about reinventing government and turning power back to the people, the hulking actor (apparently as much under the spell of Wilson as President Bush was in the grip of Cheney) quickly transformed the governor's office into a crude Marxist caricature of an "executive committee" of the ruling class.

His much ballyhooed plan to revamp state government (or rather "blow up the boxes" thereof) was openly written by lobbyists for big corporations such as Hewlett-Packard, EDS, Microsoft, and various giant HMOs. (Its brilliant planks included a loony recommendation to save money by speeding the euthanization of lost animals in shelters—a proposal that even the governor's own children protested.) In a bold statement of his priorities, Schwarzenegger took money from K–12 education to offset the lost revenue from the car license fee that he rescinded as a favor to auto dealers and SUV owners. He then reneged on his promise to eventually restore the $3 billion in education cuts, brazenly lying about his negotiations with school officials.

This declaration of war against teachers and kids was punctually followed by attacks on nurses, firefighters, disabled people, and Latinos. With Scrooge-like zeal, he targeted the state's health-care programs for the poor, proposing among other savings that jobless disabled people be required to pay part of their medical premium. In a dumb replay of Pete Wilson's crusade against undocumented immigrants in the early 1990s, Schwarzenegger greeted the sociopath Minutemen on the border as "heroes" (President Bush denounced them as "vigilantes"). The bully in the governor's mansion, who derided his critics as "girlie men," also vetoed a popular bill to raise the minimum wage by one dollar, parroting the Chamber of Commerce's claim that it would drive business out of state. In the meantime his corporate allies, thinly disguised as the nonprofit Citizens to Save California, raised a huge campaign treasury to promote four interlocked ballot initiatives to curb public-employee political contributions, cap public spending (including schools), eviscerate teacher tenure, and take away the Democrats' legislative control over redistricting.

With Wilson and the Chamber of Commerce as cheerleaders and clowns, Schwarzenegger ventured everything on a November 2005 special election. At each campaign stop and rally, however, he was heckled by crowds of angry nurses, firefighters, and teachers. Accustomed only to public adoration, he was visibly shaken by the public-employee militancy that hounded him across the state and contested his phony populist image. Election night was a complete catastrophe: in the debris of the four defeated initiatives, exit surveys found the governor's own popularity had fallen by more than 25 percentage points. Indeed polls showed the superstar being defeated for reelection by virtually unknown Democrats such as state treasurer Phil Angelides.

The pathetic case of Gray Davis aside, few politicians in California history had ever squandered so much popularity so quickly, or suffered such a humiliating ass-kicking (by nurses and girlie men, no less). In such circumstances, the Nixons and their ilk sulk, throw tantrums, and plot revenge. Arnie, however, did something more extraordinary: he apologized to the public for the special election, fired the Republican chief of staff (Patricia Cleary) that he had borrowed from Pete Wilson, and in one incredible acrobatic leap became the advocate of a centrist Democratic dream program of spending gazillions on schools, freeways, canals, and alternative energy. Indeed, incredulous Democrats rejected his initial proposal for a $68 billion spending blitz as too much of a Keynesian good thing.

Behind the scenes, beauty was reprogramming the beast: which is to say that the governor's politically savvy wife Maria Shriver was applying all her Kennedy-clan magic to resurrect Arnie's plummeting popularity. To the horror of the Grover Norquist followers and mega-church fundamentalists who dominate the California Republican Party, Chief of State Cleary was replaced by Susan Kennedy, a lesbian Democrat who had been one of Gray Davis's top aides. At the same time, however, Shriver hired two Republican top guns, Matthew Dowd and Steve Schmidt, from the 2004 Bush campaign (that is to say, the same guys who had murdered Kerry with incessant accusations of being a "flip-flopper") to manage Arnie's reelection.

Veteran political pundits like the *Sacramento Bee*'s Daniel Weintraub and *Body Politic* blogger Joe Scott marveled at Shriver's audacity in reassembling her husband from such a promiscuous mix of right-wing and left-wing parts. Schwarzenegger was no less impressive in the sheer nonchalance with which he proclaimed his made-over politics. When critics complained about his seemingly radical agenda switch, the governor just smiled and shrugged his shoulders: "I always like to win. I don't get hung up on ideology. Whatever it takes, I will do."

In perspective, as state librarian and historian emeritus Kevin Starr has pointed out, Schwarzenegger has reverted to the tried-and-true formula of bipartisan big government pioneered by Earl Warren in the 1940s, perfected by Pat Brown in the late 1950s and early 1960s, and continued by Ronald Reagan (the biggest tax-raiser in state history) in the early 1970s.(142) Indeed, "back to the Golden Age" seemed to be Schwarzenegger's new slogan as he increased state spending by almost 10 percent and unveiled a huge bond measure to buy new freeways, schools, and flood control dikes. The $20 billion for transportation improvements, in particular, was a powerful palliative for the big construction firms, land developers, and car dealers who otherwise might have revolted against Arnie's retreat from the (Pete) Wilsonian politics of welfare-slashing and union-busting.

Democrats, meanwhile, got as much as they might have expected from Gray Davis or Cruz Bustamante. To the delight of environmental groups (and the Silicon Valley venture capitalists who will be its chief beneficiaries) Schwarzenegger endorsed a bill to cut greenhouse gas emissions and subsidize sustainable energy alternatives, while simultaneously criticizing the Bush administration's refusal to act on global warming. He also started repaying the money he had stolen from the schools, affirmed support for an increase in the minimum wage, endorsed comprehensive immigration reform, and hinted that he would crusade for comprehensive health plan coverage for all Californians. Finally, his corporate-inspired plan to "blow up government" was quietly retired to the criticism of the mice in the state Library.

While ideological Republicans and the official "anti-Arnold,"

Democratic challenger Phil Angelides watched in consternation, the 2006 campaign became a bipartisan love-in as Senate President Don Peralta and Assembly Speaker Fabian Núñez—the chief Democrats—accompanied the governor in a statewide tour to promote his $37 billion infrastructure initiative. After a few dinners at Schwarzenegger's Brentwood mansion, Núñez in particular became embarrassingly star-struck and started oozing his admiration for the governor to anyone who would listen. In the meantime, the state's most charismatic and highly ranked Democrat, Los Angeles Mayor Antonio Villaraigosa, used every occasion to praise the governor, whose support he needed for his controversial school takeover bill. (Villaraigosa, with ambitions to inherit the governor's mansion after Arnold is termed-out in 2010, also had everything to gain from Angelides' defeat). Finally, the public-sector unions who had spent nearly $80 million· to defeat Schwarzenegger's November 2005 initiatives hardly roused themselves a year later.

Angelides, in a word, was orphaned by his own party, and his supporters complained bitterly about the prominent Democrats who were AWOL. They also tore their hair at Angelides' failure to gain "traction" from wedge issues like education in the aftermath of the governor's astonishing volte-face. Yet the most gigantic and obvious contradiction of the Schwarzenegger campaign was precisely the issue that Angelides lacked the guts to visit: the absence of a fiscal foundation for renewed "Golden Age" spending.

As in the late 1990s at the height of the dot-com boom, California government in 2005–06 was again financing itself with one-off capital-gains windfalls such as the public sale of Google and the rapid turnover of multimillion-dollar homes. Schwarzenegger was brazenly buying his way back into popularity with plastic: generating huge bonded debts (the interest on the $37 billion infrastructure initiative will be a staggering $36 billion) that will inevitably drive the state back to the verge of bankruptcy as long as real estate and corporate profits remain grossly undertaxed and Proposition 13 (1978) remains a fetter on future generations.

Angelides was unwilling to talk about this thousand-pound gorilla in the room because it would have forced him either to oppose new state infrastructure or, worse, to concede the necessity of raising taxes on corporations and the rich. Raising taxes, of course, is the issue that every "centrist" Democrat desperately wants to avoid dealing with. As a result, Angelides was "terminated" in another overwhelming Schwarzenegger victory, and the governor and the Democratic legislative leaders are now locked in an overspending embrace that will last only as long as the current housing bubble. In the next recession, the fiscal quicksands will quickly swallow the putative Golden Age.

(Arnie—converted, it seems, almost overnight into a zealous and erudite follower of John Maynard Keynes—reassures skeptics that the state is borrowing more than enough money to ignore the structural deficit and sustain the binge. "There will be so much construction activities going on that where the private sector will fall off, the public sector will pick up. With our infrastructure bonds, we will again stimulate the economy.")

Should any of this matter much to anyone outside of California or does it suffice to say, "Forget it, Jake, it's Chinatown"? For his part, Schwarzenegger immediately proclaimed that his reelection was the shape of things to come in national politics: the New Centrism that will bridge all gaps and end the poisonous partisan rancor of the age of Rove. (The erstwhile Republican governor also cheered the Democratic conquest of Congress as a parallel return to the ruling center.) Of course these are exactly kind of sound bites that one would expect to hear from Susan Kennedy working in tandem with two former Bush campaign strategists at the behest of Maria Shriver—especially in the midst of a wild, bipartisan spending spree.

But fusion cuisine (like the economic bubble that sustains it) may only be a passing fad in politics. What will endure, however, is the feral—no, monstrous—ambition that elevated Schwarzenegger from

Austrian farm boy to Hollywood megastar to governor of the nation's largest and most powerful state. Arnie once told an interviewer that he has had a "recurrent dream that he was king of all the Earth." Is there any reason to think that our other monstrous messiahs—Hillary Clinton, Barack Obama, Rudy Giuliani, and John McCain—don't have the same dream?

(November 2006, unpublished)

PART FOUR

DARK WATER RISING

It was easy to foresee,
but it was impossible to prevent,
the impending evils.

—Gibbon

TWENTY-EIGHT

OUR SUMMER VACATION: 50,000 DEAD

Europe's murderous heat wave of July and August (2003) has killed at least thirty-five thousand people: the highest toll in any "natural" disaster since the great Messina earthquake of 1908 (sixty thousand dead) and the equivalent of more than ten World Trade Center catastrophes. *(By 2006 the official mortality figures for summer 2003 had been revised to more than fifty thousand.)*(90) In France, where fifteen thousand died, it was the hottest summer since Charlemagne, but that fact alone (and however startling) doesn't explain why two thousand people, mainly elderly and poor, were allowed to die each day at the height of *Le Canicule* in early August. To understand what happened during Europe's long, hot summer, we need to recall the scandal eight years earlier over unnecessary heat deaths in Chicago.

In July 1995 the administration of Mayor Richard M. Daley in Chicago was the accomplice in the murder of more than seven hundred of its senior citizens. As temperatures climbed above 40 degrees Celsius, the city's airless tenements and skid row hotels became charnel houses. Thousands of poor, elderly, mainly Black people were mortally stricken. By the second day of the heat wave, overcrowded hospitals were closing their doors to the critically ill and paramedics were unable to respond to the deluge of emergency calls. Medical workers warned of a death epidemic and begged for help.

But the Daley Jr. machine bunkered itself in denial and inaction. Heat mortality among the forgotten poor received less attention than previous winter snow days, which caused few deaths but greatly in-convenienced suburban commuters and Loop businesses. Thus the fire department refused to call in more staff or ambulances, while the police ignored requests to canvass tenements for isolated seniors. City Hall, meanwhile, stonewalled the media: "what disaster?" As bodies overflowed the morgue into the streets, the mayor complained to re-porters. "It's hot. But let's not blow it out of proportion.... Every day people die of natural causes."

The Chicago "heat catastrophe," as it is now officially called, was of course anything but a "natural" disaster. As radical sociologist Eric Kli-nenberg explains in his brilliant 2002 book, *Heat Wave: A Social Au-topsy of Disaster in Chicago*, "these deaths were not an act of God."(81) He demonstrates, instead, that they were the preventable consequences of poverty, racism, social isolation, and criminal civic negligence. Kli-nenberg's approach is generally shared by public health analysts. In-deed, the lessons of Chicago 1995 were enshrined in authoritative studies published by the U.S. Centers for Disease Control and the *New England Journal of Medicine*. These reports, now widely adopted in North American cities, advocate early warning systems, the immediate opening of neighborhood "cooling centers," door-to-door searches for ill seniors, adequate summer staffing of hospitals, and the subsidization of air-conditioning in low-income apartments.(134)

This literature is scientifically canonical, easily accessible on the In-ternet, and well known to European professionals. The lesson of Chi-cago, in other words, screams from the bookshelf. There was no excuse for not heeding it. Yet this August, the vulnerable poor were again massacred by analogous social conditions and Chicago-like re-sponses. In France, for example, the right-wing health minister, Jean-Francois Mattei continued his vacation—"tennis, anyone?"—while thousands of his fellow citizens perished. Heroic lethargy was also the response of the Berlusconi government in Italy, which also lied to the press and suppressed heat death statistics.

While the Euro-right blames the 35-hour-week and the collapse of family values for these atrocities, the left must be relentless in holding neoliberal policies accountable. Socialists must demand the kind of "social autopsy"—of which Klinenberg provides an admirable model—that lays bare the causative roles of poverty, unaffordable housing, and underfunded public services, as well as the appalling collapse of intergenerational solidarity. In the face of this small mountain of corpses, moreover, it can no longer be taken for granted that European neoliberalism is actually more "compassionate" than its more raptor-like American cousin. After all, it takes a pretty big hole in the vaunted social safety net for thirty-five thousand people to fall through.

But what of the strange Augusts yet to come? How should socialist politics address the increasingly violent interaction between environmental change and the late-capitalist city? There is growing evidence, for instance, of a sinister synergy between heat stress, traffic, and air pollution. The post-Chicago studies generally focused on hyperthermia and dehydration, paying little attention to air quality per se. But French scientists now believe that high ozone levels were a key factor in as many as three thousand deaths. August holiday gridlock now may be deadly in a double sense. This is why groups like Greenpeace are renewing calls for temporary or permanent traffic moratoriums in major urban centers.

August, moreover, was a vivid illustration of the kind of "unnatural" history that we must come to expect as the norm. This will not be a history slowly unreeling itself in tidy linear progression, as in biographies of Victorian liberals. More likely, the dialectic of global warming and neoliberalism—especially the Bushite doctrine of "consuming all the good things of the earth in our lifetime"—will produce a nonlinear roller-coaster ride between unpredictable disasters. Global capitalism is the runaway train on which we're all held hostage. And each extreme summer may be inching us closer to the precipice of catastrophic environmental change.

(October 2003, *Socialist Review*)

TWENTY-NINE

THE VIEW FROM HUBBERT'S PEAK

Angry truckers celebrated this May Day (2004) by blocking freeways in Los Angeles and container terminals in Oakland and Stockton. With diesel fuel prices in California soaring to record levels in recent weeks, the earnings of independent container-haulers have dropped below the poverty line. Lacking the power of big trucking companies to pass rising fuel costs on to customers, the port drivers—many of them immigrants from Mexico—have had little choice but to share some of their pain with the public. In one action, abandoned big rigs blocked the morning commute just south of downtown Los Angeles on Interstate 5. Tens of thousands of motorists became temporary hostages of the fuel crisis. As one exasperated commuter complained to a radio station, "This is really the end of the world."

Perhaps it is. Although real (inflation-adjusted) fuel prices are still well below their 1981 maximum, a large and ever-growing chorus of voices, ranging from former British environment minister Michael Meacher to *National Geographic* magazine, are shouting from the rooftops that the age of cheap oil is ending. Even if the current oil prices rise, are slowed, or are reversed by higher OPEC outputs, we will soon arrive—petroleum pundits claim—at the genuine summit of "Hubbert's peak." M. King Hubbert was a celebrated oil geologist who in 1956 correctly prophesied that U.S. petroleum production would peak in the early 1970s, then irreversibly decline. In 1974 he likewise predicted that world oilfields would achieve their maximum output in 2000—a figure later revised by his acolytes to 2006–10.

If the curve of global oil production is indeed near the point of descent, as these experts believe, it has epochal implications for the world economy. More expensive oil will undercut China's energy-intensive boom, return OECD countries to the bad old days of stagflation, and accelerate the environmentally destructive exploitation of low-grade oil tars and shales. Most of all, it will devastate the economies of oil-importing Third World countries. Poor farmers will be unable to afford artificial fertilizers, just as poor urban-dwellers will be unable to afford bus fares or winter heating oil. (Already rising oil prices have brought chronic blackouts to cities throughout the South.)

The only certain beneficiaries of this coming economic chaos will be the big five oil corporations and their corrupt partners—the Nigerian generals, Saudi princes, Russian kleptocrats, and their ilk. Crude oil truly will become black gold. The rising value of an increasingly scarce resource is a form of monopoly rent, and a permanent regime of $50 per barrel (or higher) crude would transfer at least $1 trillion per decade from final consumers to oil producers. In plain English, this would be the greatest robbery by a rentier elite in world history.

The oilmen in the White House, of course, have the best view of the terrain on the far side of Hubbert's peak. No wonder, then, that a map of the War on Terror corresponds with such uncanny accuracy to the geography of oilfields and proposed pipelines. From Kazakhstan to Ecuador, American combat boots are sticky with oil. To cite two recent examples: first, the Malaysian foreign minister warned in May that Washington was exaggerating the threat of terrorist piracy in order to justify the deployment of forces in the Straits of Malacca—the choke-point of East Asia's oil supply.

Second, Christian Miller, reporting in the *Los Angeles Times*, revealed that U.S. Special Forces, as well as the CIA and private American security contractors, are integrally involved in the ongoing reign of terror in Colombia's Arauca province. The aim of "Operation Red Moon" is to annihilate the left-wing ELN guerrillas threatening the oilfields and pipelines operated by L.A.-based Occidental Petroleum. The result, Miller reports, has been a slow-motion massacre: "Mass arrests of politicians and union leaders have become common. Refugees fleeing combat have streamed into local cities. And killings have soared as right-wing paramilitaries have targeted left-wing critics."(106)

Latin America (Mexico, Venezuela, Colombia, and Ecuador) supplies more oil to the United States than does the Middle East and, from the very beginning, the White House has defined the War on Terror as including counter-insurgency in the Western hemisphere. Is there a pattern here? Indeed, is there a U.S. master plan for the control of oil in an age of diminishing supply and soaring prices? Obvious questions that you don't have to be a conspiracy theorist to wonder about, but just don't ask a Democrat for answers.

Although most ordinary Americans have little difficulty connecting the dots linking blood to oil, the Democrats, with few exceptions, refuse to ask any deep or probing questions about the economic architecture of the New American Empire. Thus John Kerry has waffled back and forth between advocating an energy version of Fortress America (via the integration of Canadian and Mexican oil resources) and complaints that the Bush administration hasn't put enough pressure on OPEC, especially Saudi Arabia, to expand production.

One of the richest members of the Senate in history, Kerry seems congenitally allergic to the kind of anticorporate populism and bold muckraking that has made Michael Moore an international anti-Bush icon. Indeed, Kerry so far has refused every opportunity to publicly interrogate the economic interests driving Bush's foreign policy, or to address public concern about the future of our oil-addicted, SUV-heavy society. As a result, the presidential campaign has the dismal appearance of a Republican primary, with Kerry running as Bush Lite. As the senator from Massachusetts constantly emphasizes, a vote for him will ensure the bipartisan continuity of the War on Terror, the Patriot Act, U.S. support for Likud, the isolation of Cuba and Venezuela, and the military occupations of Iraq and Afghanistan.

At this point, only the Nader campaign genuinely offers political space to demand the United States get out of Iraq and to contest Washington's broader interventionist agenda. Only Nader is likely to press the attack on the corporate puppeteers of both political parties. At the same time, it would be utopian to expect Nader—an old-fashioned progressive who has just won the endorsement of the former Perot voters and Jesse Ventura supporters in the Reform Party—to offer a coherent critique of the brave new world being fashioned in the twilight of cheap oil and the dawn of global warming. That's a job description for socialists.

(May 2004, *Socialist Review*)

THIRTY

THE MONSTER AT THE DOOR

As in a classic 1950s sci-fi thriller, our world is imperiled by a terrifying monster. Scientists try to sound the alarm, but politicians ignore the threat until it's too late. Indifference ultimately turns into panic, and panic into catastrophe.

The monster is H5N1, the lethal avian flu that first emerged in 1997 in Hong Kong and is now entrenched in half a dozen Southeast Asian countries. It has recently killed scores of farmers and poultry workers who have had direct contact with sick birds. For seven years, researchers have warned that H5N1 would eventually fall in love with a human influenza virus in the body of a sick person (or possibly a pig) and produce a mutant offspring that could travel at pandemic velocity from human to human. Ironically, in our "culture of fear"—with the Bush administration ceaselessly ranting that the terrorist apocalypse is nigh—the least attention is given to the threat that is truly most threatening.

On September 14, Dr. Shigeru Omi of the World Health Organization (WHO) tried to shake complacency with an urgent warning that human-to-human transmission of avian flu was a "high possibility." Two weeks later, grim-faced Thai officials revealed that the dreaded viral leap had already occurred. A young mother, who had died on September 20, had probably contracted the virus directly from her dying child.

A crucial threshold has been crossed. Of course, as Thai officials hastened to point out, one isolated case doesn't make a pandemic. Human-to-human avian flu would need a certain critical mass, a minimum initial incidence, before it could begin to decimate the world. The precedent always invoked to illustrate how this might happen is the 1918–19 influenza pandemic—the single greatest mortality event in human history. In only twenty-four weeks, a deadly avian flu strain killed between 2 and 5 percent of humanity (50 million to 100 million people).

But some researchers worry that H5N1 is actually an even more deadly threat than H1N1 (the 1918 virus). First of all, this flu—at least in its bird-to-human form—is a far more vicious killer. In 1918–19, 2.5 percent of infected Americans died. In contrast, more than 70 percent of this year's avian flu cases (30 out of 42) have perished. Moreover, H5N1 appears to be immune to at least three of the four antiviral drugs on the market.

Secondly, as the WHO has repeatedly emphasized, the avian flu seems to have conquered an ecological niche of unprecedented dimension. The rise of factory poultry farming in Asia over the last decade and the dangerously unhygienic conditions in farms and processing plants have created a perfect incubator for the new virus. Additionally, in the face of desperate WHO efforts to geographically contain the avian pandemic by destroying infected bird populations, the virus has literally taken flight. H5N1 has been identified in dead herons, gulls, egrets, hawks, and pigeons. Like the West Nile virus, it has wings with which it can cross oceans and potentially infect bird populations everywhere. In August, furthermore, the Chinese announced that the avian strain had been detected in pigs. This is a particularly ominous development since pigs, susceptible to both bird and human flu, are likely crucibles for genetic "reassortment" between viruses. Containment seems to have failed.

Thirdly, a new pandemic will use modern transportation. The 1918–19 virus was slowed by oceangoing transport and the isolation of rural society. Its latter-day descendant could jet-hop the globe in a week. Finally, the mega-slums of Asia, Africa, and Latin America are like so many lakes of petrol awaiting the spark of H5N1.

What are the front lines of defense against such an unthinkable catastrophe? One of the most urgent tasks is to ensure that poultry workers in Southeast Asia receive ordinary flu vaccinations in order to prevent possible mixing of human and avian genes. But seasonal flu vaccine is mostly consigned to the richer countries, and Thai officials have complained that they cannot obtain enough donated doses to conduct systematic vaccination. Furthermore the recent closure of drug company Chiron's contaminated UK production facility eliminates a fifth of the global flu vaccine stock at precisely the moment when it is urgent to reinforce the vaccination program in Southeast Asia.

A prototype H5N1 vaccine is under development, but only in quantities to safeguard frontline public health and safety workers in the United States, Europe, and Japan. Drug companies compete furiously in the market to cure minor ills, but lack profit incentives to increase the output of vital vaccines and antivirals. As the *New York Times* emphasized on September 30, there has been a disastrous "mismatch of public health needs and private control of production of vaccines and drugs." Indeed last April, at a historic WHO-convened summit about global defenses against a possible pandemic, leading experts expressed their deep pessimism about existing preparations.

"The consultation concluded that supplies of vaccine, the first line of defense for preventing high morbidity and mortality, would be grossly inadequate at the start of a pandemic and well into the first wave of international spread," the WHO reported. "Limited production capacity largely concentrated in Europe and North America would exacerbate the problem of inequitable access." "Inequitable access" is, of course, a euphemism for the death of a large segment of humanity—a callous triage already prepared in advance of the H5N1 plague by indifference to Third World public health.

This is the moral context of the deafening silence about the H5N1 threat in the current U.S. presidential debate. Only Ralph Nader has been awake to the peril. In a letter to President Bush in August, he re-peated scientific warnings that the "The Big One" was coming and urged a "presidential conference on influenza epidemics and pan-demics" to confront "the looming threats to the health of millions of people." It has become fashionable, of course, in some "progressive" circles to excoriate Nader's presence in the campaign as divisive ego-ism. But who else has warned us about the monster at the door?

(November 2004, *Socialist Review*)

THIRTY-ONE

POOR, BLACK, AND LEFT BEHIND

The evacuation of New Orleans in the face of Hurricane Ivan looked sinisterly like Strom Thurmond's version of the Rapture. Affluent white people fled the Big Easy in their SUVs, while the old and car-less—mainly Black—were left behind in their below-sea-level shot-gun shacks and aging tenements to face the watery wrath.

New Orleans had spent decades preparing for inevitable submer-sion by a monster storm surge. Civil defense officials conceded they had ten thousand body bags on hand to deal with the worst-case sce-nario, yet no one seemed to have bothered to devise a plan to evacuate the city's poorest or most infirm residents. The day before the hurri-cane hit the Gulf Coast, New Orlean's daily, the *Times-Picayune*, ran an alarming story about the "large group mostly concentrated in poorer neighborhoods" who wanted to evacuate but couldn't. Only at the last moment, with winds churning Lake Pontchartrain, did mayor Ray Nagin reluctantly open the Louisiana Superdome and a few schools to desperate residents. He was reportedly worried that lower-class refu-gees might damage or graffiti the Superdome.

In the event, Ivan the Terrible spared New Orleans, but official cal-lousness toward poor Black folk endures. Over the last generation City Hall and its entourage of powerful developers have relentlessly at-tempted to push the poorest segment of the population—blamed for the city's high crime rates—across the Mississippi River. Historic Black public-housing projects have been razed to make room for upper-income town houses and a Wal-Mart. In other housing projects, residents are routinely evicted for offenses as trivial as their children's curfew violations. The ultimate goal seems to be a tourist theme-park New Orleans—one big Garden District—with chronic poverty hidden away in bayous, trailer parks, and prisons outside the city limits.

But New Orleans isn't the only case study in what Nixonians once called the politics of "benign neglect." In Los Angeles, county supervisors have just announced the closure of the trauma center at Martin Luther King Jr. Hospital near Watts. The hospital, located in the epicenter of L.A.'s gang wars, has one of the nation's busiest ERs for the treatment of gunshot wounds. The loss of its trauma center, according to paramedics, could "add as much as 30 minutes in transport time to other facilities." The result, almost certainly, will be a spate of avoidable deaths. But then again the victims will be Black or brown and poor.

As the fortieth anniversary of the 1965 Civil Rights Act approaches, the United States seems to have returned to degree zero of moral concern for the majority of the descendants of slavery and segregation. Whether the Black poor live or die seems to merit only haughty disinterest and indifference. Indeed, in terms of the life and death issues that matter most to African Americans—structural unemployment, race-based super-incarceration, police brutality, disappearing affirmative action, and failing schools—the present presidential election might be taking place in the 1920s.

But not all the blame can be assigned to the current occupant of the former slaveowners' mansion at the end of Pennsylvania Avenue. The mayor of New Orleans, for example, is a Black Democrat (even if he did support Bush in 2000) and Los Angeles County is a famously Democratic bastion. No, the political invisibility of people of color is a strictly bipartisan endeavor.

On the Democratic side, it is the culmination of the long crusade waged by the Democratic Leadership Council (DLC) to exorcize the specter of the 1980s Rainbow Coalition. The DLC, of course, has long yearned to bring white guys and fat cats back to a Nixonized Democratic Party. Arguing that race had fatally divided Democrats, the DLC has tried to bleach the party by marginalizing civil rights agendas and Black leadership. African Americans, it is cynically assumed, will remain loyal to the Democrats regardless of the treasons committed against them. They are, in effect, hostages. Thus the sordid spectacle— portrayed in *Fahrenheit 9/11*—of white Democratic senators refusing to raise a single hand in support of the Black Congressional Caucus's courageous challenge to the stolen election of November 2000.

The Kerry campaign, meanwhile, steers a straight DLC course toward oblivion. No Democratic presidential candidate since Eugene McCarthy has shown such patrician disdain toward the Democrats' most loyal and fundamental social base. While Condi Rice hovers tight-lipped and constant at Dubya's side, the highest ranking, self-proclaimed "African American" in the Kerry camp is Teresa Heinz (born a wealthy colon in Mozambique). This crude joke has been compounded by Kerry's semi-suicidal reluctance to mobilize Black voters. As Rainbow Coalition veterans like Ron Waters have bitterly pointed out, Kerry has been absolutely churlish about financing voter registration drives in African-American communities.

Ralph Nader was cruelly accurate when he warned recently that "the Democrats do not win when they do not have Jesse Jackson and African Americans in the core of the campaign." In truth, Kerry, the erstwhile war hero, is running away as hard as he can from the sound of the cannons, whether in Iraq or in America's equally ravaged inner cities. The urgent domestic issue, of course, is unspeakable socioeconomic inequality, newly deepened by fiscal plunder and catastrophic plant closures. But inequality still has a predominant color or, rather, colors: black and brown.

Kerry's apathetic and uncharismatic attitude toward people of color will not be repaired by last-minute speeches or campaign staff appointments. Nor will it be compensated by his super-ardent efforts to woo Reagan Democrats and white males with his war stories from the ancient Mekong. A party that in every real and figurative sense refuses to shelter the poor in a hurricane will not mobilize the moral passion necessary to overthrow King George.

(September 2004, *Socialist Review*)

THIRTY-TWO

A RAINY DAY IN TIJUANA

Juana Tapia lost her two daughters—eight-year-old Martha and thirteen-year-old Maria—to the sudden rush of water and debris that blew their shanty apart like an explosion. The little girls didn't have time to scream. Neighbors helped Juana and her husband claw through the muck, but they couldn't locate the children. Later the *bomberos* (firefighters) came and dug out the crumpled bodies. The neighborhood was chaos, mud, and inconsolable grief. A few blocks away a five-year-old boy was also swept away and drowned, while hundreds of homes had been damaged or destroyed.

This could have been Sumatra or Sri Lanka, but it was San Antonio de los Buenos, a poor *colonia* on the southern fringe of the border city of Tijuana in mid-January. The Tapias are rag-pickers who earn a living from a nearby municipal dump. They have lived in San Antonio for nine years and, unlike many of their newly arrived neighbors, they were scared of the rain. Immediately after New Year's Day, a powerful weather system, fueled by moist tropical air from Hawaii, laid siege to Southern California and northern Baja California. Nearly a year's average of rain fell in a furious two-weeklong onslaught.

Winter storms are dreaded in Tijuana, because the great majority of the population of 1.5 million live in self-built colonias that cling precariously to the sides of eroding hills or squat on bare mesas. Although Tijuana is still a porno-fantasy for many gringos, forever associated with the gambling and vice that U.S. gangsters brought south during

Prohibition, the real city earns its living as a manufacturing platform for giant Japanese and Korean corporations. The maquiladoras—factories exporting to the United States under NAFTA—are located in modern, well-designed industrial parks, indistinguishable from their counterparts north of the border, with broad paved streets and good storm drainage.

The colonias, on the other hand, can wait decades for piped water and sewers. Paved streets might take a lifetime. Although the maquiladoras pay nugatory municipal taxes, they consume the greater part of the city's budget. The Tijuana working class, in other words, subsidizes wealthy foreign corporations. Left to fend for themselves, *colonos* cope as best they can with the rutted streets, bare dirty hills, and the clouds of suffocating dust that engulf much of the city. To protect their homes from the winter rains, they build ingenious terraces out of old tires packed with dirt.

But two or three times each decade, typically in an El Niño year, storms arrive that overwhelm the defenses of even the sturdiest colonias, Tijuana's barren hillsides dissolve into torrents of mud, and the usually dry Tijuana River becomes a toxic Mississippi. Over the course of past winters, vast numbers of homes have been destroyed and scores, perhaps hundreds, killed. In the late 1970s the government used a flood emergency as an opportunity to evict several thousand colonos, replacing their ruined homes with maquiladoras.

Although San Diego is contiguous with Tijuana, forming an extraordinary binational metropolis, the English-language media paid little attention to the death of the Tapia children, or, for that matter, to several drownings in the sewage-choked Tijuana River. One could plead that we gringos were simply more absorbed by own picturesque tragedies: like the beach community near Santa Barbara that was crushed by a landslide that geologists had long warned was inevitable. But, in truth, we simply take it for granted that poor *Tijuaneses* will live in the dirt and die in the mud. Doesn't it happen almost every year?

The real "global disaster" story has little to do with earthquake faults, subduction zones, angry volcanoes, super-cell storms, and other aspects of the Earth's ordinary metabolism. Instead it is about the plight of San Antonio de los Buenos multiplied a hundred-thousand-fold. Two years ago, U.N. Habitat published landmark research that claimed that a billion people now dwell in the slums of the cities of the South—a number that will double by 2020. Once upon a time, newcomers might have hoped to squat on the agricultural edge of the city, but well-drained flat land is now everywhere scarce and expensive. Poor urban migrants, as a consequence, have been forced to colonize sites that the market rejects as undevelopable because of toxicity or natural hazard.

Progressive urban planners often advocate something called "hazard zoning" to exclude development and population from dangerous floodplains, swamps, unstable hillsides, fire-prone brushlands, and liquefaction zones. Capitalist urbanization in the Third World works by exactly the opposite principle: concentrating huge densities of poor, vulnerable people in the most unstable and hazardous sites. Informal urbanization, as a result, everywhere multiplies, sometimes by a decimal order of magnitude or more, the inherent natural hazards of urban environments.

The rest of the world usually only sees the consequences when the body counts are in the thousands: the 1999 flash floods in Venezuela, the 2000 collapse of a "garbage mountain" in Manila, the 2001 Gujarat earthquake, the 2002 arsenal explosion in Lagos, and now the tsunami catastrophe in the Indian Ocean. Hidden from view is the global epidemic of small-scale, chronic disaster that only rarely deserves the adjective "natural." It is the global housing crisis, not plate tectonics or El Niño, that hands out death sentences to the poor.

(February 2005, *Socialist Review*)

THIRTY-THREE

DROWNING ALL ILLUSIONS

The tempest that destroyed New Orleans was conjured out of tropical seas and an angry atmosphere 125 miles offshore of the Bahamas. Labeled initially as "Tropical Depression 12" on August 23, it quickly intensified into "Tropical Storm Katrina"—the eleventh named storm in one of the busiest hurricane seasons in history. Making landfall near Miami on the 24th, Katrina had grown into a small hurricane—Category 1 on the Saffir-Simpson Hurricane Scale—with 125 km per hour winds that killed nine people and knocked out power to one million residents.

Crossing over Florida to the Gulf of Mexico where it wandered for four days, Katrina underwent a monstrous and largely unexpected transformation. Siphoning vast quantities of energy from the Gulf's abnormally warm waters—3 degrees centigrade above their usual August temperature—Katrina mushroomed into an awesome, top-of-the-scale Category 5 hurricane with 290 km per hour winds that propelled tsunami-like storm surges nearly 10 meters in height. (*Nature* later reported that Katrina absorbed so much heat from the Gulf that "water temperatures dropped dramatically after it had passed, in some regions from 30° C to 26° C.")(132) Horrified meteorologists had rarely seen a Caribbean hurricane replenish its power so dramatically, and researchers debated whether or not Katrina's explosive growth was a portent of global warming's impact on hurricane intensity.

Although Katrina had dropped to Category 4 (210–249 km per hour winds) by the time it careened ashore in Plaquemines Parish, Louisiana, near the mouth of the Mississippi River on early Monday, August 29, it was small consolation to the doomed oil ports, fishing camps, and Cajun villages in its direct path. In Plaquemines, and then again on the Gulf Coast of Mississippi and Alabama, Katrina churned the bayous with relentless wrath, leaving behind a devastated landscape that looked like a watery Hiroshima.

Metropolitan New Orleans, with its 1.3 million inhabitants, was originally dead center in Katrina's way, but the hurricane veered to the right after landfall and its eye passed 55 kilometers to the east of the metropolis. The Big Easy—largely under sea level and bordered by the salt-water embayments known as Lake Pontchartrain (on the north) and Lake Borgne (on the east)—was spared the worst of Katrina's winds but not its waters. Hurricane-driven storm surges, funneled by the notorious ship canal known as MRGO, broke through the notoriously inadequate levees that guard Black-majority eastern New Orleans as well as adjacent white blue-collar suburbs in St. Bernard Parish. There was no warning and the rapidly rising waters trapped and killed hundreds of unevacuated people in their bedrooms, including thirty-four elderly residents of a nursing home.

Later, probably around midday, a flood wall gave way at the 17th Street Canal, soon followed by other breaches on the London Avenue and Orleans canals, allowing Lake Pontchartrain to pour into city's low-lying central districts. Although New Orleans's most famous tourist assets, including the French Quarter and the Garden District, and its most patrician neighborhoods, like Audubon Park and Lakeshore, are built on high ground and survived most of the inundation, the rest of the city was flooded to its rooftops or higher—damaging or destroying more than 250,000 housing units. Locals promptly dubbed it "Lake George" after the president who failed to build new levees or come to their aid after the old ones had burst.

Although Bush later claimed that "the storm didn't discriminate," every aspect of the catastrophe was in fact shaped by inequalities of class and race. In addition to unmasking the fraudulent claims of the Department of Homeland Security to make Americans safer, the "shock and awe" of Katrina also exposed the devastating consequences of the federal neglect of majority Black and Latino big cities and their vital infrastructures. The staggering incompetence of the Federal Emergency Management Agency (FEMA) demonstrated the folly of entrusting life-and-death public mandates to clueless political appointees and ideological foes of "big government." And the speed with which Washington suspended the prevailing wage standards of the Davis-Bacon Act and swung open the doors of New Orleans to corporate looters like Halliburton, the Shaw Group, and Blackwater Security—already fat from the spoils of the Tigris—contrasted obscenely with FEMA's deadly procrastination over sending water, food, and buses to the multitudes trapped in the stinking hell of the Louisiana Superdome.

But if New Orleans—as many of its bitter exiles now believe—was allowed to die as a result of governmental incompetence and neglect, the blame also squarely falls on the Governor's Mansion in Baton Rouge and, especially, City Hall on Perdido Street. Mayor C. Ray Nagin—a wealthy African-American cable television executive who was elected in 2002 with 87 percent of the white vote—was ultimately responsible for the safety of the estimated one-quarter of the population that was too poor or infirm to own a car. His stunning failure to mobilize resources to evacuate car-less residents and hospital patients—despite warning signals from the city's botched response to the threat of Hurricane Ivan in September 2004—reflected more than personal ineptitude: it was also a symbol of the callous attitude among New Orleans's elites, both white and Black, toward their poor neighbors in the back-swamp districts and rundown housing projects. Indeed, the ultimate revelation of Hurricane Katrina—striking the Gulf Coast shortly after the fortieth anniversary of the Voting Rights Act of 1965—was how comprehensively the promise of equal rights for poor African Americans has been dishonored and betrayed by every level of government.

Where's the Cavalry?

The death of New Orleans, of course, had been forewarned; indeed no disaster in American history had been so accurately predicted in advance. Although Homeland Security secretary Michael Chertoff would later claim that "the size of the storm was beyond anything his department could have anticipated," this was flatly untrue. If scientists were surprised by Katrina's sudden burgeoning to super-storm dimensions, they had grim confidence in exactly what New Orleans could expect from the landfall of a great hurricane. "The sad part," one researcher lamented after Katrina had passed, "is that we called this 100 percent."

Since the nasty experience of Hurricane Betsy in September 1965—a Category 2 storm that inundated many of the eastern parts of Orleans Parish that were drowned again by Katrina—the vulnerability of New Orleans to wind-driven storm surges has been intensively studied and widely publicized. In 1998, after another close call with Hurricane Georges, research was ramped up, and a sophisticated computer study by Louisiana State University warned of the "virtual destruction" of the city by a Category 4 storm approaching from the southwest.(23) New Orleans's levees and stormwalls are only designed to withstand a Category 3 hurricane, but even that threshold of protection was revealed as illusory in computer simulations adopted last year by the Army Corps of Engineers. The continuous erosion of southern Louisiana's barrier islands and bayou wetlands (an estimated annual shoreline loss of 60 to 100 square kilometers) increases the height of storm surges as they arrive at New Orleans, while the city itself, along with its levees, is slowly sinking. As a result even a Category 3 hurricane, if slow moving, would now flood most of the city.(147) Global warming and sea-level rise will only make the "Big One"—as folks in New Orleans, like their counterparts in Los Angeles, call the local apocalypse—even bigger.

Lest politicians have difficulty understanding the implications of such predictions, other studies modeled the exact extent of flooding as well as the expected casualties in the event of direct hit. Supercomputers kept cranking out the same horrifying numbers: 160 square kilometers or more of the city under water with eighty thousand to one hundred thousand dead—the worst disaster in American history. In light of these studies, FEMA in 2001 warned that a hurricane flood in New Orleans was one of the three mega-catastrophes most likely to strike the United States in the near future (along with a California earthquake and a terrorist attack on Manhattan). Shortly afterward, *Scientific American* published an account of the flood danger ("Drowning New Orleans") which, like a subsequent award-winning series in the *Times-Picayune* in 2002 ("Washing Away"), was chillingly accurate in its warnings.(51, 103) Last year, after meteorologists predicted a strong upsurge in hurricane activity, federal officials carried out an elaborate disaster drill ("Hurricane Pam") which again reconfirmed that casualties would be likely in the tens of thousands.

The Bush administration's response to these frightening forecasts was to rebuff Louisiana's urgent requests for more flood protection: the crucial Coast 2050 project to revive protective wetlands—the culmination of a decade of research and negotiation—was shelved and levee appropriations, including the completion of defenses around Lake Pontchartrain, were repeatedly slashed. In part, this was a consequence of new priorities in Washington that squeezed the budget of the Army Corps: a huge tax cut for the rich, the financing of the war in Iraq, and, ironically, the costs of "Homeland Security." Yet there is undoubtedly a brazen political motive as well: New Orleans is a Black-majority, solidly Democratic city whose voters frequently wield the balance of power in state elections. Why would an administration so relentlessly focused on partisan warfare seek to reward this thorn in Karl Rove's side by authorizing the $2.5 billion that senior Army Corps officials estimate would be required to build a Category 5 protection system around New Orleans?

Indeed when the head of the Army Corps of Engineers, a former Republican congressman, protested in 2002 against the way that flood-control projects were being shortchanged, Bush removed him from office. Last year the administration also pressured Congress to cut $71 million from the budget of the Army Corps's New Orleans district despite warnings of the epic hurricane seasons close at hand. (To be fair, Washington has spent a lot of money on Louisiana, but largely on non-hurricane-related public works that benefit shipping interests and hard-core Republican districts).

In addition to underfunding coastline restoration and levee construction, the White House also mindlessly vandalized FEMA. Under Director James Lee Witt (who enjoyed Cabinet rank), FEMA had been the showpiece of the Clinton administration, winning bipartisan praise for its efficient dispatch of search and rescue teams and prompt provision of federal aid after the 1993 Mississippi River floods and the 1994 Los Angeles earthquake. When Republicans took over the Agency in 2001, however, it was treated as enemy terrain: the new director, former Bush campaign manager Joe M. Allbaugh, decried disaster assistance as "an oversized entitlement program" and urged Americans to rely more upon the Salvation Army and other faith-based groups. Allbaugh punctually cut back many of the key flood and storm mitigation programs before resigning in 2003 to become a highly paid consultant to firms seeking contracts in Iraq. (An inveterate ambulance-chaser, he recently reappeared in Louisiana as an insider broker for firms looking for lucrative reconstruction work in the wake of Katrina.)

Since its absorption into the new Department of Homeland Security in 2003 (with corresponding loss of its representation in the Cabinet), FEMA has been repeatedly downsized as well as ensnared in new layers of bureaucracy and patronage. Last year FEMA employees wrote to Congress that "emergency managers at FEMA have been supplanted on the job by politically connected contractors and by novice employees with little background or knowledge."(136) A prime example was Allbaugh's successor and protégé, Michael Brown, a Republican lawyer with no emergency management experience and a phony resume, whose previous job was representing the wealthy owners of Arabian horses. Under Brown, the Agency continued its metamorphosis from an "all hazards" approach to a monomaniacal emphasis on terrorism. Three-quarters of the federal disaster preparedness grants that FEMA formerly used to support local earthquake, storm, and flood prevention has now been diverted to various counterterrorism scenarios. The Bush administration, in effect, has built a Maginot Line against hypothetical threats from al-Qaeda while neglecting levees, storm walls and pumps.

Thus there was every reason for anxiety, if not panic, when Max Mayfield, the director of the National Hurricane Center in Miami, warned President Bush (still vacationing in Texas) and Homeland Security officials in a videoconference on Sunday, August 28, that Katrina was poised to devastate New Orleans. Yet FEMA Director Brown—faced with the possible death of one hundred thousand locals—exuded breathless, arrogant bravado: "We were so ready for this. We planned for this kind of disaster for many years because we've always known about New Orleans..." For months Brown and his boss, Homeland Security secretary Michael Chertoff, had trumpeted the new National Response Plan that would ensure unprecedented coordination among government agencies during a major disaster.

But as the floodwaters swallowed New Orleans and its suburbs, it was difficult to find anyone to answer a phone, much less take charge of the relief operation. "A mayor in my district," an angry Republican congressman told the *Wall Street Journal*, "tried to get supplies for his constituents, who were hit directly by the hurricane. He called for help and was put on hold for 45 minutes. Eventually, a bureaucrat promised to write a memo to his supervisor." Although state-of-the-art communications were supposedly the backbone of the National Response Plan, frantic rescue workers and city officials were plagued by the breakdown of phone systems and the lack of a common bandwidth. At the same time they faced immediate shortages of all the critical logistics—food rations, potable water, sandbags, generator fuel, satellite phones, portable toilets, buses, boats, and helicopters—that FEMA should have pre-positioned in New Orleans. Most fatefully, Homeland Security secretary Chertoff inexplicably waited a full twenty-four hours after New

Orleans had been flooded to upgrade the disaster to an "incident of national significance"—the legal precondition for moving the federal response into high gear.

Far more than the reluctance of the president to return to work, or the vice president to interrupt his mansion-hunting trip, or the secretary of state to end her shoe-buying expedition in Manhattan—it was the dinosaur-like slowness of the brain of Homeland Security to register the magnitude of the disaster that doomed so many to die clinging to their roofs or hospital beds. Lathered in premature and embarrassing praise from the president for their heroic exertions, both Chertoff and Brown were more like sleepwalkers. As late as Thursday (September 2), Chertoff astonished an interviewer on National Public Radio by claiming that the scenes of death and desperation inside the Superdome, which the entire world was watching on television, were just "rumors and anecdotes." FEMA director Brown, meanwhile, was blaming the victims, claiming that most deaths were the fault of "people who did not heed evacuation warnings," although he knew that "heeding" had nothing to do with the lack of an automobile or confinement in a wheelchair.

Despite claims by Secretary of Defense Donald Rumsfeld that Iraq had nothing to do with Katrina, the absence of more than one-third of the Louisiana National Guard and much of its heavy equipment crippled rescue and relief operations from the outset. FEMA often obstructed rather than facilitated relief: preventing civilian aircraft, for instance, from evacuating hospital patients and delaying authorizations for out-of-state National Guard and rescue teams to enter the New Orleans area. As an embittered representative from devastated St. Bernard Parish told the *Times-Picayune*: "Canadian help arrived before the U.S. Army did."

A Conservative New Jerusalem

New Orleans's City Hall could have used Canadian help as well: the emergency command center on its ninth floor was put out of operation early in the emergency by a shortage of diesel fuel to run its back-

up generator. Indeed for two days, Mayor Nagin and his aides were utterly cut off from the outside world by the failure of both their land
lines and cellular phones. This collapse of the city's command-and-
control apparatus is puzzling in view of the $18 million in federal
grants that the city had spent since 2002 in training exercises to deal
with precisely such contingencies. Even more mysterious was the relationship between Nagin and his state and federal counterparts. As the
mayor later summarized it, the city's disaster plan was "get people to
higher ground and have the feds and the state airlift supplies to them,"
yet Nagin's director of homeland security, Colonel Terry Ebbert, astonished journalists with the admission that "he never spoke with
FEMA about the state disaster blueprint."

Nagin later ranted with justification about FEMA's failure to pre-
position supplies or to promptly rush buses and medical supplies to the
Superdome. But evacuation planning was, first and above all, a city responsibility; and earlier planning exercises and surveys had shown that
at least one-fifth of the population would be unable to leave New Orleans without assistance. Indeed, in September 2004 Nagin had been
roundly criticized for making no effort to evacuate poor residents as
their better-off neighbors drove off in advance of Category 3 Hurricane
Ivan (which fortunately veered away from the city at the last moment).
In response the city produced (but never distributed) thirty thousand
videos targeted at poor neighborhoods that urged residents "don't wait
for the city, don't wait for the state, don't wait for the Red Cross…leave."
In the absence of official planning to provide evacuation buses or, better, trains, such advice seem to imply that poor people had to start walking. (When, after the breakdown of sanitation and order in the
Superdome, hundreds of people did attempt to escape the city by walking across a bridge into the white suburb of Gretna, they were turned
back by panicky local police who fired over their heads.)

It is inevitable that many of those left behind in their drowning
neighborhoods will interpret City Hall's unconscionable negligence in
the context of the bitter economic and racial schisms that have long

made New Orleans the most tragic city in the United States. It is no secret that New Orleans's business elites and their allies in City Hall
would like to push the poorest segment of the population—blamed for
the city's high crime rates—out of the city. Historic public-housing
projects have been razed to make room for upper-income townhouses
and a Wal-Mart. In other housing projects, residents are routinely
evicted for offenses as trivial as their children's curfew violations. The
ultimate goal seems to be a tourist theme-park New Orleans—Las
Vegas on the Mississippi—with chronic poverty hidden away in bayous, trailer parks and prisons outside the city limits.

Not surprisingly, some advocates of a whiter, safer New Orleans see
a divine plan in Katrina. "We finally cleaned up public housing in New
Orleans," a leading Louisiana Republican confined to Washington lobbyists. "We couldn't do it, but God did." Likewise, Mayor Nagin boasted
of his empty streets and ruined neighborhoods, "this city is for the first
time free of drugs and violence, and we intend to keep it that way." Indeed a partial ethnic cleansing of New Orleans will be a fait accompli
without massive local and federal efforts to provide affordable housing
for the tens of thousands of poor renters who are now dispersed across
the country in refugee shelters. Already there is intense debate about
transforming some of poorest low-lying neighborhoods like the Lower
Ninth Ward into water retention ponds to protect the wealthier parts of
the city. As the *Wall Street Journal* has rightly emphasized, "that would
mean preventing some of New Orleans's poorest residents from ever
returning to their neighborhoods."(22)

As everyone recognizes, the rebuilding of New Orleans and the rest
of the afflicted Gulf region will be an epic political dogfight. Already
Mayor Nagin has staked out the claims of the local gentrifying class by
announcing that he will appoint a sixteen-member blue ribbon reconstruction commission evenly split between whites and Blacks, although
the city is more than 75 percent African American. New Orleans's
"white-flight" suburbs (the social springboards for neo-Nazi David
Duke's frightening electoral successes in the early 1990s), meanwhile,

will fiercely lobby for their cause, while Mississippi's powerful Republican establishment has already warned that it will not play second fiddle to Big Easy Democrats. In this inevitable clash of interest groups, it is unlikely that New Orleans's traditional Black neighborhoods—the true hearths of the city's joyous sensibility and jazz culture—will be able to exercise much clout.

The Bush administration meanwhile hopes to find its own resurrection in a combination of rampant fiscal Keynesianism and fundamentalist social engineering. Katrina's immediate impact on the Potomac, of course, was such a steep fall in the president's popularity—and collaterally, of the U.S. occupation of Iraq—that Republican hegemony itself seemed suddenly under threat. For the first time since the Los Angeles riots of 1992, "Old Democrat" issues like poverty, racial injustice, and public investment temporarily commanded public discourse, and the *Wall Street Journal* warned that Republicans had "to get back on the political and intellectual offensive" before liberals like Ted Kennedy could revive New Deal nostrums such as a massive federal agency for flood control and shoreline restoration along the Gulf Coast.

Accordingly, the Heritage Foundation hosted meetings late into the night at which conservative ideologues, congressional cadre, and the ghosts of Republicans past (like Edwin Meese, Nixon's former attorney general) hashed out a strategy to rescue Bush from the toxic aftermath of FEMA's disgrace. New Orleans's floodlit but empty Jackson Square became the eerie backdrop for the president's September 15 speech on hurricane reconstruction. It was an extraordinary performance. Bush sunnily reassured the 2 million victims of Katrina that the White House would pick up most of the tab for the estimated 200 billion dollars' worth of flood damage: deficit spending on a scale that would have given even Keynes vertigo. (The president is still proposing another huge tax cut for the superrich.) He then wooed his political base with a dream list of long-sought-after conservative social reforms: school and housing vouchers, a central role for churches, an "urban homestead" lottery, extensive tax breaks to businesses, the creation of a

Gulf Opportunity Zone, and the suspension of annoying government regulations (which in the fine print turn out to include prevailing wages in construction and environmental regulations on offshore drilling).(156)

For connoisseurs of Bush-speak, the Jackson Square speech was a moment of exquisite déjà vu: had not similar promises been made on the banks of Euphrates? As Paul Krugman cruelly pointed out, the White House, having tried and failed to turn Iraq "into a laboratory for conservative economic policies" would now experiment on traumatized inhabitants of Biloxi and the Ninth Ward.(86) Congressman Mike Pence, a leader of the powerful Republican Study Group, which helped draft the president's reconstruction agenda, emphasized that Republicans would turn the storm rubble into a capitalist utopia. "We want to turn the Gulf Coast into a magnet for free enterprise. The last thing we want is a federal city where New Orleans once was."(156)

Symptomatically, as the *New York Times* recently pointed out, the Army Corps in New Orleans is now led by the same official who formerly oversaw contracts in Iraq.(111) The Lower Ninth Ward may never exist again, but already the barroom and strip-joint owners in the French Quarter are relishing the fat days ahead, as the Halliburton workers, Blackwater mercenaries, and Bechtel engineers leave their federal paychecks behind on Bourbon Street.

(October 2005, *Le Monde Diplomatique*)

THIRTY-FOUR

AT THE CORNER OF
NEW ORLEANS AND HUMANITY

A few blocks from the badly flooded and still-closed campus of Dillard University, a wind-bent street sign announces the intersection of Humanity and New Orleans. In the nighttime distance, the downtown skyscrapers on Poydras and Canal Streets are already ablaze with light, but a vast northern and eastern swath of the city, including the Gentilly neighborhood around Dillard, remains shrouded in darkness.

The lights have been out for six months now, and no one seems to know when, if ever, they will be turned back on. In greater New Orleans about 125,000 homes remain damaged and unoccupied, a vast ghost city that rots in darkness while *les bon temps* return to a guilty strip of unflooded and mostly affluent neighborhoods near the river. Such a large portion of the Black population is gone that some radio stations are now switching their formats from funk and rap to soft rock.

Mayor Ray Nagin likes to boast that "New Orleans is back," pointing to the tourists who again prowl the French Quarter and the Tulane students who crowd Magazine Street bistros; but the current population of New Orleans on the west bank of the Mississippi is about the same as that of Disney World on a normal day. More than 60 percent of Nagin's constituents—including an estimated 80 percent of the African Americans—are still scattered in exile with no obvious way home.

In their absence, local business elites, advised by conservative think tanks, "New Urbanists" and neo-Democrats, have usurped almost every function of elected government. With the City Council largely shut out of their deliberations, mayor-appointed commissions and outside experts, mostly white and Republican, propose to radically shrink and reshape a majority-Black and Democratic city. Without any mandate from local voters, the public-school system has already been virtually abolished, along with the jobs of unionized teachers and school employees. Thousands of other unionized jobs have been lost with the closure of Charity Hospital, formerly the flagship of public medicine in Louisiana. And a proposed oversight board, dominated by appointees of President Bush and Governor Kathleen Babineaux Blanco, would end local control over city finances.

Meanwhile, Bush's pledge to "get the work done quickly" and mount "one of the largest reconstruction efforts the world has ever seen" has proved to be the same fool's gold as his earlier guarantee to rebuild Iraq's bombed-out infrastructure. Instead, the administration has left the residents of neighborhoods like Gentilly in limbo: largely without jobs, emergency housing, flood protection, mortgage relief, small-business loans, or a coordinated plan for reconstruction.

With each passing week of neglect—what Representative Barney Frank has labeled "a policy of ethnic cleansing by inaction"—the likelihood increases that most Black Orleanians will never be able to return. As the *New York Times* observed in early February (2006), Katrina "barely merited a mention" in the president's State of the Union address, and "New Orleans has all but dropped off the map of national priorities." Mayor Nagin has become so desperate for assistance that he has begged for help from foreign countries, including France and Jordan.

Yet, even as pundits rant about the foolishness of locals wanting to return to their below-sea-level homes, it has become clear that federal negligence, not wrathful nature, was most responsible for killing New Orleans.

Dereliction of Duty

"Not just human error was involved.
There may have been malfeasance."
—Forensic engineer on the levee breaches(133)

Humanity Street was flooded on August 29 by a breach in the London Avenue Canal, which—like the Orleans and 17th Street canals further west—provides a lake outfall for storm water pumped from low-lying residential districts like Gentilly that were originally swamplands.

After Katrina, the Army Corps of Engineers and the Orleans Parish Levee Board claimed the northern portion of the city had drowned because a hurricane-driven storm surge of biblical magnitude had overtopped the flood walls that the agencies jointly build and maintain along New Orleans's canals. "The intensity of the storm," said Corps commander Lieutenant General Carl Strock on September 2, "simply exceeded the design capacity of this levee."(125) Later in testimony before Congress, representatives of the two bureaucracies continued to blame a "Category 4 or 5 surge" despite evidence from an American Society of Civil Engineers investigation that water levels, in fact, were "well below the top height of the floodwalls [sic]" (designed to withstand a Category 3 hurricane) and that the breaches were the results of design and construction flaws, not monster waves.(113)

Now, thanks to further research by a team of forensic engineers sponsored by the National Science Foundation (NSF) as well as by inspired muckracking by the press, there is stunning evidence that federal authorities were well aware that the city's levee system was fatally compromised by incompetent design and shoddy construction as well as by chronic underfunding that left critical holes in the city's defenses.

In the cases of the 17th Street and probably London Avenue canals, for example, flawed soil analyses, which ignored dangerously unstable layers of swamp peat, led project engineers to build walls that were too weak and poorly anchored to resist shifts in the underlying soil. When the Army Corps's Vicksburg office—the highest level of engineering authority on the entire Mississippi system—discovered these potentially catastrophic faults in a 1990 design review, their New Orleans colleagues apparently shrugged off the warning without any attempt the remediate the unstable structures.(99)

In the case of the Orleans Canal flood wall—which NSF investigators describe as having "basically failed before the storm began"—a large (and ultimately fatal) gap had been left to prevent water pressure from bursting the walls of an ancient pumping station. Despite urgent appeals by both the Corps and the Levee Board, the Bush administration refused to authorize $10 million to rebuild the pumping station and complete the flood wall. (As a Democratic stronghold controlling the balance of power in Louisiana elections, New Orleans is obviously not a favorite charity of a Republican White House.)

Meanwhile, as everyone knew it would, the funneling effect of the notorious Mississippi River Gulf Outlet (MRGO)—a little-used ship channel expensively maintained by the Army Corps—amplified Katrina's storm surge by as much as 40 percent as it raced toward the Industrial Canal and the Lower Ninth Ward. "Hurricane Pam," an interagency planning exercise in 2004, confirmed this scenario and accurately predicted extensive flooding throughout the city's eastern flank. Yet the Corps, in obeisance to shipping interests, had for years rejected urgent local demands to close MRGO.(65)

In the face of growing evidence of its negligence, the Army Corps has only compounded suspicion by withholding crucial documents from the NSF team and repeatedly blocking their access to levee breach sites. Likewise, Republicans in congressional hearings have tried to deflect the blame for the Katrina fiasco from the Army Corps to the Orleans Parish Levee District, which they depict as a corrupt patronage machine that cares less about flood control than a lucrative subsidiary that includes a marina, amusement park, and gambling boat. This caricature may be largely true, but it is almost irrelevant since the Army Corps and its top boss, Secretary of Defense Donald Rumsfeld, bear the ultimate legal responsibility for flood protection and the design standards of the city's levees and flood walls. By tradition, the Corps is supposed to represent the gold standard in American engineering; instead, it now faces the disgrace of losing New Orleans (as well as having squandered billions in the failed "rebuilding of Iraq").

Lie and Stall

"The worst fears of many policymakers are being realized....
Bureaucratic delays have caused the recovery effort
to be appallingly slow and inefficient."
—Senator Tom Coburn (R-OK)(74)

False promises are a Bush dynasty tradition. In the spring of 1992, President George H. Bush toured the burnt-out rubble in South Central L.A., reassuring residents that Washington had "an absolute responsibility to solve inner-city problems." In response to the Rodney King riots, the White House promised major initiatives to aid Los Angeles and other neglected big cities. But presidential compassion quickly turned back into indifference as Republican leaders in Congress blocked every effort to "reward the rioters."(140)

Likewise, after his bungling initial response to Katrina, Bush impersonated FDR and Lyndon Johnson when he reassured the nation in his September 15 Jackson Square speech that "we have a duty to confront [New Orleans's] poverty with bold action.... We will do what it takes, we will stay as long as it takes to help citizens rebuild their communities and their lives."

In the event, the White House sat on its pledges all autumn, mumbling homilies about the limits of government, while its conservative attack dogs in Congress offset Gulf relief with $40 billion worth of cutbacks in Medicaid, food stamps, and student loans. Republicans also rebelled against aid for a state that was depicted as a venal Third World society, a failed state like Haiti, out of step with national values. "Louisiana and New Orleans," according to Idaho Senator Larry Craig, "are the most corrupt governments in our country and they always have been.... Fraud is in the culture of Iraqis. I believe that is true in the state of Louisiana as well."(36)

Democrats, apart from the Congressional Black Caucus, did pathetically little to counter this backlash or to hold Bush's feet to the fire over his Jackson Square pledge. The promised national debate about urban poverty never took place; instead, New Orleans, like a great derelict ship, drifted helplessly in the treacherous currents of White House hypocrisy and conservative contempt.

An early, deadly blow was Treasury Secretary John Snow's refusal to guarantee New Orleans municipal bonds, forcing Mayor Nagin to lay off three thousand city employees on top of the thousands of education and medical workers already jobless. The Bush administration also blocked bipartisan measures to increase Medicaid coverage for Katrina evacuees and to give the State of Louisiana—facing an estimated $8 billion in lost revenues over the next few years—a share of the income generated by its offshore oil and gas leases.

Even more egregious was the flagrant redlining of Black neighborhoods by the Small Business Administration (SBA), which rejected a majority of loan applications by local businesses and homeowners. An analysis by the *New York Times* in mid-December concluded that "the [SBA] loans that have been approved so far appear to be flowing to wealthy neighborhoods in New Orleans but not to poor ones."(44) At the same time, a bipartisan Senate bill to save small businesses with emergency bridge loans was sabotaged by Bush officials, leaving thousands to face bankruptcy and foreclosure.

As a result, the economic foundations of the city's African-American middle class (those with public-sector jobs and small businesses) have been swept away by deliberate decisions made in the White House and presumably overseen by the domestic-policy troika of Dick Cheney, Andrew Card, and Karl Rove. Similarly, FEMA's excruciating failure to provide temporary housing within the city prevented blue-collar Orleanians, exiled in Baton Rouge, Houston, and Atlanta, from returning to jobs in reconstruction and revived tourism. In six months, FEMA had installed barely one-seventh of the trailers it had promised to New Orleans and even police officers were still homeless.

In the absence of federal or state initiatives to employ locals or provide adequate temporary housing, low-income Blacks are probably permanently losing their niches in the construction and service sectors to more mobile outsiders. "With jobs lost, shuffled and solicited," Christine Hauser reported last fall, "the workforce crisis is changing the very demography of New Orleans. With schools still closed, for example, families have migrated to other states to look for work and stability . Many of the newer workers here are younger and single, able to double up in apartments. Better-off and more mobile workers, some commuting from nearby areas, have begun to replace workers who could not afford cars."(66)

In stark contrast to its neglect of neighborhood relief, the White House has made Herculean efforts to reward its own base of large corporations and political insiders. Representative Nydia Velazquez, who sits on the House Small Business Committee, pointed out that the SBA has allowed large corporations to get $2 billion in federal contracts while excluding local minority contractors. Likewise, the so-called Gulf Opportunity Zone has primarily benefited larger companies outside the disaster area. A typical example, according to veteran Louisiana political analyst John Maginnis, is "apartment developers in Baton Rouge and Lafayette, who were able to raise rents to meet growing demands from displaced residents, and who now can have virtually free money to build more units."(96)

But the paramount beneficiaries of Katrina relief aid—to no one's surprise—have been the giant Republican engineering firms KBR (a Halliburton subsidiary) and the Shaw Group, which enjoy the services of lobbyist Joe Allbaugh (a former FEMA director and Bush's 2000 campaign manager). FEMA and the Army Corps of Engineers, while unable to explain to Governor Blanco last fall exactly how they were spending money in Louisiana, have tolerated levels of profiteering that would raise eyebrows even on the war-torn Euphrates. Some of this largesse, of course, is guaranteed to be recycled as GOP campaign contributions.

FEMA, for example, has paid the Shaw Group $175 per square (100 square feet) to install tarps on storm-damaged roofs in New Orleans. Yet the actual installers earn as little as $2 per square, and the tarps are provided by FEMA. Similarly, the Army Corps pays prime contractors about $20 per cubic yard of storm debris removed, yet some bulldozer operators receive only $1. (The cleanup, moreover, is proceeding so slowly that by February contractors have removed only 6 million out of an estimated 50 million cubic yards of debris in the city.)(128)

Every level of the contracting food chain, in other words, is grotesquely overfed except the bottom rung, where the actual work is carried out. While the Friends of Bush mine gold from the wreckage of New Orleans, many disappointed recovery workers—often Mexican or Salvadoran immigrants camped out in city parks and derelict shopping centers—can barely make ends meet.

The Big Kiss-Off

"Lawmakers need to understand that for New Orleans the words 'pending in Congress' are a death warrant requiring no signature."
—*New York Times*(112)

In the fractious, take-no-prisoners world of Louisiana politics, broad solidarity of interest is normally as rare as a boulder in a bayou. Yet Katrina created an unprecedented bipartisan consensus around twin demands for Category 5 hurricane protection and mortgage relief for damaged homes. From conservative Republicans to liberal Democrats, there has been unanimity that the region's recovery depends on federal investment in new levees and coastal restoration, as well as financial rescue of the estimated two hundred thousand homeowners whose insurance coverage has failed to cover their actual damage. (There has been no equivalent consensus and little concern for the right of renters—who constituted 53 percent of the population before Katrina—and of public-housing tenants to return to their city.)

Comprehensive Category 5 protection for the New Orleans region had actually been mandated by the Johnson administration after Hurricane Betsy flooded parts of New Orleans in 1965, but key elements of the plan, including storm gates on the canal outfalls on Lake Pontchartrain, were subsequently scuttled, and others, like the Orleans Canal flood wall, were left unfinished. By the 1990s, annual appropriations for hurricane protection were consistently less than the urgent requests from the Army Corps and local governments.

Yet even as the federal commitment to southern Louisiana was waning, the storm-surge danger to New Orleans was steadily increasing as its protective delta dissolved into the Gulf of Mexico. Catastrophic coastal erosion at the rate of one acre every twenty-four minutes is partly a consequence of the Army Corps's monumental dam-building and streamlining of river flow, which reduces the delta's vital diet of sediment; but even more so, it is the by-product of the constant, promiscuous dredging and canal-cutting by the oil and gas industries. (51) In both cases, the ultimate safety of New Orleans and surrounding parishes had been compromised to accommodate powerful, nonlocal economic interests (upriver agribusiness, shipping companies, and energy corporations) without any mechanism to recycle revenues into compensatory coastal restoration and urban flood control.

In 1998, after a terrifying close call with Hurricane Georges, a coalition of agencies and governments including the Army Corps, EPA, and all twenty coastal parishes united around Coast 2050, a comprehensive $14 billion plan to rebuild barrier islands and restore vanishing wetlands. Experts agreed that the protection of New Orleans required in addition the modernization and relocation of the city's storm pumps, massive flood gates on the lake, the construction of truly robust levees, and the closure of the infamous MRGO. The combined cost of coastal restoration and new hurricane fortifications has been estimated at $30 billion over a generation.

Before Katrina, there was never the slightest chance that a Republican White House or GOP-dominated Congress would give consideration to spending so much money to protect the Deep South's "bluest," most Democratic city. Then after the deluge, the president's Jackson Square speech seemed to signal a new dispensation: Coast 2050 and Category 5 levees were suddenly topics of serious discussion. Bipartisan

Louisiana delegations rushed off to the Netherlands to see what a truly serious national commitment to coastal protection could achieve.

Yet the Louisianans quickly discovered, as had the Angelenos before them, that Bush Inc. was offering little more than empty words and a few bottles of snake oil. By early November it was clear that saving New Orleans was no longer high on the administration agenda, if it had ever been. When reporters asked if the president supported Category 5 levees, his spokespeople pointedly refused to give a direct answer. Washington was rumored to be suffering from "Katrina Fatigue," with little congressional enthusiasm for flushing billions down the supposed "black hole" of bayou corruption. When Louisiana delegates lobby for flood protection, a reporter noted, "they often are met with skepticism, ignorance and outright hostility"—attitudes that the newly appointed Gulf recovery czar, Texas banker and Bush mega-contributor Donald Powell, did nothing to dispel.

To locals, of course, Washington was brazenly blaming the victim (all the more so, in light of the exposes about the Army Corps's negligence), and, as the *Times-Picayune* complained, "They [Congress] act as if we wore our skirts too short and invited trouble." One of New Orleans's few outspoken allies, the editorial page of the *New York Times*, pointed out that the thirty-year bill for protecting New Orleans would equal "barely one-third the cost of the $95 billion in tax cuts passed just last week by the House of Representatives."(112) Louisianans added that they wouldn't need to beg if they received the same share of offshore oil and gas royalties that states like California and Texas have traditionally derived from land-based oil exploration.

But both points were moot. As Congress headed toward its Christmas adjournment, the Louisiana delegation was in panic mode: A Category 5 plan had disappeared from serious discussion, and there were doubts about whether the damaged levees would be repaired before hurricane season returned. (In early March engineers monitoring the progress of the Army Corps's work complained that the use of weak, sandy soils and the lack of concrete "armoring" insured that the levees would again fail in a major storm.)

Congress ultimately voted to provide $29 billion for Gulf Coast relief. Yet as the *Washington Post* reported, "All but $6 billion of the measure merely reshuffled some of the $62 billion in previously approved Hurricane Katrina aid. The rest was funded by a 1 percent across-the-board cut of non-emergency, discretionary programs."(73) The Pentagon won approval for a whopping $4.4 billion in base repairs and other professed Katrina-related needs, but Congress cut out the $250 million allocated to combat coastal erosion. Meanwhile, Mississippi's powerful Republican troika—Governor Haley Barbour and Senators Trent Lott and Thad Cochran—persuaded fellow Republicans to support $6.2 billion in discretionary housing aid for Louisiana and $5.3 billion for Mississippi.

Louisiana Democrats blushed in gratitude to their Mississippi colleagues, but it was truly the devil's bargain, with red-state Mississippi getting five times as much aid per distressed household as pink-state Louisiana. Although the administration took credit for doubling spending on levees to $3.1 billion, it was sheer sleight of hand since $1.4 billion in Louisiana Community Development Block Grants (CDBG) assistance had been shifted to flood control; all for the sake of providing (as the *Times-Picayune* pointed out) "the Category 3 hurricane protection the New Orleans area was supposed to have before Katrina revealed structural inadequacies in the system."

Louisiana received another blow on January 23, when Bush rejected GOP Representative Richard Baker's plan calling for a federally guaranteed Louisiana Reconstruction Corporation, which would bail out homeowners by buying distressed properties and packaging them in larger parcels for resale to developers. Local Republicans as well as Democrats howled in rage, and the future of southern Louisiana was again thrown into chaos. Although the Administration eventually promised an additional $4.2 billion in housing aid, the appropriation continues to be fought over by Texas and other jealous states.

Ancient Calumnies

"I hate the way they portray us in the media. If you see a
black family, it says they're looting. See a white family,
it says they're looking for food."
—Kanye West

The Republican hostility to New Orleans, of course, runs deeper and is nastier than mere concern with civic probity (America's most corrupt city, after all, is located on the Potomac, not the Mississippi). Underlying all the circumlocutions are the same antediluvian prejudices and stereotypes that were used to justify the violent overthrow of Reconstruction 130 years ago.

Let us return for a moment to the symbol-laden corner of New Orleans and Humanity. Humanity Street and the adjacent 610 freeway constitute a local social divide: to the south are older working-class neighborhoods largely composed of weary bungalows and "shotgun" duplexes, with occasional apartment buildings and public-housing projects. North of Humanity, however, are attractive subdivisions of brick-facade homes: part of a sprawling Black middle-class universe that includes Pontchartrain Park with its golf course and country club as well as the generic Home Depot and Days Inn suburbia of New Orleans East, across the Industrial Canal.

Usually it is the poor who are invisible in the aftermath of urban disasters, but in the case of New Orleans it has been the African-American professional middle class and skilled working class. In the confusion and suffering of Katrina—a Rorschach test of the American racial unconscious—most white politicians and media pundits have chosen to see only the demons of their prejudices. The city's complex history and social geography have been reduced to a cartoon of a vast slum inhabited by an alternately criminal or helpless underclass, whose salvation is the kindness of strangers in other, whiter cities. Inconvenient realities like Gentilly's red-brick normalcy—or, for that matter, the pride of homeownership and the exuberance of civic activism in the blue-collar Lower Ninth Ward—have not been allowed to interfere with the belief, embraced by New Democrats as well as old Republicans, that Black urban culture is inherently pathological.

Thus the national media shamelessly and uncritically purveyed the spectacle of a flooded city under the terrorist rule of thugs, rapists, and zombies—a hallucination, to be fair, that originated in the hysteria of Mayor Nagin and top police officials. Lurid images of a rampaging underclass, in turn, "changed troop deployments, delayed medical evacuations, drove police officers to quit, grounded helicopters" and left a toxic legacy in public opinion. Terrified members of New Orleans's oligarchy, like regional transit head James Reiss, helicoptered in machine-gun-toting Israeli security guards to protect their Audubon Place mansions.(34) Yet the mayhem was largely urban myth: in late September New Orleans's police superintendent Eddie Compass confessed to the *New York Times* that "we have no official reports to document any murder. Not one official report of rape or sexual assault."(41)

But the truth will never slacken the thirst of conservative fundamentalists like the Cato Institute's David Boaz, intent on blaming the Katrina catastrophe on a welfare state that "so destroyed wealth and self-reliance in the people of New Orleans that they were unable to fend for themselves in a crisis."(14) Nor will it stop Joel Kotkin, writing in the *American Enterprise* magazine, from libeling "isolated, immobile African-American remnants mired in urban poverty," or prevent David Brooks from claiming with self-righteous certainty that "if we just put up new buildings and allow the same people to move back into their old neighborhoods, then urban New Orleans will become just as rundown and dysfunctional as before."(18, 83)

Such calumnies reproduce ancient caricatures—Blacks running amok, incapable of honest self-government—that were evoked by the murderous White League when it plotted against Reconstruction in New Orleans in the 1870s. (The League's platform declared that "where the white race rules, the negro is peaceful and happy; where the black rules; the negro is starved and oppressed." It promised to restore "that just and legitimate superiority in the administration of our State affairs to which we are entitled by superior responsibility, superior numbers and superior intelligence.")(61) Indeed, some civil rights veterans fear that the 1874 Battle of Canal Street, a bloody League-organized insurrection against a Republican administration elected by Black suffrage, is being refought—perhaps without pikes and guns, but with the same fundamental aim of dispossessing Black New Orleans of economic and political power. Certainly, a sweeping transformation of the racial balance of power within the city has been on some people's agenda for a long time.

The Krewe of Canizaro

"As I wish, thus I command."
—Motto of Comus

Power and status in New Orleans have always been defined by membership in secretive Mardi Gras "krewes" and social clubs, with the Krewe of Comus and the Boston and Louisiana Clubs at the apex. "Perhaps more than any other city in America," historian John Barry has written, "New Orleans was [is] run by a cabal of insiders.... Looking on as if from behind a two-way mirror, these insiders watched and judged and decided."(9)

In the early 1990s civil rights activists, led by feisty Councilmember Dorothy Mae Taylor, finally forced the token desegregation of Mardi Gras, and some of the clubs reluctantly admitted a few African-American millionaires. Despite some old-guard holdouts (like Comus, which preferred to stop parading rather than integrate), Uptown seemed to be adjusting, however grudgingly, to the reality of Black political clout.(61) But as post-Katrina events have brutally clarified, if the oligarchy is dead, then long live the oligarchy.

While elected Black officials protest impotently from the sidelines, a largely white elite has wrested control over the debate about how to rebuild the city. This de facto ruling krewe includes Jim Amoss, editor

of the New Orleans *Times-Picayune;* Pres Kabacoff, developer-gentri-
fier and local patron of the New Urbanism; Donald Bollinger, ship-
yard owner and prominent Bushite; James Reiss, real estate investor
and chair of the Regional Transit Authority (i.e., the man responsible
for the buses that didn't evacuate people); Alden McDonald Jr., CEO
of one of the largest Black-owned banks; Janet Howard of the Bureau
of Government Research (originally established by Uptown elites to
oppose the populism of Huey Long); and Scott Cowen, the aggressively ambitious president of Tulane University.

But the dominating figure and kingpin is Joseph Canizaro, a
wealthy property developer who is a leading Bush supporter with
close personal ties to the White House inner circle. He is also the
power behind the throne of Mayor Nagin, a nominal Democrat (he
supported Bush in 2000) who was elected in 2002 with 85 percent of
the white vote. Finally, as the former president of the Urban Land Institute, Canizaro mobilizes the support of some of the nation's most
powerful developers and prestigious master planners.

In a city where old money is often as reclusive as Anne Rice's vampires, Canizaro poses as a brave civic leader unafraid to speak bitter
but necessary truths. As he told the Associated Press about the Katrina
diaspora last October: "As a practical matter, these poor folks don't
have the resources to go back to our city just like they didn't have the
resources to get out of our city. So we won't get all those folks back.
That's just a fact."(6)

Indeed it is a "fact" that Canizaro has helped shape into reigning
dogma. The number of displaced residents returning to the city is obviously a highly variable function of the resources and opportunities
provided for them, yet the rebuilding debate has been premised on
suspicious projections—provided by the RAND Corporation and
endlessly repeated by Nagin and Canizaro—that in three years the city
would recover only half of its August 2005 population.

Many Orleanians cynically wonder whether such projections aren't
actually goals, since the likes of Canizaro, Reiss, and Kabacoff have

complained for years about the city's "teaming underclass and atten-
dant high crime rate," the percentage of residents in public-housing
projects, and the proliferation of derelict and abandoned homes.(145)
Faced with the dire fiscal consequences of white flight to suburban Jefferson and St. Tammany's parishes, as well as three decades of deindus-
trialization (which gives New Orleans an economic profile closer to
Newark than Houston and Atlanta) they have argued that the city has
become a soul-destroying warehouse for underemployed and poorly
educated African Americans, whose real interests—it is claimed—
might be better served by a Greyhound ticket to another town. As
Kabacoff argued in 2003, "if a city is going to be healthy, you need to
disperse your poor and concentrate your wealth. In New Orleans, we
concentrate our poor and disperse our wealth."(146)

Katrina, from this elite perspective, offers an almost utopian opportunity to resurrect New Orleans freed of its burden of poverty and
crime. As one real-estate magnate chortled to a European reporter:
"The hurricane drove poor people and criminals out of the city, and
we hope they don't come back. The party's finally over for these people, and now they're going to have to find someplace else to live."(59)
Although Canizaro and Kabacoff would never express themselves this
crudely, both have long crusaded for replacing older, centrally situ-
ated public-housing projects like St. Thomas (Lower Garden District)
and Iberville (across from the French Quarter) with New Urbanist inspired mixed-income neighborhoods. Urban revitalization, in so
many words, requires a triage of the burdensome poor.

Kabacoff's 2003 redevelopment of the St. Thomas public housing
project as River Garden, a largely market-rate faux Creole subdivi-
sion, has become the prototype for the smaller, wealthier, whiter city
that Mayor Nagin's Bring New Orleans Back commission (with
Canizaro as head of the crucial urban planning committee) proposes
to build. "Mayor Ray Nagin suggested, in one of his often impulsive
public addresses," the *Times-Picayune* reported in November, "that
the River Garden brand of New Urbanism should be the model for rebuilding the presumably soon-to-be-bulldozed portions of the Big

Easy. His assertions were soon echoed by Housing and Urban Development Secretary Alphonso Jackson, who vowed that River Garden would be the rebuilding model when other flooded public housing developments are razed."(102)

Despite years of protest, St. Thomas was bulldozed in 2000 and its 1,700 tenants were relocated elsewhere. River Garden, which was built with federal HOPE VI program funds, symbolized the Clinton-era approach to breaking up intractable concentrations of Black poverty by bulldozing public housing and using housing vouchers to "empower" residents to move elsewhere in the city (often to even poorer neighborhoods and more miserable housing). HOPE VI was originally envisioned as one-for-one replacement of public housing but quickly became a stealth strategy of gentrification that has given politically connected developers like Kabacoff access to sites with extraordinary redevelopment potential. (Nationally, HOPE VI is estimated to have caused a net loss of fifty thousand affordable housing units.)(121) In the case of River Garden only a handful of original project tenants have met the criteria for remaining in subsidized units, but land values in the adjacent parts of the Lower Garden District have soared.

Underlying the New Urbanism of River Garden is a dogmatic belief that low-income Black neighborhoods, trapped in multigenerational "cultures of poverty," are incapable of self-improvement, waste scarce public investment, and don't generate significant social capital. Although a 10 percent to 30 percent quota of low-income residents may sound revolutionary if applied to Beverly Hills, "mixed income" in the context of New Orleans's housing projects means mass eviction, tempered only by new homes for a minority of the "deserving poor" (to use a Victorian term). Kabacoff fervently argues that a low ratio of poor tenants is the sine qua non to ensure the viability of rebuilt neighborhoods: "with 30 percent affordable (mothers and children), you are pushing the envelope."(94)

Planned Shrinkage

"A massive redlining plan wrapped around a giant land grab."
—Former New Orleans mayor Mark Morial(50)

The awkwardly acronymized BNOB—Bring New Orleans Back—
is perhaps the most important elite initiative in New Orleans since the
famous "Cold Water Committee" (which included Kabacoff's father)
mobilized in 1946 to overthrow the "Old Regulars" and elect reformer
deLesseps Morrison as mayor. BNOB grew out of a notorious meeting
between Mayor Nagin and New Orleans business leaders (dubbed by
some "the forty thieves") that Reiss organized in Dallas twelve days
after Katrina devastated the city. The summit excluded most of New
Orleans's elected Black representatives and, according to Reiss as
characterized in the *Wall Street Journal,* focused on the opportunity to
rebuild the city "with better services and fewer poor people."(34)

Fears that a municipal coup d'etat was in progress were scarcely
mollified when at the end of September the mayor charged BNOB
with preparing a master plan to rebuild the city. Although the seven-
teen-member commission was racially balanced and included City
Council president Oliver Thomas as well as jazz musician Wynton
Marsalis (telecommuting from Manhattan), the real clout was exer-
cised by committee chairs, especially Canizaro (urban planning),
Cowen (education), and Howard (finance), who lunched privately
with the mayor before the group's weekly meeting. This inner sanc-
tum was reportedly necessary because the full-panel meetings did not
allow a frank discussion of "tough issues of race and class."(127)

BNOB might have quickly imploded but for a shrewd outflanking
movement by Canizaro, who persuaded Nagin to invite the Urban
Land Institute (ULI) to work with the commission. Years earlier
Canizaro had brought the ULI to help convince St. Thomas residents
to seek the HOPE VI funding that eventually resulted in Kabacoff's
River Garden and the displacement of most tenants. Although the
ULI is the self-interested national voice of corporate land developers,

Nagin and Canizaro welcomed the delegation of developers, architects, and ex-mayors as a heroic cavalry of expertise riding to the city's rescue. In a nutshell, the ULI's recommendations reframed the historic elite desire to shrink the city's socioeconomic footprint of Black poverty (and Black political power) as a crusade to reduce its *physical* footprint to contours commensurate with public safety and a fiscally viable urban infrastructure.

Upon these suspect premises, the outside "experts" (including representatives of some of the country's largest property firms and corporate architects) proposed an unprecedented triage of an American city, in which low-lying neighborhoods would be targeted for mass buyouts and future conversion into a greenbelt to protect New Orleans from flooding. As a visiting developer told BNOB: "Your housing is now a public resource. You can't think of it as private property anymore."(25)

Keenly aware of inevitable popular resistance, the ULI also proposed a Crescent City Rebuilding Corporation, armed with eminent domain, that would bypass the City Council, as well as an oversight board with power over the city's finances. With control of New Orleans schools already usurped by the state, the ULI's proposed dictatorship of experts and elite appointees would effectively overthrow representative democracy and annul the right of local people to make decisions about their lives. For veterans of the 1960s civil rights movement, especially, it reeked of disenfranchisement pure and simple, a return to the paternalism of plantation days.

The City Council, supported by a surprising number of white homeowners and their representatives, angrily rejected the ULI plan. Mayor Nagin—truly a cat on a hot tin roof—danced anxiously back and forth between the two camps, disavowing abandonment of any area while at the same time warning that the city could not afford to service every neighborhood. But state and national officials, including HUD Secretary Alphonso Jackson, applauded the ULI scheme, as did the editorial page of the *Times-Picayune* and the influential Bureau of Government Research. Additional support came from Beltway carpetbaggers like

James Glassman of the American Enterprise Institute ("Those areas should return to marshland"), Ron Utt of the Heritage Foundation ("Should we think about a New Orleans that shrinks back to its original and more viable core?"), and Nicole Gelinas of the Manhattan Institute ("I would submit that the entire structure of the elected school board should be dismantled").(13) New Orleans was treated like a failed state, a domestic Haiti.

Faced with such a formidable coalition of plutocrats, newspaper editors, policy wonks, even environmentalists in favor of downsizing New Orleans, and with their grassroots memberships scattered in exile across the southern tier, the ULI's opponents (including local churches, unions, and activist groups like ACORN) had enormous difficulty making their voices heard. The *Times-Picayune,* as well as the major national dailies, relentlessly sermonized that New Orleans was faced with the choice between the anarchy of its irresponsible elected Council or the wisdom of Canizaro and the ULI elders. Yet throughout December, as the committees worked on their final reports, there was considerable nervousness among its original instigators that the BNOB might bow to popular opinion and pull its punch.

Just before Christmas, the Bureau of Government Research issued a position paper *(Wanted—A Realistic Development Strategy),* which warned that the city faced further disaster if it allowed politics, rather than "physical and demographic realities" to determine "exactly which parts of the city can be rebuilt and when." "Unless the city's plan addresses the mismatch between the city's footprint and its population by initially directing development into more compact areas, the outcome will be random, scattered development in a sea of blight."(21)

The BNOB recommendations presented by Canizaro in January faithfully hewed to the ULI framework: They included an appointed redevelopment corporation, outside the control of the City Council, that would act as a land bank to buy out heavily damaged homes and neighborhoods with federal funds, wielding eminent domain as needed to retire low-lying areas to greenbelt ("Black people's neighborhoods into white people's parks," someone commented) or to assemble "in-fill" tracts for mixed-income development à la River Garden.(17) Other committees recommended a radical diminution of the power of elected government: for example, eliminating the City Council's ability to override decisions by the Planning Commission, consolidating seven elected assessors' offices into a single appointed office, and transferring financial control to a banker-dominated oversight board like Felix Rohatyn's MAC, which ruled New York in the 1970s.

On the crucial question of how to decide which neighborhoods would be allowed to rebuild and which would be bulldozed, BNOB endorsed the concept of forced buyouts but equivocated over process. Instead of the ruthless map that the Bureau of Government Research wanted, Canizaro and colleagues proposed a Rube Goldberg–like temporary building moratorium in tandem with neighborhood planning meetings that would poll homeowners about their intentions. Only those neighborhoods where at least half of the pre-Katrina residents had made a commitment to return would be considered serious candidates for CDBGs and other financial aid.

Canizaro presented the report to Nagin in front of a public audience on January 11. The mayor said, "I like the plan," and he complimented the commissioners for "a job well done." The *Times-Picayune* predictably homilized (in editorials in the December 27 and January 15 issues) that the "death of neighborhoods is an uncomfortable idea for many people, and understandably so, but it may be unavoidable in the aftermath of Katrina." But that "doesn't have to mean," the editors added, "that New Orleans becomes a lesser version of itself. The city can be rebuilt with the same charm."

But most locals found little charm in the Canizaro report. "I will sit in my front door with my shotgun," one resident warned at a jammed meeting in the Council chambers on January 14, while another demanded, "Are we going to allow some developers, some hustlers, some land thieves to grab our land, grab our homes, to make this a Disney World version of our homes, our lives?" Predictably, Nagin panicked and eventually disavowed the building moratorium. Soon afterward the White House torpedoed the Baker plan and left BNOB with only the state-controlled CDBG appropriation to finance its ambitious vision of New Orleans regrouped around a dozen new River Gardens linked by a high-speed light-rail line.

But Canizaro doesn't seem unduly worried. He has reassured supporters that the ULI/BNOB plan can go forward with CDBGs alone if necessary. In addition, he knows that independent of the local political weather, there are powerful external forces—lack of insurance coverage, new FEMA flood maps, refusal of lenders to refinance mortgages, and so on—that can make permanent the exodus from redlined neighborhoods. Moreover, as anyone versed in the realpolitik of modern Louisiana knows, nothing is finally decided in New Orleans until some good ol' boys (and girls) in Baton Rouge have their say.

Power Shift

"We are concerned that there are both a land grab and a power grab going on."
—NAACP(53)

Even before the last bloated body had been fished out of the fetid waters, conservative political analysts were writing gleeful obituaries for Black Democratic power in Louisiana. "The Democrats' margin of victory," said Ronald Utt of the Heritage Foundation, is "living in the Astrodome in Houston." Others pointed excitedly to the new math: subtract the Ninth Ward of New Orleans and Senator Mary Landrieu and numerous other Democrats, big and small, would likely be unemployed.(53) Thanks to the Army Corps's defective levees, the Republicans stand to gain another Senate seat, two Congressional seats, and probably the governorship. The Democrats would also find it impossible to reproduce Bill Clinton's 1992 feat, when he carried Louisiana by almost exactly his margin of victory in New Orleans. With a ruthless psephologist like Karl Rove in the White House, it is inconceivable that such considerations haven't influenced the shameless Bush response to the city's distress.

But there have been Machiavellian celebrations in Baton Rouge as well. As Representative Charlie DeWitt, a conservative Democrat from rural Lecompte, gleefully told a reporter from California: "This state has changed politically. I think it's going to be probably one of the most conservative states in the South." A political analyst from Shreveport added: "Even good people are quietly sitting back, not lending their support to the rebuilding of New Orleans. What you're seeing is a lot of people snickering and winking and nodding..."(8)

Presumably some of this "snickering and winking" has been happening just across the parish borders. New Orleans has always vied with Detroit when it comes to the violent antipathy of white-flight suburbs toward its Black central city, so it is not surprising that representatives from Jefferson Parish (which elected Klan leader David Duke to the state legislature in 1989) and St. Tammany Parish have particularly relished the post-Katrina shift in metropolitan population and electoral power. Both parishes are in the midst of housing booms that may consolidate the hollowing out and decline of New Orleans. In December, for example, giant KB Homes of California announced a partnership with the Shaw Group to start phase-one construction of twenty thousand homes on the West Bank of Jefferson Parish: a move clearly designed to preempt the rebuilding of flood-damaged white-collar neighborhoods in New Orleans across the river. Similarly, across Lake Pontchartrain, there has been a "feeding frenzy" in St. Tammany's "desperation [real estate] market" where the population is predicted to surge 30 percent in the next few years.(63) Likewise, zero-vacancy Baton Rouge is rushing to build enough subdivisions, apartments, and offices to accommodate tens of thousands of expatriates from downriver.

For her part, Governor Blanco, a Democrat, has expressed little concern about this fundamental reconfiguration of Louisiana's major metropolitan area. Indeed, her immediate, Bush-like responses to Katrina were to help engineer a state takeover of New Orleans schools and to slash $500 million in state spending while sponsoring tax breaks (in the name of economic recovery) for oil companies awash in profits. The Legislative Black Caucus was outraged at Blanco's "complete lack of vision and leadership" and went to court to challenge her right to make cuts without consulting lawmakers. But Blanco, supported by rural conservatives and corporate lobbyists, remained intransigent, even openly hostile, to Black Democrats whose support she had previously courted. Representative Cedric Richmond (D-New Orleans), the chair of the Black Caucus, interpreted the confrontation as evidence of a post-Katrina political realignment. "It would appear that the administration is moving to the right." He promised, however, that the Caucus would "continue to speak for the people whose voice is ignored, and that's poor people—not just African Americans, but poor people across the state."(8)

But poor people have no voice inside the Louisiana Recovery Authority, whose gaggle of university presidents and corporate types appointed by Blanco is even less beholden to Black New Orleans voters and their representatives than the Canizaro krewe. The twenty-nine-member LRA board, dominated by representatives of big business, has only one trade unionist and not a single grassroots Black representative. Moreover, in contrast to Nagin's commission, the LRA has the power to decide, not merely advise: It controls the allocation of the FEMA funds and CDBGs that Congress has provided for reconstruction.

According to interviews in the *Times-Picayune,* leading members of the LRA believe that the sheer force of economic disincentives will shrink the city around the contours proposed by the Urban Land Institute.(129) The authority has thus refused to disburse any of its hazard mitigation funds to areas considered unsafe, and presumably will be equally hardheaded in the allocation of CDBG spending. At a special session of the legislature Governor Blanco emphasized that the state, not local government or neighborhood planning committees, will retain control over where grants and loans go. Blanco has announced that she wants to set aside $4.4 billion of the CDBGs to help homeowners throughout the state, with another $1 billion for afford-able housing: far too little to rebuild New Orleans, much less to heal the wounds of a dozen other devastated coastal parishes. In the absence of further federal aid, the threat of a triage controlled by rural and suburban legislators hangs ominously over the city. As advertising executive Sean Reilly, an LRA appointee from Baton Rouge, told the *New York Times* (January 8): "Someone has to be tough, to stand up and to tell the truth. Every neighborhood in New Orleans will not be able to come back safe."

But the elites may have overlooked the Fats Domino factor.

"No Bulldozing!"

"The battle for New Orleans has now become a guerrilla struggle fought block by block and house by house."
—ACORN organizer Wade Rathke(124)

Like hundreds of other flood-damaged but structurally sound homes, Fats Domino's house wears a defiant sign: Save Our Neighborhood: No Bulldozing! The R&B icon, who has always stayed close to his roots in working-class Holy Cross, knows his riverside neighborhood and the rest of the Lower Ninth Ward are prime targets of the city-shrinkers. Indeed, on Christmas Day the *Times-Picayune*—declaring that "before a community can rebuild, it must dream"—published a vision of what a smaller-but-better New Orleans might look like: "Tourists and schoolchildren tour a living museum that includes the former home of Fats Domino and Holy Cross High School, a multiblock memorial to Katrina that spans the devastated neighborhood."(26)

"Living museum" (or "holocaust museum," as a Black friend bitterly observed) sounds like a bad joke, but it is the elite view of what African-American New Orleans should become. In the brave New Urbanist world of Canizaro and Kabacoff, Blacks (along with that other colorful minority group, Cajuns) will reign only as entertainers and self-caricatures. The high-voltage energy that once rocked juke joints,

housing projects, and second-line parades will now be safely embalmed for tourists in a proposed Louisiana Music Experience in the
Central Business District.

But this minstrel-show version of the future must first defeat a remarkable local history of grassroots organization. The Crescent City's
best-kept secret—in the mainstream press, at least—has been the
resurgence of trade-union and community organizing since the mid-
1990s. Indeed, New Orleans, the only southern city in which labor was
ever powerful enough to call a general strike,(4) has become an important crucible of new social movements. In particular, it has become the
home base of ACORN, a national organization of working-class
homeowners and tenants that counts more than nine thousand New
Orleans member-families, mostly in triage-threatened Black neighborhoods. ACORN's membership has been the engine behind the tu-
multuous, decade-long struggle to unionize downtown hotels as well
as the successful 2002 referendum to legislate the nation's first municipal minimum wage (later overthrown by a right-wing state Supreme
Court). Since Katrina, ACORN has emerged as the major opponent of
the ULI/BNOB plan for shrinking the city. Its members find themselves again fighting many of the same elite figures who were opponents of hotel unionization and a living wage.

ACORN founder Wade Rathke scoffs at the RAND Corporation
projections that portray most Blacks abandoning the city. "Don't believe those phony figures," he told me over beignets at Cafe du Monde
in January. "We have polled our displaced members in Houston and
Atlanta. Folks overwhelmingly want to return. But they realize that
this is a tough struggle, since we have to fight simultaneously on two
fronts: to restore people's homes and to bring back their jobs. It is also
a race against time. The challenge is, You make it, you take it. So our
members are voting with their feet."

Not waiting for CDBGs, FEMA flood maps, or permission from
Canizaro, ACORN crews and volunteers from across the country are
working night and day to repair the homes of one thousand member-
families in some of the most threatened areas. The strategy is to con-

front the city-shrinkers with the incontestable fact of reoccupied, viable neighborhood cores.

ACORN has allied with the AFL-CIO and the NAACP to defend worker rights and press for the hiring of locals in the recovery effort. Rathke points out that Katrina has become the pretext for the most vicious government-supported attack on unions since President Reagan fired striking air-traffic controllers in 1981. "First, suspension of Davis-Bacon [federal prevailing wage law], then the state takeover of the schools and the destruction of the teachers' union, and now this." He points to a beat-up green garbage truck rattling by Jackson Square. "Trash collection in the French Quarter used to be a unionized city job, SEIU members. Now FEMA has contracted the work to a scab company from out of state. Is this what Bring New Orleans Back means?"

ACORN also went to court to insure that New Orleans's displaced, largely Black population would have access to out-of-state polling places, especially in Atlanta and Houston, for the scheduled April 22 city elections. When a federal judge rejected the demand, ACORN organizer Stephen Bradberry said it's "so obvious that there's a concerted plan to make this a whiter city." The NAACP agrees, but the Justice Department denied its request to block an election that is likely to transfer power to the artificial white majority created by Katrina.

While ACORN is trying to bring its members home, a coalition of smaller groups, including the Peoples' Hurricane Relief Fund (with a genealogy that goes back to SNCC and the New Orleans chapter of the Black Panther Party), the Common Ground collective, and the New Orleans Green Party, as well as progressive law students and activists from across the country, have been battling proposed demolitions in the Lower Ninth Ward. After Christmas, the city stealthily attempted to bulldoze more than one hundred "public hazard" homes without any effort to locate or notify their owners. Local activists and volunteer workers rushed to put their bodies in the way, winning time for veteran civil-rights lawyer Bill Quigley to file suit against the city for its blatant violation of due progress. As both sides were keenly aware, it was the just the first skirmish in the coming struggle against mass demolitions and neighborhood triage.

It would be inspiring to see in this latest battle of New Orleans the birth pangs of a new or renewed civil rights movement, but gritty local activism has yet to be echoed in meaningful solidarity by the labor movement, so-called progressive Democrats, or even the Congressional Black Caucus. Pledges, press statements, and occasional delegations, yes; but not the unfaltering national outrage and sense of urgency that should attend the attempted murder of New Orleans on the fortieth anniversary of the Voting Rights Act. In 1874, as historian Ted Tunnell has pointed out, the failure of Northern Radicals to launch a militant, armed riposte to the white insurrection in New Orleans helped to doom the first Reconstruction.(149) Will our feeble response to Hurricane Katrina now lead to the rollback of the second?

(February 2006; shorter version in the *Nation*, April)

The lights are still out in most of Gentilly. By New Year's Day 2007 less than one hundred New Orleans homeowners had received federal grants for reconstruction. The expert engineering autopsies, along with published hearings by bipartisan House and Senate committees, have confirmed the Army Corps's responsibility for the flood-wall breaches as well as deepening public understanding of the catastrophic failure of Homeland Security in every aspect of the response. (Since the federal government for the most part is immune to legal action, any remediation awaits further hearings by the new Democratic majority in Congress.) Meanwhile, more than half of the city's 2001 population remains in exile (many of them now evicted from emergency housing elsewhere) and, of the returnees, a recent poll indicates that one-third were planning to leave as soon as possible. The BNOB plan was shelved after furious community opposition and replaced by a patchwork local planning process with no guarantee of state and federal support. Hundreds of outside architects, planners, and miscellaneous experts have "reenvisioned" New

Orleans in scores of schemes and plans, but on-the-ground progress has been betrayed by the criminal slowness of the government response. The contrast with the reconstruction boom in Mississippi (or for that matter, in suburban Jefferson and St. Tammany parishes) only reinforces the perception that New Orleans—a citadel of African-American electoral power—has been deliberately murdered.

THIRTY-FIVE

SISTER CATARINA

The genesis of two Category 5 hurricanes (Katrina and Rita) in a row over the Gulf of Mexico is an unprecedented and troubling occurrence. But for most tropical meteorologists the truly astonishing "storm of the decade" took place in March 2004. Hurricane Catarina—so named because it made landfall in the southern Brazilian state of Santa Catarina—was the first recorded South Atlantic hurricane in history.

Textbook orthodoxy had long excluded the possibility of such an event; experts claimed that sea temperatures are too low and wind shear too powerful to allow tropical depressions to evolve into cyclones south of the Atlantic Equator. Indeed, forecasters rubbed their eyes in disbelief as weather satellites downlinked the first images of a classical whirling disc with a well-formed eye in these forbidden latitudes.

In a series of recent meetings and publications, researchers have debated the origin and significance of Catarina. A crucial question is this: was Catarina simply a rare event at the far outlier of the normal bell curve of South Atlantic weather (in the same sense, for example, as Joe DiMaggio's incredible 56-game hitting streak in 1941—an analogy made famous by Stephen Jay Gould) *or* was Catarina a "threshold" event, signaling some fundamental and abrupt change of state in the climate system?

Scientific discussions of environmental change and global warming have long been haunted by the specter of nonlinearity. Climate models, like econometric models, are easiest to build and understand when they are simple linear extrapolations of well quantified past behavior with causes maintaining a consistent proportionality to their effects. But all the major components of global climate—air, water, ice, and vegetation—are actually nonlinear: at certain thresholds they switch from one state of organization to another, with catastrophic consequences for species too finely tuned to the old norms. Until the early 1990s, however, it was generally believed that these major climate transitions took centuries if not millennia to accomplish. Now, thanks to the decoding of subtle signatures in ice cores and sea-bottom sediments, we know that global temperature and ocean circulation can change abruptly—in a decade or even less.

The paradigmatic example is the so-called Younger Dryas event, 12,800 years ago, when an ice dam collapsed, releasing an immense volume of meltwater from the shrinking Laurentian ice sheet into the Atlantic Ocean via the instantly created St. Lawrence River. The freshening of the North Atlantic suppressed the northward conveyance of warm water by the Gulf Stream current and plunged Europe back into a thousand-year ice age.

Abrupt switching mechanisms in the climate system, like relatively small changes in ocean salinity, are augmented by causal loops that act as amplifiers. Perhaps the most famous example is the sea-ice albedo: the white, frozen Arctic Ocean reflects heat back into space, thus providing positive feedback to cooling trends; alternatively, shrinking sea ice increases heat absorption and accelerates planetary warming.

Thresholds, switches, amplifiers, chaos—contemporary geophysics assumes that the Earth's history is inherently revolutionary. This is why many prominent researchers—especially those who study topics like ice-sheet stability and North Atlantic circulation—have always had qualms with the consensus projections of the Intergovernmental Panel on Climate Change (IPCC), the world authority on global warming.

In contrast to Bushite flat-earthers and shills for the oil industry, their skepticism has been founded on the fear that the IPCC models fail to adequately allow for catastrophic nonlinearities like the Younger Dryas or Hurricane Catarina. Where other researchers model late twenty-first-century climate upon the precedents of the Altithermal (the hottest phase of the current Holocene, 8,000 years ago) or the Eemian (the previous and warmer interglacial episode, 120,000 years ago), they toy with the possibilities of runaway warming returning the earth to the torrid chaos of the Paleocene-Eocene Thermal Maximum (PETM, 55 million years ago) when extreme and rapid heating of the oceans led to massive extinctions.

Dramatic new evidence has emerged recently that we may be headed, if not back to the dread and almost inconceivable PETM, then at least toward a much harder landing than envisioned by the IPCC. As I flew toward Louisiana and the carnage of Katrina three weeks ago, I perused the August 23 issue of *EOS*, the newsletter of the American Geophysical Union. I was quickly transfixed by an article entitled "Arctic System on Trajectory to New, Seasonally Ice-Free State," coauthored by twenty-one scientists from almost as many universities and research institutes.(115) Even two days later, walking among the ruins of the Lower Ninth Ward, I found myself worrying more about the *EOS* article than the disaster surrounding me.

The article begins with a recounting of trends familiar to any reader of the Tuesday science section of the *New York Times*: for almost thirty years Arctic sea ice has been thinning and shrinking so dramatically that "a summer ice-free Arctic Ocean within a century is a real possibility." It adds, however, the new observation that this process is probably irreversible: "surprisingly, it is difficult to identify a single feedback mechanism within the Arctic that has the potency or speed to alter the system's present course."

An ice-free Arctic Ocean has not existed for at least one million years and the authors warn that the Earth is inexorably headed toward a "super-interglacial" state "outside the envelope of glacial-interglacial fluctuations that prevailed during recent Earth history." They emphasize that within a century global warming will probably exceed the Eemian temperature maximum and thus all the models that have used this as a likely scenario.

We are living, in other words, on a runaway train that is picking up speed as it passes the stations marked "Altithermal" and "Eemian." "Out of the envelope," moreover, means that we are not only leaving behind the serendipitous climatic parameters of the Holocene—the last ten thousand years of mild, warm weather that has favored the explosive growth of agriculture and urban civilization—but also of the late Pleistocene that fostered the evolution of *Homo sapiens* in eastern Africa. Other researchers undoubtedly will contest the extraordinary conclusions of the *EOS* article and—we must hope—suggest counteracting forces to the sea-ice albedo catastrophe. But for the time being, at least, research on global change is pointing toward worst-case scenarios.

All of this, of course, is a perverse tribute to industrial capitalism and extractive imperialism as geological forces so formidable that they have succeeded in scarcely more than two centuries—indeed, mainly in the last fifty years—in knocking the Earth off its climatic pedestal and propelling it toward the nonlinear unknown.

The demon in me wants to say: party and make merry. No need now to worry about Kyoto, recycling your aluminum cans, or using too much toilet paper, when we'll soon be debating how many hunter-gatherers can survive in the scorching deserts of New England or the tropical forests of the Yukon. The good parent in me, however, screams: how is it possible that we can now contemplate with scientific seriousness whether our childrens' children will themselves have children? Let Exxon answer that in one of their sanctimonious ads.

(October 7, 2005, *Los Angeles Times*)

PART FIVE

OLD FLAMES

He hoped to kindle anew the war of the slaves,
which was but lately extinguished, and seemed to need
but a little fuel to set it burning again.

—Plutarch on the rebellion of Spartacus

THIRTY-SIX

ARTISANS OF TERROR

Mike Davis interviewed by Jon Wiener for *Radical History*

JW: I've heard through the grapevine that you are working on a book about terrorism.

MD: My day job currently is a grassroots history of Los Angeles in the sixties. But I have also been busy on an extracurricular project entitled (after a poem in *Mother Earth*) "Heroes of Hell." It aims be a world history of revolutionary terrorism from 1878 to 1932.

JW: Why did you choose those specific dates as bookends?

MD: 1878 is the inception of the "classical" age of terrorism: the half century during which the bourgeois Imaginary was haunted by the infamous figure of the bomb-throwing Nihilist or Anarchist. Beginning in 1878, in fact, Bakuninists of several nationalities and their cousins, the Russian Narodniki, embraced assassination as a potent, if last-ditch, weapon in the struggle against autocracy.

The calendar of that year is extraordinary. In January, Vera Zasulich wounds General Trepov, the sadistic jailer of the Narodniki. In April, Alexander Solovev makes his attempt on the czar, the beginning of the royal game hunt that will culminate in Alexander II's assassination by Peoples' Will in 1881. In May and June there are the successive attacks on the aged kaiser in Berlin by the anarchists Holding and Nobiling, which provide Bismarck with his long-sought-after pretext for repressing the utterly innocent German social democrats. In the fall, meanwhile, Moncasi tries to kill Alfonso XII of Spain, and Giovanni Passanante, hiding a dagger in a red flag, slashes at King Umberto of Italy. The year ends with a hysterical encyclical from Pope Leo XIII on the "deadly pestilence of Communism."

The debut of modern terrorism, I should emphasize, followed in the wake of defeated hopes for popular uprisings in Russia, Andalusia, and the Mezzogiorno. (The Italian Bakuninists did briefly establish a Che-like guerrilla *foco* in the Matese Mountains above Naples for a few weeks in 1877.) Terrorism, in other words, was one response to the double failure of old-style urban Blanquism and rural Garibaldeanism. There is an obvious parallel with the contemporary experience of the Irish Revolutionary Brotherhood: after the betrayal and suppression of the great Fenian conspiracy, a secret cadre turned from insurrection to individual assassination as well as the first dynamite campaign against English cities.

JW: And 1932 as a finale?

MD: 1932 is the last in a series of desperate but unsuccessful attempts by Italian anarchists, direct descendants of Passanante, to assassinate Mussolini. Fascism and Stalinism succeed—where previous regimes failed—in bringing anarchism (and in Russia, the powerful Social Revolutionary [SR] movement) to the brink of extinction. The classical *attentat* is rendered powerless in the face of the modern totalitarian state, although faint embers of the Spanish FAI will persist through the 1950s to help reignite "propaganda of the deed" with a bang in the 1960s. But that is a story for another volume.

JW: What put you on the track of Malatesta, Ravachol, and Durruti? Is this a political and intellectual response to 9/11?

MD: Only after the fact and, then, reluctantly. The real occasion of this project was reading Pierre Broué's magnificent *Histoire de L'Internationale Communiste* (1997). Like Victor Serge and Isaac Deutscher, Broué writes in the almost extinct idiom of the Left Opposition. His history is a passionate—at times almost unbearably poignant—engagement with the Shakespearean tragedy of the revolutionary generation decimated by Stalin and Hitler. He rescues the memory—the courage and moral grandeur—of hundreds of extraordinary women and men.

Broué inspired me to look at an even more out-of-fashion and politically incorrect group: the avenging angels who stalked kings and robber barons with bomb or dagger in hand. They tend to be the pariahs of the left (even of "respectable" anarchism) as well as demons of the right. I want to understand the moral architecture of their universe as well as the repercussions of their acts. In doing so, of course, I am now unavoidably drawn into the periphery of debates about that sinister catch-all category: Terrorism.

JW: Are you hoping to revise previous historiography or is this breaking new ground?

MD: Fortunately, I have giant shoulders to stand on. Anarchism—including its violent denominations—has had superb national historians: Abel Paz (Spain), Jean Maitron (France), Paul Avrich (United States), and Osvaldo Bayer (Argentina). Their work should be familiar to all radical historians, although Maitron's *History of the Anarchist Movement in France* and Bayer's *Rebellion in Patagonia*, like Broué's Comintern book, have inexplicably failed to find English translations.

One must be extremely modest in the face of such achievements. On the other hand, there is not yet any synoptic account that encompasses the world scope of anarchist and social-revolutionary terrorism. The key actors were fervent internationalists (sometimes claiming Esperanto as their first language!) who conceived themselves engaged in common combat against capital and state. (A popular slogan, ascribed to a Russian who blew himself up in the Bois de Vincennes in Paris, was "take revenge on the bourgeoisie wherever they are!") Chinese and Japanese anarcho-terrorists, for example, were directly inspired by Russian heroes, while veterans of the European underground end up planting bombs or doing bank jobs in the New

World. American anarchists, in turn, crossed the Atlantic to take revenge on the despots of the Old World. My project is a global audit, ranging from Chicago to Canton, Latvia to Patagonia.

JW: Hasn't Walter Laqueur written about the history of terrorism on a broad international canvass?

MD: Indeed, Laqueur has a reputation as *the* historian, or historical interpreter, of classical and contemporary terrorism. But his major work, *The Age of Terrorism* (1987), epitomizes everything that is intellectually shabby about "Terrorism Studies" (or, alternatively, what might be called the Hoover Institution paradigm). To begin with, he immolates himself with spectacular self-contradictions. One moment, he is claiming that "psychologically interesting, the *ere des attentats* was of no great political significance"; the next, he is blaming the same "propagandists of the deed" for most of the carnage of the twentieth century—e.g., the failure of "peaceful reform" [*sic*] in Russia, the rise of the Iberian dictatorships, the massacre of Armenians, and so on. Like most "experts" on terrorism, he reifies violence on the left in abstraction from the ruling-class and state violence to which it was almost always a reaction. The image of totally autonomous, self-propelled Terror—the political equivalent of Satanism—has always had a certain sublimity, but it is myth. Revolutionary terrorism was completely embedded in decadal cycles of class struggle and repression, and in cultures of plebian anger. The Nihilist who so enthralled *fin de siècle* writers like Conrad and Henry James, and continues to provide a stipend to academics like Laqueur, is pure phantom.

JW: Tell us more about this reciprocal spiral of class violence.

MD: Anyone who attempts to work on this terrain must carefully heed the warnings of Eric Hobsbawm and Arno Mayer. Hobsbawm, in an essay on "Political Murder," reminds us that "violence" is an entirely problematic concept, usually defined from the administrative and legal position of the ruling classes and excluding the epic but everyday violences of poverty and exploitation. Mayer, who in *The Fu-*

ries attempts to reinstate the dialectical relationship between instigatory counterrevolutionary and reactive revolutionary violence, writes that "Terror(ism) invites interpretations that are variously overdetermined, monocausal, demonizing, and didactic."

JW: Okay, this sounds like historiographical commonsense. But what is the specific historical site of "classical terrorism"?

MD: In a phrase, the Mur des Fédérés. This is the infamous wall in Père-Lachaise cemetery against which the last Communards were executed. As Eugene Pottier, the author of the *Internationale*, put it in a contemporary poem: "Your history, bourgeoisie, is written on this wall. It is not a difficult text to decipher." Thiers's slaughter of thirty thousand working-class and bohemian Parisians, to the almost universal approval of middle-class opinion, was the moral watershed in European labor history. As Mayer emphasizes, it was essentially a colonial massacre brought home to the metropolis. Together with other subsequent atrocities—like the mass executions in Russia, the murder of Internationalists in Cadiz in 1873, the violent suppression of the 1877 strike wave, and the Haymarket hangings—it convinced many revolutionaries that terror had to be fought with terror. If victory seemed impossible, better then, vengeance. Labor historians tend to be uncomfortable with the occasions when workers were not victims, but sought to even the score with individual employers and rulers.

If the escalation of class violence by republican as well as absolutist rulers was the *necessary* condition for this new terrorism, causal sufficiency, as I mentioned earlier, was provided by the frustration of Bakuninist and Narodnik hopes for large-scale uprisings in the Mediterranean and Russian countrysides. In the generation from the death of the Commune to the first International May Day in 1890, revolutionaries were vexed by the immaturity of social conditions to sustain large-scale class struggle. The European artisanate was in its final death agony from the Pale to Sicily, yet the modern industrial proletariat, except in England, was not yet fully born. Strikes were usually crushed or led to small violent cataclysms like that depicted by

Zola in *Germinal*. Gains in suffrage, meanwhile, were easily annulled by antisocialist laws or confiscated by corruption (as in Spain and the United States). In this context, the Social Democratic strategy—Marx and Engels's counsel of patient organizing and the gradual accumulation of forces—seemed maddeningly slow, especially for young artisans forced to choose between starvation, emigration, or crime.

JW: Terrorism, then, was a pathology of structural transition, of delayed modernization?

MD: It is tempting to simplify matters and say that the anarcho-terrorism of the 1880–1900 period was the Ghost Dance of the European artisanate, with Ravachol as Wovoka or the Mahdi. Certainly this has been a traditional approach to understanding the popular, episodically violent anarchism of Andalusia, yet as Temma Kaplan demonstrated in a major revisionist study, the millenarian interpretation collapses under careful scrutiny or, at least, yields to a more rational-actor model.

Similarly, traditional attempts to portray anarchists as criminal madmen or publicity-hungry megalomaniacs—beginning with the Italian criminologist Lombroso in the 1890s—are disproved by the sober, exemplary characters of such figures as Bresci (the assassin of King Umberto) or Durruti (whose Robin-Hood-like feats defy credulity). Even Czolgosz, the killer of McKinley, who has always been portrayed as a "lunatic" by historians, was quite sane, as well as extraordinarily modest and dignified in bearing. As James Clarke has shown, Czolgosz was seeking revenge for the massacre several years earlier of nineteen [some accounts say twenty one] Slavic miners in Latimer, Pennsylvania. (When some of the wounded had asked for water, deputies replied: "We'll give you hell, not water, hunkies!")

If the criminological approach is bankrupt in the study of anarchism, this doesn't mean that there weren't significant overlaps between terrorism and the late Victorian underworlds. But the violent anarchists of the 1880s and early 1890s represent less a criminalization of the labor movement than an unprecedented politicalization of the

criminal strata of the urban proletariat. (There are interesting similarities to the Black Panthers' orientation to the street proletariat in the
late 1960s.) In post-1871 Montmartre and Belleville, as Maitron and
others have shown, there was a fascinating continuum between anarchism, bohemia, proletarian subculture, and criminality. In the 1890s,
one of the most popular songs in the cabarets was *La Ravachol*: "Lady
Dynamite that dances so fast, let us dance and sing.... and dynamite!"

It was a very different articulation of class location and politics
than the Parisian lumpens whom Marx denounced as shock troops of
Bonapartism in 1848–50. The *attentat*—in the full sense that it was
used in *Père Peinard* and the underground press of the period—en-
compassed both the act of revolutionary vengeance against the class
oppressor *and* routine expropriations that allowed Ravachol, say, to
wear new suits or purchase books. A common moral economy—apparently embraced by a significant minority of the Parisian working
class—justified both assassination and theft on class grounds.

JW: But can you generalize from this Parisian instance?

MD: No, although it has fascinating counterparts in Berlin, Barcelona,
and Buenos Aires, especially in the 1920s. My research is structured
around a provisional typology and periodization. In my reading, revolutionary terrorism is largely retributive, although sometimes messianic. It is useful to distinguish four distinctive types of elitist
revolutionary violence. *Moral-symbolic* terrorism was typically carried
out by lone wolves (*solitarios*) like Ravachol or Bresci with the support
of a few friends or by autonomous cells (groupuscules or *grupitos*)
with never more than a score of members. On this scale there was no
capacity to sustain long campaigns, so the terrorist sequence typically
involved an act of revenge, the execution of the avenger, then further
revenge for his death. Sometimes this cycle was repeated.

Thus in Paris in 1892, Ravachol avenges massacred workers in
Fourmies with a series of bombings of prosecutors and judges. After
he is executed, Meunier blows up the Restaurant Very, Leautheir stabs
the first bourgeois he meets on the street (it turns out to be the Ser-

bian minister), and Valliant bombs the Chamber of Deputies. When Valliant is guillotined, he is avenged by Henry who blows up the Café Terminus and a police station. Henry's arrest enrages the art critic Feneon, who plants a bomb in the chic Café Foyot, which ironically only wounds the anarchist Tailhade, who nonetheless approves of the attack. Finally Caserio, claiming justice for Valliant and Henry, stabs to death the president of France, Sadi Carnot. A similar cycle of vengeance—originally in response to the repression of the Jerez uprising in 1892—takes place simultaneously in Barcelona. Both lead to mass trials of anarchist sympathizers (including writers and editors) and repressive legislation. In Barcelona the defendants are imprisoned in the infamous Montjuich fortress and are hideously tortured. This, of course, only supplies more fuel for revenge.

JW: This sounds like the West Bank today.

MD: There are certainly similarities on the supply-and-demand side. Indeed from the 1890s, every ruling-class crime seems to summon a "hero from hell" to avenge dead strikers or executed revolutionaries. The relentless slogan of Russian anarchists was *smert za smert*, death for death. Thus Frick was shot for Homestead; Canovas del Castillo, the Spanish prime minister, was killed in revenge both for dead anarchists and the executed Filipino patriot Rizal; King Umberto was assassinated for the hundreds killed by his troops during the 1898 bread riots; McKinley was killed for Latimer; the prince of Wales was sniped at in Brussels in 1900 as an anarchist response to the deaths of thousands of Boer women and children; likewise King Leopold was shot at in 1902 for his Congo atrocities; ex-governor Stuenenberg was blown up for the Coeur d'Elene outrages; a Spanish anarchist took aim at General Renard, who slaughtered 2,500 Chilean nitrate miners in 1907; Colonel Falcon, who killed May Day demonstrators in Buenos Aires in 1909, was punctually given an anarchist send-off as was, thirteen years later, General Varela, the butcher of Patagonia; four New York anarchists blew themselves up with the bomb they intended to use against Rockefeller for the Ludlow Massacre; Count Sturgkh was shot in Vienna (by the son of a leading socialist) as antiwar protest; Australian IWWs fought conscription with arson, while the Galleanisti in the United States used letter bombs; in 1920 Wall Street was bombed for the Palmer Raids; Petlura, the butcher of Ukrainian Jews, fell before an anarchist bullet in Paris in 1926; and, a year later, the Bank of Boston in Buenos Aires was blown up in retaliation for the electrocution of Sacco and Vanzetti.

This is only a partial declension. Anarchists also killed the empress of Austria, several more Spanish prime ministers, and made innumerable attempts on other monarchs, including the Persian shah and the Japanese mikado. In the Russian Empire, the eye-for-an-eye spiral became almost uncountable. If tens of thousands of insurgents were cut down by Cossack sabers or died on the scaffold, then *several thousand* czarist officials, from lowly policemen to grand dukes, were shot, stabbed, or blown up in an estimated twenty thousand separate terrorist acts between 1902 and 1917. European and American terrorism was craft work; Russian terrorism was mass production. But for this reason it clearly constitutes a separate type.

JW: Explain.

MD: *Strategic terrorism* in Russia, which was also emulated by the Chinese anarchists in 1907–12, sought to cripple the autocratic state: either to force liberal reforms from the top down (the aim of Narodnaya Volya in 1879–82) or to open a breach that could be stormed by revolutionary peasants and workers (the goal of the Socialist Revolutionaries and their splinter groups, as well as various Polish, Latvian, and Armenian revolutionary formations, in 1902–1908). Symbolic justice was an integral dimension, but the true goal was the decimation of the human infrastructure of despotism. Although the struggle was carried out by small cells, the ties to truly mass parties gave Russian terrorism a formidable stamina that distinguished it from the amateurish and episodic attentats of European and American anarchists. On the other hand, as the Social Democrats constantly pointed out, the Socialist Revolutionaries' Combat Organization became the tail that wagged the dog. Terrorism became an end unto itself: a veritable "theodicy of violence" in the words of one historian.

JW: What were the other two types of classical terrorism?

MD: *Expropriatory terrorism* consisted of two subspecies. On one hand, there were the celebrated bands of anarcho-outlaws like Jacob's "Workers of the Night" and the Bonnot Gang (which included the young Victor Serge) in Paris, and Severino Di Giovanni's desperados in Buenos Aires. They thrived as much from notoriety as from loot, and self-consciously "performed" in the gaze of the popular press. On the other hand, there were the far more anonymous although no less legendary groups who robbed banks on behalf of their left-wing parties or unions. The most famous example was the mixed cell of Lettish Socialist Revolutionaries, anarchists, and Bolsheviks—under the leadership of the mysterious "Peter the Painter"—who perpetrated the "Tottenham Outrage" in 1909, the "Houndsditch Murders" in 1910, and then blazed away with their Mausers at Winston Churchill and the Scots Guards during the "Sidney Street Siege" in 1911. But there were other notable instances: Russian Socialist Revolutionaries and anarchists did bank jobs all over Europe, and Durruti and Ascaso were Spanish anarchism's Butch Cassidy and the Sundance Kid as they blazed a trail across Cuba, Mexico, and Argentina in the early 1920s.

Defensive terrorism arose in conditions of semi-civil war when employers and the state were engaged in systematic murder of union or radical leaders while maintaining a facade of electoral democracy. This was the situation in Barcelona from 1917–21 and in parts of Germany in 1919–23. Thus the *pistoleros* of the Catalan employers were countered by Durruti, the Ascaso brothers and other fearless CNT *justicieros*; while in Saxony, Max Höelz led a famous band of anarcho-communist fighters—the Red Army of Vogtland—which robbed banks, sacked noble estates, drove the paramilitary police out of factories, kidnapped bosses, liberated political prisoners, and, finally, fought the Reichswehr from barricades during the insurrectionary March Action. Similarly, there were instances, both during the 1905

Revolution and the Civil War, when Jewish revolutionaries—Bundists, anarchists, and so on—used assassination or a well-placed bomb to deter pogromists. (A French jury, incidentally, acquitted the Jewish anarchist Sholom Schwartzbard after he shot Petlura, the Ataman of the Ukranian whites, outside a Latin Quarter bistro in 1926.)

JW: This sounds very romantic, but surely the balance sheet of each of these types of terrorism must be negative. Didn't every bomb and bullet ultimately ricochet against the mass workers movements?

MD: As Debray pointed out years ago, "the revolution revolutionizes the counterrevolution." Terrorism, by analogy, revolutionizes state repression, and, indeed, in some cases was instigated by the secret police for the express purpose of legitimizing a state of emergency. The mass left, indeed the working class as a whole, was repeatedly victimized for the "heroic" deeds of a few. And despite the traditional disclaimers of its theoreticians, terror substitutes the messianic role of the self-sacrificial individual—or the magical totemism of the attentat—for the conscious movement of the masses. This is why Lenin called the terrorism of the Socialist Revolutionaries (SRs) the "opium of intellectuals." Likewise, Trotsky—perhaps the first true sociologist of the phenomenon—warned that terrorism was too "absolutist," too messianic a form of struggle to coexist with the democratic workers' movement.

Yet the classical socialist critique of anarchist and populist terrorism was never simplistic or completely consistent. Marx, for example, excoriated the Bakuninists yet deeply admired Narodnaya Volya (as did many European liberals) and believed that the assassination of the czar might actually speed history in the right direction. Lenin, despite the ferocity of his attacks on the SRs (whom Kautsky by the way supported), was relentless in urging Social Democrats to adopt terrorist methods to resist the pogroms and Cossack terror that followed the defeat of the Moscow insurrection in December 1905. And Trotsky, while scornful of the "minister after minister, monarch after monarch, Ivan after Ivan" agenda of the SRs, argued that revenge was a powerful and positive revolutionary emotion. "Whatever moral eunuchs and

Pharisees may say," he wrote, "the feeling of revenge has its right. The working class has greater moral probity because it does not look with dull indifference at what is happening in this, the best of all worlds."

Moreover, if one attempts to draw up a cooly objective balance sheet, not all terrorist acts in the nineteenth and early twentieth century end up in the debit column. Some historians of the first Chinese Revolution, for example, credit the anarchist "Eastern Assassination Corps" (built on the model of the Socialist Revolutionaries' Combat Organization) with accelerating the decomposition of Qing power. In the same period, the killing of the Portugese king and crown prince in Lisbon in 1908 by anarcho-republican Carbonari undoubtedly cleared the path for the October Revolution of 1910. And the assassination of notorious warmongers and murderers of the poor sometimes resonated fully with popular demands for revolutionary justice: as in the celebrated deeds of Zasulich, Bresci, Spiridonova, Radowitzy, Adler, Durruti, and Schwartzbard. One might also regret that the Italian anarchists did not succeed in killing Mussolini or that the KPD after 1933 was so dogmatically opposed to assassination.

The problem, of course, is that such methods are—forgive me—literally "hit and miss" and most likely to boomerang against the revolutionary groups that authorize their use. Consider the most "successful" single terrorist action in European history: the bombing of the Sveta-Nedeia Cathedral in Sophia in 1925. A joint team of communists and left-wing agrarians managed to plant a bomb during the funeral service for a general killed a few days before in an anarchist ambush. Although King Boris did not attend, most of the Bulgarian ruling class gathered in the cathedral. The huge explosion killed eleven generals as well as the mayor of Sophia, the chief of police, and 140 other eminent people. It was the only example of classical terrorism I can think of that was carried out by a member party of the Comintern. And its aftermath was debacle: a renewed reign of terror that decimated the Bulgarian left.

JW: The examples you cite, even if forgotten today, all generated lurid headlines in their time. I am sure they must add up to an impressive pile of illustrious corpses. But how about more anonymous, less reported forms of violence: say, the murder of factory foremen? Were the famous *attentats* just the tip of the iceberg or its bulk?

MD: I think radical historians are more willing than in the past to focus on popular retaliation and proletarian self-defense. There is a growing recognition, for instance, that Black folk in the Jim Crow South fought back frequently, guns in hand, against racist terror, and that not all the bodies in the bayou were African American. Likewise, Chicano historians are beginning to appreciate the importance of the Plan de San Diego and the insurrectionary tradition of South Texas. But we are still a long way from understanding the extent or role of working-class counter-violence in workplace struggles. Certainly the *intransigenti* who considered Ravachol a holy figure or subscribed to Galleani's bloodthirsty *Cronaca Sovversiva* deemed killing the boss a highly admirable act. And during strikes, American workers—especially—have hardly needed any ideological instigation to shoot back at Pinkertons or the militia. But, not surprisingly, we have few testimonies from the workers' side about these illegal and violent aspects of the labor movement. This is still largely terra incognita, although Paul Avrich's brilliant excavation of the secret history of the American Galleanisti (*Sacco and Vanzetti: the Anarchist Background*) is an inspiration.

JW: Where do you draw the line between revolutionary terrorism per se and the various violent national liberation movements in contemporary Ireland, the Balkans, East Asia?

MD: There is, of course, a considerable overlap in ideology and cadre, as well as plentiful instances of collaboration. The Irish, to be sure, were scarcely anarchists, but their expertise, courage, and tenacity were admired from Catalonia to China. On the other hand, the Armenian Dashnaki and Pilsudski's OSB (the Polish socialist combat organization that could mobilize more than five thousand fighters) are clearly part of my story. Their nationalism, like that of the revolutionary Letts and Finns, had not yet compromised their anticapitalist politics. More difficult to arbitrate, because of their ideological hetereodoxy are such groups as the Portugese Carbonari (which seem to have alloyed Mazzinian republicanism with elements of Spanish anarchism), the Serbian revolutionaries (nationalism again spiced with anarchism), and those most feared of contemporary terrorists, the Macedonians. IMRO (the Macedonian Internal Revolutionary Organization) is perhaps a sui generis phenomena, but repeatedly demonstrated its solidarity with the Russian SRs and Social Democrats. No one built a better bomb, not even the Irish.

JW: How big was the political base of classical terrorism? Do we have any way of ascertaining the popularity of your "heroes of hell"?

MD: The anarchists themselves, not to mention the secret police, were very interested in such a census and produced several estimates. In Spain in the 1890s, for example, there were probably twenty-five thousand active anarchists and fifty thousand sympathizers who occasionally attended a meeting or subscribed to a newspaper. Almost all were in Catalonia, Valencia, or Andalusia. Only 10 percent of these, according the writer Gil Maestre, were *anarquistas de accion*, i.e., propagandists of the deed. In *fin de siècle* Paris, the advocates of the attentat certainly didn't number more than five hundred in a score of groupuscules with perhaps ten thousand sympathizers. There were probably a similar number in Buenos Aires, the Southern Hemisphere's capital of left-wing terrorism. On the other hand, the illegal and terroristic Russian Socialist-Revolutionary Party in 1907 claimed forty five thousand members and three hundred thousand serious sympathizers.

Beyond this it is hard to know how to measure contemporary working-class opinion. Certainly the Social Democrats, and later the anarcho-syndicalists, waged relentless propaganda warfare against terrorism (although seldom to the extremes of the communist and socialist parties in Western Europe in the 1970s). But I wager that many of their members had emotional sympathies with the terrorists, or, at least, agreed with Severine, the editor of *Le Cri du Peuple*, when he declared—in the course of a bitter polemic with the anarchist "pope" Jean Grave, who had come to denounce "revolutionary crime"—that he was "with the poor *always*, despite their errors, despite their faults, despite their crimes."

THIRTY-SEVEN

STREET ILIAD

One icy night in 1855, the celebrated street brawler John Morrissey walked into a Broadway saloon and spat in the face of Bill "The Butcher" Poole, the even more renowned goliath of New York streets. Poole, who led a murderous mob of anti-Catholic "Know Nothings," was the archfoe of Morrissey and other Irish gang leaders in the pay of Tammany Hall. Morrissey tried to blow Poole's brains out with his pistol but it misfired and Butcher Bill was preparing to "bone the Irishman's cutlet" when the police intervened.

Later that night Poole and some companions returned to the same saloon where they were attacked by the rest of Morrissey's gang. In fighting style of the period, there was berserk mayhem with bowie knives, antique pistols, and much chewing of ears and noses. Poole was shot in the heart, but lingered for two weeks before gasping his famous last words: "Good-bye, boys, I die a true American!" Five thousand admirers marched in his funeral procession and Poole became a martyr symbol for anti-immigrant nativists.

The legend of "Bill the Butcher," generally forgotten after the Civil War, was colorfully resurrected in 1927 by Herbert Asbury in *The Gangs of New York*.(5) Although of dubious accuracy as social history, Asbury's gang genealogy of Manhattan is unquestionably wonderful storytelling: an urban counterpart to the Homeric epic or Icelandic saga. Like the rivalry of Achilles and Hector, the heroic combat between Morrissey and Poole (or, later in the book, between Monk Eastman and Paul Kelly) has beguiled generations of readers—not least among them, Jorge Luis Borges and Luc Sante.

Now *The Gangs of New York* provides both a title and loose narrative framework for Martin Scorsese's $120 million film. Daniel Day-Lewis, who reportedly roused himself to the role by listening nonstop to Eminem CDs, plays Bill the Butcher, while Leonardo DiCaprio is the vengeful son of an Irish immigrant killed by the gang chieftain. The film portrays the epic street battles, two years after the historical Poole's murder, between the Irish Dead Rabbits and the native-Protestant Bowery Boys. It ends in the apocalypse of the July 1863 Draft Riots, the bloodiest urban insurrection in American history, with regiments recalled from Gettysburg, firing grapeshot point-blank at mobs of Irish slum-dwellers.

The film's startling claim is that "America was born in the streets," or, rather, in these street wars. Scorsese, of course, is the greatest contemporary fabulist of New York's mean streets, and *Gangs of New York* is his urban creation myth, explaining the origins of the world that would eventually be inherited by his petty thieves, "made" guys, taxi drivers, child prostitutes, prizefighters, crooked cops, Times Square hustlers, and Italian-American movie directors.

But is this Manhattan Iliad real history? The short (and generous) answer is that it is half the story. The violent rivalries between native American workers and the Irish immigrant poor did provide internal combustion for the great engine of Tammany Hall (the Manhattan Democratic Party) and its endlessly skillful manipulations of an ethnically and confessionally divided working class. Indeed street gangs, along with volunteer fire companies, were the true grass roots of the ethnic spoils contest that passed for "democracy" in the city with the largest mass electorate in the mid-Victorian world.

But the streets of Manhattan in the 1850s and 1860s were also an epic battleground between capital and labor. While Morrissey and Poole were leading their tribes to war at the behest of unscrupulous political bosses, other immigrants—English Chartists, Irish Fenians, and German communists—were struggling alongside American-born trade unionists to build a united labor movement. This is the untold story within Asbury's and Scorsese's "secret history" of nineteenth-century New York.

Gotham's most radical constituency—the immigrant artisans and industrial workers of Kleindeutschland (Little Germany)—scarcely figure in the big-screen drama. These Lower East Side Germans (a third of the city's population by 1870) were the most class-conscious section of the working class—equally opposed to gang leaders, political bosses, and racist demagogues as well as to the uptown plutocracy. Indeed, this German New York, to quote its leading historian, was "the first stronghold of socialism in American history."(109)

Scorsese's film opens in 1846, when as many German as Irish immigrants were pouring into the waterfront slums and tenement districts of New York. Likewise, tens of thousands of young Yankees were leaving their hardscrabble farms and canal towns for the booming railroad workshops, shipyards, and slaughterhouses of Manhattan Island. The traditional plebian population, with its long radical "producerist" traditions, had to confront the competition of these new immigrants at the same time that their trades were being deskilled or replaced by machine production.

The resulting social turbulence, magnified by the Crash of 1857, cannot be compressed into a single narrative; the reality was dialectical not allegorical. While Irish and "American" gangs were bloodying each other in the alleys of the Bowery, the Irish labor leader James McGuire, the German communist Albert Komp, and the native radical Ira B. Davis were organizing thousands of the unemployed into the militant American Workers League. When the bourgeois press begged the militia "to shoot down any quantity of Irish or Germans" as necessary to break the movement, native workers defiantly stood shoulder to shoulder with immigrants in Tompkins Square.

Although the great capitalists of the day—Astor, Vanderbilt, Grinnell, Belmont, and so on—despised Tammany Hall and its Irish allies

("Rum and Rowdyism" was the slogan of the time), they feared gangs less than unions, a divided working class less than a united labor movement. Defeated in their attempt to impose their own order on the city in the 1850s (a political crisis that included the famed "Dead Rabbit Riots"), the city's mercantile elite on the eve of the Civil War was moving toward an accommodation with populist Mayor Fernando Wood and Democratic boss William Tweed.

Two groups resisted assimilation into this solution. One was the radical wing of the labor movement, solidly rooted among the Red 48s and socialists of Kleindeutschland, whose strategic goal was an independent labor party. Many of them were both abolitionists and anticapitalists. The other was the Irish poor—the day laborers and sweatshop workers—whose appalling misery (brilliantly depicted by Scorsese) was now compounded by wartime inflation and inflamed by the horrific losses of Irish regiments in Virginia. The Irish were also alarmed by pro-Confederate propaganda that warned of a tidal wave of freed slaves in Northern labor markets if the Union won.

These two groups—the labor vanguard and the slum poor—played contrasting roles in the 1863 insurrection. The draft lottery that July was universally scorned by Northern workmen as an institutionalization of class privilege, since the well-heeled could buy exemptions for $300. Accordingly, the massive demonstration and strike on Monday morning July 13 was largely led by uptown Irish and German industrial workers, supported by volunteer fire companies.

By early evening, however, the trade unions had lost leadership to street gangs and Confederate sympathizers who directed the wrath of the Irish poor against both the mansions of the rich and the hovels of African Americans. The Colored Orphans Asylum was burned to the ground and Blacks were hounded down and hideously murdered. The Germans and, indeed, many Irish workers (especially those who had long lived side by side with Blacks in the Five Points) recoiled from the carnage and either took no part or actively opposed the pogrom.

The hysterical upper classes, meanwhile, demanded a retaliatory bloodbath in the slums. Six thousand federal troops, many of them Irish New Yorkers, dutifully cleared the streets with grapeshot and bayonet. The heroes of Gettysburg became the butchers of New York. In scenes that foreign observers repeatedly compared to the June 1848 massacres in Paris, scores of rag-clad Irish women and children were cut down alongside their menfolk in last-ditch street battles.

Scorsese certainly has a poetic license to depict the great riot as the climax of the Age of Gangs. Indeed, it was the direct outgrowth of the political role of street violence in dividing New York workers by religion and race. But this catastrophe scarcely annihilated class consciousness or petrified history into a predetermined trajectory.

The direct aftermath was a massive campaign, largely led by socialists, to rebuild an independent and nonsectarian labor movement. As one historian has emphasized, "the massive strikes for an eight-hour workday in spring 1872 were the sober denouement to the draft riots." Out of these struggles, in turn, arose the powerful New York branch of the First International, the pioneer Workingwoman's Association, the "red specter of the Commune" at Tompkins Square in 1874, and, ultimately, the radical mayoral campaign of Henry George that came within a hairsbreadth of overthrowing Tammany Hall.

Certainly we should enjoy Scorsese's Homeric tale—especially its vivid reimagining of 1850s Manhattan as a Third World city—but we should not forget that socialists and class fighters, not gangsters, left the biggest footprints on the real streets of old New York.

(January 2003, *Socialist Review*)

THIRTY-EIGHT

SAVING PRIVATE IVAN

The decisive battle for the liberation of Europe began sixty years ago this month (June 1944) when a Soviet guerrilla army emerged from the forests and bogs of Belorussia to launch a bold surprise attack on the mighty Wehrmacht's rear. The partisan brigades, including many Jewish fighters and concentration-camp escapees, planted forty thousand demolition charges that devastated the vital rail lines linking the seven hundred thousand soldiers of German Army Group Center to their supply bases in Poland and Eastern Prussia.

Three days later, on June 22, 1944, the third anniversary of Hitler's invasion of the Soviet Union, Marshal Zhukov gave the order for the main assault on German front lines. Twenty-six thousand heavy guns pulverized German forward positions. The terrifying screams of the Katyusha rockets were followed by the roar of four thousand tanks and the battle cries (in more than forty languages) of 1.6 million Soviet soldiers. Thus began Operation Bagration (named after a Russian hero of 1812), an assault over a five-hundred-mile-long front.

This Red blitzkrieg—the response to Eisenhower's request for a major "diversion" to cover the Allied landings in Normandy—broke the German front at five strategic points, unleashing Soviet armored task forces deep into the rear of German positions where they annihilated 130,000 Nazi soldiers in the first week alone. By late August, more than fifty German divisions, including some of the most famous units on the

Eastern Front, had been destroyed and White Russia had been completely liberated. In the end, Hitler stripped elite reserves from Western Europe to temporarily stem the Soviet tide on the banks of the Vistula outside Warsaw.

As a result, American and British troops faced few of the veteran Panzer divisions that were originally deployed to drive them back into the sea; much less did they have to deal with reinforcements sent from the east as Eisenhower had feared. Tens of thousands of Allied lives were thus saved by Soviet courage and sacrifice. But what American has ever heard of the exploits of Yermakov's 23rd Guard Corps, Malyshev's 4th Shock Army, or the partisans in the Pripyat Marshes? June 1944 signifies Omaha Beach, not the breakthrough south of Vitebsk or the tank race to Borisov. You will not find Operation Bagration in any textbook of modern American history.

Yet the Soviet summer offensive—that "great military earthquake" as the eminent historian Jon Erickson called it(48)—was several times larger than Operation Overlord (the invasion of Normandy), both in the scale of forces engaged and the direct cost to the Germans. Indeed, an American military historian, Walter Dunn Jr., has characterized Bagration—not the epic battles of Stalingrad or Kursk, much less El Alamein—as "the worst defeat suffered by the German Army in World War II."(43) By the end of summer, the Red Army had reached the gates of Warsaw as well as the Carpathian passes commanding the entrance to Central Europe. Soviet tanks had caught Army Group Centre in steel pincers and destroyed it, while another huge Nazi army had been encircled and would eventually be annihilated along the Baltic coast. The road to Berlin had been opened.

Thank Private Ivan.

It does not disparage the brave men who died in the North African desert or the cold forests around Bastogne to recall that almost 80 percent of the Wehrmacht is buried not in French fields or beneath Saharan sands but on the Russian steppe. In the struggle against Nazism, approximately forty "Ivans" died for every "Private Ryan." Scholars now believe that approximately 28 million Soviet soldiers and citizens perished during World War II, including 3.3 million Red Army prisoners who were deliberately starved to death by the Germans in 1941–42.* Yet the ordinary Soviet soldier—the tractor mechanic from Samara, the actor from Orel, the miner from the Donetsk, and the high-school girl from Leningrad—is invisible in the current celebration and mythologization of the "greatest generation."

It is as if the so-called New American Century of George W. Bush cannot be fully born without exorcizing the central role played by Soviet citizens in last century's epochal victory against fascism. Indeed, most Americans are shockingly clueless about the relative burdens of combat and death in World War II. And even the minority who understand something of the enormity of the Soviet sacrifice tend to visualize it in terms of crude stereotypes of the Red Army: a barbarian horde driven by feral revenge, a frenzy for rape, and primitive Russian nationalism. (Indeed the conventional American image is little different from Goebbels's official stereotype of Soviets as "motorized robots.") Only GI Joe and Tommy are seen as truly fighting for civilized ideals of freedom and democracy.

It is thus all the more important to recall that—despite Stalin, the NKVD, and the massacre of a generation of Bolshevik leaders—the Red Army still retained powerful elements of revolutionary fraternity. In its own eyes, and that of the slaves it freed from Hitler, it was the greatest liberation army in history. Moreover, the Red Army of 1944 was still a Soviet army. The generals who led the breakthrough on the Dvina included a Jew (Chernyakovskii), an Armenian (Bagramyan), and a Pole (Rokossovskii). In contrast to the class-divided and racially segregated American and British forces, command in the Red Army was an open, if ruthless, ladder of opportunity.

---

* This other, forgotten holocaust of Red soldiers is scarcely recognized by most American war historians or "holocaust scholars." It is a measure of their neglect that Christian Streit's groundbreaking analysis of the German treatment of Soviet prisoners—*Keine Kameraden* (Stuttgart 1978)—caused a famous debate in Germany but has never been translated into English.

Anyone who doubts the revolutionary élan and rank-and-file hu-manity of the Red Army should consult the extraordinary memoirs of K. S. Karol (*Between Two Worlds*) and Primo Levi (*The Reawaken-ing*).(77, 91) Both hated Stalinism but loved the ordinary Soviet sol-dier and saw in her/him the seeds of socialist renewal. They testify to the radical transformative impact of the Red Army's victories in 1944 and 1945 upon ordinary Ivans and Ivanas, leading to the emergence of a critical popular culture that obviously terrified Stalin and his hench-men. The tragic result of this reawakening, of course, was the dictator's postwar purge of such incomparable Soviet heroes as Marshal Zhukov and Leopold Trepper (the leader of the famed "Red Orchestra" spy net-work in Germany and occupied Europe), as well as the liquidation of thousands of Eastern European Communists (with service in the In-ternational Brigades in Spain a virtually guaranteed death warrant).

The American "victory" in the Cold War has visited yet more in-famies and lies upon the graves of the Red Army. So, after George Bush's recent demeaning of the memory of D-Day to solicit support for his war crimes in Iraq and Afghanistan, I've decided to hold my own private commemoration.

I will recall, first, my Uncle Bill, the salesman from Columbus, hard as it is to imagine such a gentle soul as a hell-for-leather teenage GI in Normandy. Second—as I'm sure my Uncle Bill would have wished—I will remember his comrade Ivan.

The Ivan who drove his tank through the gates of Auschwitz and battled his way into Hitler's bunker. The Ivan whose courage and tenacity overcame the Wehrmacht, despite the deadly wartime errors and crimes of Stalin. Two ordinary heroes: Bill and Ivan. Obscene to celebrate the first without also commemorating the second.

(June 2004, *The Guardian*/London)

THIRTY-NINE

THE GHOST SHIRTS

On September 1, 1934, millions of cotton spindles stopped spinning. Across the Southern Piedmont mill whistles blew, but workers didn't come to work. The most exploited industrial workforce in the U.S.— the "lint heads" of the Carolinas, Tennessee, Georgia, and Alabama— was on strike.

As mill owners appealed frantically for injunctions, tear gas, and the National Guard, a vast peaceful army of textile workers demolished the image of southern labor as culturally servile and unorganizable. With voices honed to spare beauty in the choirs of mountain Baptist churches, they sang powerful hymns of solidarity instead. And they were robustly answered (often in Portuguese, Italian, or French) by the mill workers of New England who joined what became the first industry-wide general strike of the 1930s. It was also the most violently repressed. Before Franklin D. Roosevelt—more concerned to appease the "lords of the loom" than to liberate their slaves—cajoled the national textile union to call off the strike, thousands had been teargassed and arrested. Thirteen—mostly in the South—had been shot dead.

Now, seventy years later, with only a handful of moist-eyed veterans left alive to remember the heroism and heartbreak of the Great Textile Strike, the cotton spindles down in Dixie have once again stopped spinning. But this time they've stopped forever.

The U.S. textile and clothing industries are dying. Since the inauguration of George W. Bush in January 2001, 350,000 jobs—almost a third of the total—have been lost. Another 400,000 jobs are expected to disappear by the end of the decade. Textile manufacture in the Piedmont, today as in 1934, is largely a monoculture, and as the mills close towns die with them. Already too many Main Streets in the upland South are populated only by thrift stores, drug-counseling services, and military recruiters.

The parallel decline of the clothing industry is likewise eroding the survival economy of recent Latino and Asian immigrants in the tenement districts of downtown Los Angeles, New York, and Miami. Soon even sweatshops will be remembered with nostalgia. Thus another large segment of the U.S. industrial working class is being fast-forwarded to that brave new world that Kurt Vonnegut predicted with such eerie prescience in his 1952 novel *Player, Piano*—a society of discarded laborers whose only option is enlistment in the imperial legions fighting wars for oil and other resources on distant frontiers.(152)

This almost invisible tragedy (who talks about plant closures on Fox News or CNBC?) is part of a larger global jobs catastrophe that follows in the wake of trade liberalization. The final quota barriers protecting American textile and garment jobs will be dismantled next January. China's soft exports to the United States have doubled since its accession to the WTO in 2001, and the *Financial Times* predicts China will grab the greater share of the global market in a breathtakingly rapid restructuring that will eliminate millions of jobs worldwide, from Danville to Dhaka. China's chief comparative advantage, as the AFL-CIO argued last March in a petition asking the U.S. trade representative to promote the rights of Chinese factory labor, grows from the government's "unremitting repression of workers' rights" and the ruthless exploitation of an estimated 100 million rural migrants.

The Bush administration, not surprisingly, rejected the AFL-CIO appeal to enforce the International Labour Organization (nonbinding) core covenants. Nor can labor expect much more solidarity from a Democratic Party that prides itself on NAFTA and the WTO. Certainly

John Edwards may strike some heroic poses outside shuttered textile plants in his home state of North Carolina, but that doesn't mean, to quote a stupid campaign slogan, that "Help is on the way." The dominant party line, as argued in the *New York Times* recently by William Gould IV (Clinton's chairman of the National Labor Relations Board), is instead to "keep labor standards out of trade agreements."

In the eyes of most leading Democrats, the epochal achievement of the Clinton years was bringing the wealth and glamour of the so-called New Economy into the party. No chance, then, that a Kerry-Edwards White House would risk biotech's intellectual property rights or Hollywood's lucrative royalties in the new capitalist China for the sake of some "lint heads" in Georgia or undocumented immigrants in Los Angeles. In the face of this free trade juggernaut, unionized textile and garment workers (since 1976 fused together in UNITE) merged this summer with HERE, the dynamic hotel workers' union. Although UNITE HERE promises to devote half its budget to new organizing, it may be too late to save the jobs imminently imperiled by trade liberalization.

Edna Bonacich (coauthor of *Behind the Label: Inequality in the Los Angeles Apparel Industry*) is both a leading academic expert and respected activist.(16) I asked her for a frank view of the situation: "UNITE will likely lose a big chunk of its membership. Already the union has shifted focus from garment workers, believing it is hopeless to organize them because of the potential flight of the industry offshore. Certainly Los Angeles, as an apparel center and magnet for immigrants, will suffer severe consequences. The victims will tend to be the newest and poorest of immigrants. Whatever of the industry remains in the U.S. is guaranteed to operate at the lowest levels of worker protection." Bonacich believes that heroic but localized fights against plant closure are doomed to failure: "This is too big an issue to handle on a piecemeal basis." She concedes that a recipe for globalized worker resistance to global capital—"the political question of our times"—remains elusive.

In *Player Piano* the remnants of the skilled working class, like the last of the Plains Indians, form a millenarian resistance movement, the "Ghost Shirts," before final defeat and disorganization. On the forgotten anniversary of an epic strike, Vonnegut's cautionary tale has an unfortunate new meaning.

(September 5, 2004, *Los Angeles Times*)

FORTY

MALCOLM—MORE THAN EVER

Forty years ago, in the winter of 1964–65, I was one of the teenage kids working in the New York City national office of Students for a Democratic Society (SDS). SDS was on the verge of the explosive growth and radicalization that would make it the campus leader of resistance against the war in Vietnam. Indeed, most of my friends in the office were working sixteen-hour days to organize the first march on Washington, D.C. (April 17, 1965) to protest Lyndon Johnson's escalation of U.S. intervention, especially his brutal bombing campaign against North Vietnam.

My assignment, however, was to organize a sit-in demonstration (March 19, 1965) at the huge Chase Manhattan Bank skyscraper in lower Manhattan. Following the 1960 Sharpeville massacre, when South African police murdered scores of unarmed protesters, Chase Manhattan led a consortium of international banks that gave loans to Pretoria and stabilized its international credit. In our eyes, the Rockefeller-controlled bank was a chief partner in apartheid and we hoped to use the demonstration to publicize Wall Street's myriad investments in racism, both in South Africa and the American South.

SDS's chief ally was the Student Nonviolent Coordinating Committee (SNCC), then embroiled in the famous voting-rights struggle in Selma, Alabama. SNCC's New York organizer was Betita Martinez, the celebrated Chicana writer, who became the sit-in's tactical planner. We also received terrific support from Africans in New York, including ex-iled members of the African National Congress as well as the younger staff members of the Tanzanian mission to the United Nations. One of the latter—the first "real" revolutionary that I had ever met—was in contact with Malcolm X and his new Organization of African-American Unity.

In early 1964 the charismatic Black Muslim leader had left the Nation of Islam with the goal of building a revolutionary organization that would link the struggles of U.S. people of color to global anticolonial and national liberation movements. After his famous pilgrimage to Mecca, Malcolm X had praised the Cuban and Chinese revolutions, and was actively engaged in strategic discussions with Marxists as well as with militant Muslims and Third World nationalists.

My Tanzanian friend, who had introduced us to other veteran Black nationalists, hoped to arrange a meeting between Malcolm and the SDS staff. The prospect filled us with awe. "Do you know who Malcolm X is?" he asked me one day while we were walking through Harlem. I dumbly shook my head. "He is your American Lenin."

Two weeks after this conversation (February 21), our Lenin was dead: shot down while addressing a rally at Manhattan's Audubon Ballroom. He was only thirty-nine years old. Malcolm's assassins were henchmen of the Nation of Islam, but historians and activists have never ceased debating the sinister roles of the FBI and the New York Police, both of which, we now know, were insidiously enflaming divisions within Black nationalist ranks.

In the meantime, the grief in Harlem and throughout Black America was truly inconsolable. At Malcolm's funeral, his close friend, the actor Ossie Davis, famously eulogized "our own Black shining Prince." "What we place in the ground," Davis told mourners, "is no more now a man—but a seed—which, after the winter of our discontent, will come forth again to meet us." Davis, a beloved progressive figure in his own right, died last month (February 4, 2005), having spent four decades defending the legacy of Malcolm X against both vilification and commercialization.

On this side of the water, of course, we are used to the periodic murder of our prophets, dissidents, and revolutionists, but Malcolm X's death has undoubtedly left the largest hole in American history. As John Simon writes in the February issue of the independent Marxist journal *Monthly Review*: Malcolm X was "arguably the most dangerous figure in this country's history to confront its ruling class."(137)

The "danger" that Malcolm X embodied—and which kept J. Edgar Hoover awake at night—was the threat of transforming a reformist civil rights movement into a radical liberation movement that saw itself as part of a global uprising of people of color. There was much contemporary white hysteria about Malcolm's rejection of dogmatic nonviolence in favor of armed self-defense, but he simply gave eloquent voice to the attitude of most working-class African Americans, who rejected turning the other cheek to murderous vigilantes and blue fascists. More radical was Malcolm's rejection of a parochial "civil rights" strategy that relied upon federal courts and the national Democratic Party in favor of an internationalist "human rights" strategy that allied the Black revolt in America to a tricontinental revolution against European and U.S. hegemony.

Malcolm X—a brilliant and dynamic thinker whose ideas were rapidly evolving in dialogue with other liberation fighters—was the principal relay between this global revolutionary dialectic and the most oppressed sectors of the American population. Murdered just six months before the great August 1965 ghetto uprising in Los Angeles, he was the only national political figure who commanded the universal admiration of youth in Northern ghettoes. And he had long been the passionate advocate of Black unity with insurgent Native Americans, Latinos, and Asians.

Malcolm X was cut down, not simply in his prime, but in the very process of profound political reorientation, on the eve of his greatest leadership. His assassination, like that of Rosa Luxemburg in 1919 or Trotsky in 1939, shifted the rails of history. If he had lived, Malcolm X, almost certainly, would have quickly galvanized African-American opposition to the genocidal war in Indochina; perhaps, as many Black radicals believe, in alliance with a left-moving Martin Luther King Jr. Likewise the volcanic ghetto uprisings of 1965 to 1968 might have attained truly "dangerous" organization and ideological direction. The FBI, in turn, might have found it more difficult to spread the venom of jealousy and disunity among Black revolutionaries.

These "what ifs" haunt radicals of my generation, for whom Malcolm X was the symbol of the alternative history that we tried, but failed, to create. For younger generations, however, the "seeds" of Malcolm's life continue to bear gloriously intransigent and subversive fruit.

(March 2005, *Socialist Review*)

FORTY-ONE

PUNCH-OUT TIME

The most famous punch in American history wasn't thrown by the Manassas Mauler or the Brown Bomber, but by the labor leader John L. Lewis. Seventy years ago, the irascible, bushy-eyebrowed president of the United Mine Workers gave carpenters union leader Big Bill Hutchinson a helluva dig in the jaw.

It was Lewis's way of saying good-bye to the American Federation of Labor and the conservative, often nativist craft unions that dominated it. The AFL refused to charter or seriously support fledgling industrial unions in rubber, auto, steel, and electrical manufacture, and Lewis openly worried that the rank-and-file revolt in basic industry might grow into a left-led challenge to the trade-union bureaucracy per se. So, he took his mine workers and the Committee for Industrial Organization out of the convention hall and back to the picket lines. Twenty years passed before a purged and de-radicalized Congress of Industrial Organization rejoined the AFL in an uneasy, often tempestuous marriage.

At the recent executive meeting of the AFL-CIO in Las Vegas (March 1–2), the leader of the Federation's largest union, Andy Stern of the Service Employees (SEIU), refrained from taking a literal poke at his old boss and AFL-CIO president, John Sweeney, but the atmosphere of dissension was reminiscent of 1935. Ten years after Sweeney's "New Directions" team took the helm of the AFL-CIO with the promise of restoring labor unity and bringing heroic energy to new organizing, the Federation is on the brink of splitting in two.

Although the last decade has witnessed memorable and successful organizing campaigns by janitors, hotel workers, and nurses, the overall balance sheet of the Sweeney era is relentless decline. Less than 8 percent of private-sector workers now belong to a union—the lowest level since 1901. As traditional manufacturing shrinks, unions have failed to make any progress in organizing either high-tech industries or the low-wage retail sector. There are no union labels on Macs, or, for that matter, on Big Macs. Meanwhile, that mega-exploiter of U.S. and Third World labor, Wal-Mart, threatens to extinguish unionism in the grocery industry.

Despite Sweeney's grandiose promise in 1995 to "organize, organize, organize," the Federation has suffered a net loss of eight hundred thousand members: a deficit that would be twice as large if the SEIU had not added eight hundred thousand to its ranks since 1996. Moreover, "rebuilding" has recently turned into rout. The crucially important Southern California grocery strike in 2003–04 was defeated, largely due to leadership incompetence, while autoworkers, machinists, and airline employees were forced to make huge concessions in jobs, benefits, and medical coverage the following year.

At the same time, most of the AFL-CIO's budget has continued to disappear down an old sinkhole: the Democratic Party. Like an addicted gambler in front of a slot machine, the AFL-CIO obsessively spends its members' dues on Democratic campaigns in the hope of an electoral payoff that never comes. Loyalty to Clinton-Gore, for instance, only brought free-trade agreements that devastated union jobs in the former industrial heartland. As a result, a majority of white working-class voters now apparently regard Republican management of the economy as the lesser of two evils. A new analysis of last November's votes shows that white workers preferred Bush over Kerry on the economy, 55 percent to 39 percent.

Stern, without breaking with two-party politics per se, has become an increasingly outspoken critic of labor's one-sided relationship with the Democrats. "Workers don't have a party right now that speaks clearly and precisely to their economic interests." At Las Vegas, he proposed to strip the national AFL-CIO of half of the dues that it collects to support Democrat candidates and Washington lobbying: the funds instead would be rebated to new organizing, with Wal-Mart as chief target.

The proposal was cosponsored by James Hoffa of the Teamsters and supported by the hotel workers, food workers, laborers, and autoworkers. Although Sweeney easily defeated this frontal challenge to his leadership by a 15 to 7 vote, the Las Vegas meeting was only a prelude to the battle royal expected at the AFL-CIO convention in July. Stern warned last summer that his 1.8 million members (mainly hospital workers and janitors) will leave the AFL-CIO if it fails to streamline its structure, force the merger of smaller unions, end jurisdictional disputes, and pour resources into the new organizing promised back in 1995. Most likely, Stern's ally, John Wilhelm of the hotel workers, will run against Sweeney at the convention. If he loses, it would presumably be the signal for the reform unions to secede and form a new national labor alliance, possibly with the participation of the already independent carpenters' union.

As in 1935, there is a temptation to portray the reformers as the "left" and the federation leadership as the "right." Certainly, as far as commitment to aggressive organizing is concerned, Stern self-consciously, even theatrically emulates Lewis's precedent. But as embittered rank-and-file coal miners and labor radicals knew back in 1935, John L. Lewis was also an autocrat who crushed dissident locals and witch-hunted socialists and communists.

Stern is scarcely a tyrant of Lewis's caliber, but he has often ridden roughshod over rank-and-file leadership in his own union. Partisans of union democracy are also worried about the top-down model of mega-mergers and organizing campaigns that allies Stern with more sinister figures like the younger Hoffa (son of the corrupt Teamster leader murdered a generation ago). Stern ceaselessly preaches the necessity of smaller unions amalgamating into larger super-unions: a sermon that inevitably alarms both craft unions and declining industrial unions. Tom Buffenbarger of the Machinists has accused Stern of "trying to corporatize the labor movement." Supporters of Stern, including the legion of young SEIU organizers recruited from Ivy League universities, respond that union density will only be rebuilt by adapting union structure to the age of Wal-Mart.

In a recent open letter, Donna Dewitt, the president of the South Carolina AFL-CIO, and Bill Fletcher, the former educational director of the AFL-CIO and a prominent Black Marxist, joined by a number of other progressive unionists, wrote that "the top-to-bottom approach to revitalizing workers' organizations will not foster meaningful membership participation and support." They also warned that an organizing offensive alone would not renew a disappearing U.S. labor movement: unions need to be in the forefront of battles against the "fortress-like society" being created in the name of the War on Terrorism.

Meanwhile, Sweeney and his supporters—including, among the big unions, the machinists, public employees, teachers, and communication workers—are still stubbornly putting the workers' rent money in the Democratic one-armed bandit. After defeating Stern's proposal to shift dues to organizing, the majority of the executive voted to double their annual investment in political and legislative programs. So, for the moment at least, the struggle within the AFL-CIO leadership has defined two clearly contrasting sets of priorities. It is now the urgent job of the new Democratic National Chairman Howard Dean to persuade Stern to pull his punches in July, lest the AFL-CIO convention actually debate—for the first time in its history—labor's dismal monogamy with the Democrats.

(April 2005, *Socialist Review*)

As expected, Stern boycotted the Chicago convention and instead joined hands with the Teamsters, UNITE HERE, and four other unions to form Change to Win (6 million members in seven unions) as an alternate pole to Sweeney's AFL-CIO (9 million in fifty-three unions). Although the worst-case scenario—the splintering of city and county labor federations—has been avoided thanks to a last-minute compromise by Sweeney, who allowed the feds to issue so-called solidarity charters to the secessionist unions, the immediate impact of the divorce (which Stern bragged was akin to the formation of the CIO) has been a dramatic surge in raiding by rival unions. The bitterest examples involve SEIU's attempts to poach upon emergent public-sector constituencies long cultivated by AFSCME, especially child-care workers in Maryland, Illinois, and Iowa.(154)

The rival federations also managed to loosely join forces to support the Democrats in the 2006 congressional elections, with SEIU—despite its avowal to put organizing first—spending hugely on a variety of candidates, DLCers as well as liberals. As Harry Kelber noted in his newsletter LaborTalk, however, the unions were utterly silent about the debacle in Iraq and the War on Terrorism. "The leaders of both labor federations… instituted a total blackout of news and information about the Iraq war, as though it is of no interest to America's working families."(79) The split, in other words, has not significantly improved labor's public politics or reclaimed the critical voice on foreign policy and other big issues that existed even in the Reuther era.

Although Stern continues to insist that Change to Win inherits the true mantle of the CIO and the militant organizing tradition, he has opened up a dialogue with corporate leaders that more directly recalls Samuel Gompers's efforts to negotiate a social contract with robber barons through the National Civic Federation at the turn of the century. Building upon the SEIU's and UNITE HERE's well-established practice of supporting their employers' sectoral political goals (urban redevelopment, reform of gambling laws, and so on) in exchange for collective bargaining, Stern is proposing in his new book (A Country That Works, 2006) to accommodate corporate demands to eliminate health-care and pension benefits in return for a united front in Congress for health-care and pension reform.(141) As in the case of Gompers and his successors William Green and George Meaney , such labor-management "partnerships" (which Europeans call "corporatism") have always been a slippery slope to class collaboration and *total defeat. Funny how old, discredited ideas rise from the grave to become "new paradigms" and "outside the envelope" thinking—perhaps someone needs to throw a punch or two at Andy Stern.*

FORTY-TWO

HAPPY BIRTHDAY, BIG BILL

Brand's Hall, Chicago, June 27, 1905. "Big Bill" Haywood pounded his gavel and brought the founding convention of the Industrial Workers of the World (IWW) to order: "This is the Continental Congress of the working class. We are here to confederate the workers of this country into a working-class movement that shall have for its purpose the emancipation of the working class from the slave bondage of capitalism."

The hall erupted in applause. In addition to Haywood's own union, the Western Federation of Miners (WFM), the delegates included coal miners from Kansas, tailors from San Francisco, pressmen from Schenectady, janitors from Chicago, longshoremen from Detroit and Hoboken, blacksmiths from Pullman, brewery workers from Milwaukee, and cloakmakers from Montreal. Keynote speakers included North America's two most famous revolutionary socialists: Eugene Debs and his old sectarian antagonist Daniel De León. Other prominent supporters included Mother Jones of the coal miners' union, and A. M. Simons, the editor of the *International Socialist Review*.

But the call for the convention had originated with the WFM. As Haywood reminded the delegates, hard-rock miners had been fighting a brutal labor war in the Rockies since 1892: "There has not been a strike in the mines by the WFM but that we have been confronted by the militia." In contrast to the American Federation of Labor (AFL) under Samuel Gompers, the WFM did not dine with robber barons, support U.S imperialism, or beg President Roosevelt to mediate industrial disputes. If necessary, its membership knew how to use the business end of a Winchester 30-30 rifle. As Haywood accurately noted, "the capitalist class of this country fear the WFM more than they do all the rest of the labor organizations."

Now the western miners had come east to help build a new "labor organization broad enough to take in all of the working class"—an organization, Haywood insisted, "formed, based, and founded on the class struggle, having in view no compromise and no surrender." The AFL, Haywood argued, was not a working-class movement, but an exclusionist cartel that represented an elite of white, native-born skilled workers. "What we want to establish at this time is a labor organization that will open wide its doors to every man [sic] that earns his livelihood either by his brain or his muscles."

In the most eloquent speech of the convention Lucy Parsons made it clear that this new solidarity must include working women, "the slaves of slaves." An ex-slave herself, and widow of Albert Parsons, one of the Chicago labor radicals executed for the Haymarket affair, she was one of the most extraordinary figures on the American left. She urged delegates to cast their eyes "to far-off Russia and take heart and courage from those who are fighting the battle there, and from the further fact that carries the greatest terror to the capitalist class throughout all the world—that the red flag has been raised."

Indeed, the reports of strikes in Moscow and mutinies in Odessa electrified the convention hall. Over the next year solidarity with the unfolding revolution in Russia would become one of the new movement's principal priorities. When the Socialist International called for global action in support of the Russians on January 22, 1906, the IWW organized mass meetings, and later sponsored a celebrated fundraising tour by Russian writer Maxim Gorky, greeting him as "a representative Industrial Unionist."

When Gorky found out that Bill Haywood and WFM president Charles Moyer had meanwhile been arrested in Idaho for the alleged murder of a strikebreaking former governor, he immediately sent them a telegram: "Greetings to you, my brother socialists. Courage! The day of justice and delivery for the oppressed of all the world is at hand." From their jail cell Haywood and Moyers replied, "Brother. The class struggle which is worldwide, the same in America as in Russia, makes us brothers indeed. Convey our best wishes to fellow workers in your native land."

Such effusions of internationalism were far more than mere sentiment. According to labor historian Philip Foner, the Wobblies' passionate solidarity with the revolt in Russia won them enthusiastic support among immigrant workers in eastern mill towns, opening the way for the IWW's key role in the epic strike wave of 1909–13 that mobilized a supposedly "unorganizable" immigrant working class into militant confrontations with the nation's largest industrial corporations. Hundreds of exiled Russian, Polish, Finnish, and Jewish revolutionaries soon became organizers and popular tribunes of the IWW, giving the movement a cosmopolitan character unprecedented in U.S. history.

On the one-hundredth birthday of the IWW, it is vital to see the IWW as it really was, and to discard the popular stereotype of the Wobblies as romantic but essentially harmless hobo anarchists. There is a tendency in American labor history, especially among well-meaning liberals and social democrats, to sentimentalize the IWW to the point of caricature. In a similar vein, some historians applaud "native" traditions of protest but denigrate or pathologize solidarities with revolts in other lands. In fact, as Foner has irrefutably demonstrated in his essential but often ignored histories, the IWW was the first U.S. labor organization of national significance to make internationalism the bedrock of its values.(54) As a result, it quickly became an extraordinary melting pot of revolutionary traditions and tactical wisdom from every corner of the Earth.

This was dramatically illustrated during the great 1909 strike that inaugurated the four-year-long uprising of the new-immigrant working class. At the notorious Pressed Steel Car Company in McKees Rocks, Pennsylvania, an average of one worker each day was killed in an industrial accident. Sixteen different nationalities toiled in the plant, and management relied on American-born craftsmen's bigotry toward immigrant "Hunkies" to keep unionism at bay. When a spontaneous strike broke out in July, both company and AFL officials expected that it would collapse in a day or two. Instead the foreign-born workforce under IWW leadership fought strikebreakers, the Coal and Iron Police, and the local constabulary for forty-five days. Thirteen strikers were killed, but the workers won their demands.

It was a stunning victory by supposedly "ignorant European peasants." In fact, as an *International Socialist Review* article explained, the internal strike committee was a miniature revolutionary international that included Italian anarchists and socialists, a Russian Social Democrat, several survivors of the "Bloody Sunday" massacre in St. Petersburg, blacklisted Swiss and Hungarian trade unionists, as well as a cadre of veteran German metal workers.

A few years later the IWW would become deeply involved in another epochal revolution in Mexico, and hundreds of Wobblies crossed the border to fight for the short-lived red republic established by Mexican anarchists in Baja California. Later when President Wilson tried to rally support for the marine landing at Veracruz, Big Bill Haywood reminded protesters in New York: "It is better to be a traitor to your country than to your class." The IWW implacably opposed U.S. intervention in World War One and fervently supported antimilitarist rebels everywhere. Not surprisingly, the organization became the principal target of government repression and patriotic vigilantism in 1917. They were, after all, truly dangerous. No labor organization in American history was less patriotic or more gloriously internationalist.

(January 2005, *Socialist Review*)

FORTY-THREE

RADICAL GRIT

In the spring of 1951 the *Nation*, the octogenarian flagship of independent radical opinion, was almost on the ropes. The refusal of its doughty publisher-editor Freda Kirchway (1937–55) to enlist the magazine in the ranks of Cold War liberalism had made it the special target of media inquisitors and anticommunist intellectuals. While Joe McCarthy hunted subversion on the banks of the Potomac, Congress for Cultural Freedom types—including Arthur Schlesinger Jr., Sidney Hook, Elliot Cohen, and Irving Kristol—circled around the *Nation* like so many hungry sharks. In a typical attack, Harvard historian Schlesinger accused Kirchway of "betraying [the magazine's] finest traditions" by publishing "week after week, these wretched apologies for Soviet despotism."(126)

A mere subscription to the *Nation* warranted suspicion of being "soft on communism," and in at least one case (Hollywood writer Edward Eliscu) buying the magazine at a newsstand was cited as a pretext for blacklisting. The magazine was banned from New York city schools, fundraising appeals brought dismal results, longtime donors refused to return Kirchway's phone calls, veteran contributing editors deserted the masthead, and its former art critic, Clement Greenberg, viciously libeled its foreign editor, Spanish Republican exile Julio Alvarez del Vayo, as a Stalinist agent. Sensing the *Nation's* vulnerability, its CIA-supported archfoes, *Commentary* and *The New Leader*, moved in for the kill with sustained campaigns of innuendo and allegations of disloyalty.

Besieged and nearly bankrupt, Kirchway asked the magazine's West Coast contributing editor, Carey McWilliams, to come to New York for a few weeks to edit an emergency civil liberties issue and to help her with fundraising. McWilliams—who had previously urged Kirchway to move the *Nation* to California away from the toxic atmosphere of the New York intelligentsia—agreed to come for a month. He stayed for more than twenty-five years.

The Los Angeles author, lawyer, and progressive activist, whose celebrated 1939 book, *Factories in the Field*, was the nonfiction counterpart to *Grapes of Wrath*, brought a tough Western grit to the ideological battlefields of Manhattan. Although several of his closest friends, including the Marxist literary scholar F. O. Matthiessen and immigrant writer Louis Adamic, were driven to suicide by McCarthyism, McWilliams was unflinching under attack: indeed, he relished political combat, even on the most unequal terrains. In California he had long brawled with such powerful semi-fascist groups as the Associated Farmers and Sons of the Golden West. During his term (1939–42) as director of migrant housing for the New Deal administration of Governor Floyd Olsen, the big growers had labeled him as "Agricultural Pest No. 1, worse than pear blight or the boll weevil" and Republican Earl Warren had campaigned for governor in 1942 with the promise that firing McWilliams would be his first act of office (McWilliams resigned first).

In accepting Kirchway's invitation, he warned of his notoriety: "I consider myself a radical democrat who might better be called a socialist, with both 'democrat' and 'socialist' being written without caps." Freda responded that she was also a "socialist of sorts"—who hadn't been a decade earlier? As Kirchway's right hand—then after 1955 as her successor—McWilliams worked ceaselessly to replenish the *Nation*'s finances and to parry attacks from the red-baiting literati. The job was grueling: in his memoir *The Education of Carey McWilliams* (1978) he writes that "I kept thinking that the crisis at the magazine, which reflected mounting tensions in the Cold War, would soon pass, but it got steadily worse. There was no time to think of anything else."(104)

In the event, McWilliams both substantially reinvented the internal culture of the *Nation* and almost singlehandedly revived the muckracking tradition in American journalism. Like a good military strategist, he believed that it was essential to move from defense to offense as quickly as possible, and to this end, he brought in crack investigative reporters like Fred J. Cook, Gene Gleason, B. J. Widick, and Mathew Josephson, to write famous exposes of the Alger Hiss prosecution, the FBI, the CIA intellectuals, the military-industrial complex, consumer culture, and much else. During the 1920s McWilliams, like so many other unknown young writers in the West and South, had benefited from the editorial patronage and friendship of H. L. Mencken and his *American Mercury*; now he returned the favor, becoming the champion of such fresh talents as Ralph Nader, Dan Wakefield, Howard Zinn, Richard Cloward, Frances Piven, and a broke and desperate soul named Hunter S. Thompson to whom McWilliams fatefully pitched the idea of a report on California motorcycle gangs.

He also struggled mightily against the no-intelligent-life-west-of-Hudson parochialism endemic to the New York scene. In addition to consistent coverage of politics on the other coast (including the many ominous facets of California conservatism), he published riveting firsthand accounts of the southern freedom movement and annual audits of its progress by Martin Luther King Jr., as well as Robert Sherrill's acid portraits of the leading Dixiecrats. Even that perennial orphan of New York liberals, Chicago and its vast Midwestern hinterland, found occasional mention in the *Nation* during the Carey years.

McWilliams had been the California left's one-man think tank during the New Deal years, and he brought to New York a singular passion for turning journalism into sociological investigation and vice versa. He opened the magazine's doors to the hugely influential C. Wright Mills—another outlaw from west of the Pecos—and launched a series of ambitious sociological explorations of the heartlands of Eisenhower-era conformity: corporate bureaucracies, consumer culture, suburban families, the fallout shelter hysteria, and, yes, college campuses. He also kept the era's greatest foreign correspondents—Alexander Werth, Edgar Snow, Basil Davidson, Isaac Deutscher, Carleton Beals, Claude Bourdet, as well as New Left historians William Appleman Williams and Gabriel Kolko—prominently on the front cover.

McWilliams, in short, not only saved the *Nation* from the hellhounds of the Cold War, he also made it into a bully pulpit where radical academics, muckracking journalists, independent Marxists, trade-union rebels, freedom riders, beatniks, and peace protesters found a common voice after the dark age of McCarthyism. Defying the notorious "generation gap," he self-consciously tried to make the magazine an intellectual bridge between the culture of 1930s activism and the emergent New Lefts of the 1960s. And, perhaps most importantly, he kept the attention of white progressives focused on the Black freedom movement and the farmworkers' revolt in California. *The Education of Carey McWilliams*, sadly out of print, remains the indispensable history of the *Nation's* most heroic years as well as a fascinating encyclopedia of its myriad contributors and characters.(104)

But Californians, as Peter Richardson reminds us in his superb new biography of McWilliams, paid a significant price for losing their most brilliant radical critic and social documentarist to the salons of the East.(126) By 1949 McWilliams had written eight books and more than one hundred articles in a single decade, including two classical studies of farm labor (*Factories in the Field* and *Ill Fares the Land*); the still-definitive introduction to the Los Angeles region (*Southern California Country*); a stunning, almost Braudelian interpretation of the main contours of California history (*California: the Great Exception*); the first book-length history of the Chicano experience (*North from Mexico*), and three landmark studies of racism and discrimination (*Brothers Under the Skin, Prejudice: Japanese-Americans, Symbol of Racial Intolerance*, and *A Mask for Privilege: Anti-Semitism in America*). *Witch Hunt: The Revival of Heresy* was published on the eve of his move to New York. But thereafter his amazing literary discipline and productivity were largely diverted to editorial chores and the generous shaping of projects carried to completion by other *Nation* writers.

Richardson's book, with its balanced perspective on his early, middle, and late years, comes at crucial juncture when even hard-core McWilliams fans are in danger of losing sight of the whole man. On the East Coast, he is largely a fond but fading memory to veterans of the *Nation* and its milieu who tend to know little about his seminal California years. Conversely, if he is again a lodestone in the West, where a major McWilliams revival—thanks to the ceaseless championing of his work by historian Kevin Starr, Sacramento journalist Peter Schrag, and "California Studies" instigator Jeff Lustig—has been under way since the early 1990s, contemporary Californian readers have little appreciation of his *Nation* tenure or his contributions to national progressive causes.

Biographies these days, of course, can meander for thousands of pages and consume a generation of research; *American Prophet* is more economic and stays focused on the literary output. Robinson, who admits that he had never heard of McWilliams until 1999, and then was astonished to discover "one of the most versatile, productive, and consequential American public intellectuals of the twentieth century," aspires to be a "fit reader" of his books and articles in the specific historical contexts of their production. The result is a fascinating portrait of activism deepened and sustained by Herculean labors of research and investigation: as McWilliams confesses in his memoir, "the fact that all my books represent efforts to relieve my ignorance on subjects of compulsive interest often prompted me to wonder if I had selected the subjects or whether it was the other way around." (104)

Certainly causes were ceaselessly finding a way to his door: Robinson, after poring through McWilliams's datebooks and diaries, is staggered by the sheer number of defense committees, solidarity campaigns, strike funds, and fundraising events that Carey found time to organize or chair. When combined with a law practice, or later, with public office, as well as a daily writing stint of one thousand words or more, activism, whether on behalf of cotton strikers, Spanish

Republicans, or the Sleepy Lagoon defendants, left little time to play *pater familis*. In his memoir, McWilliams devotes less than a paragraph to his adult family life: marriages and children, he implies, are a private sphere, off-limits to public scrutiny. As a dutiful biographer, Robinson roots through McWilliams's closets but finds little evidence of anything more than a failed first marriage, too much time at the office, and a penchant for occasional rowdy binges with writer friends (but Carey was always sober and hard at work the next morning).

McWilliams, as Robinson demonstrates, was a chip off the old (Scots-Irish) block: raised on a sprawling Colorado cattle ranch by busy parents who had little time for expressive affection but gave their sons early scope for responsibility and independence. Carey grew up with the hands and imbued their egalitarian cowboy ethos of irreverence, hard work, and self-reliance. In the unpredictable moral meteorology of Hollywood in the 1940s and Manhattan in the 1950s, when one's closest friends and most deeply held beliefs could be forfeited in a day, McWilliams was Yosemite granite, with unwavering loyalty to old friends and youthful convictions.

By sheer coincidence, I read *American Prophet* in tandem with Cormac McCarthy's *No Country for Old Men*. McCarthy's new novel, compounded out of equal portions of sentimental nostalgia and apocalyptic violence, is a lament for the loss of those chivalric qualities—honor, duty, discretion, courage, and, alas, kindness—that once supposedly typified frontier knights like the novel's Sheriff Bell, now obsolete in a world of insolent punks and robot-like assassins. We tend to think of these public funerals for America's lost nobility of character—*Saving Private Ryan* and *The Greatest Generation* also come to mind—as ceremonies of the right, moral deceits to cover up actual histories of racism and carnage, but there may be other, alternative dimensions to this national nostalgia.

Carey McWilliams, I am sure, would have reminded McCarthy (or Spielberg, for that matter) that the finest embodiments of moral courage in American history were the Abolitionists, the Wobblies, the

Abraham Lincoln Battalion, and the Student Nonviolent Coordinating Committee. In the storms of the mid-twentieth century, McWilliams himself was as unbending as Wendell Phillips had been in the 1850s and 1860s. Indeed, as one of his sons—the historian Wilson Carey McWilliams—points out in a beautiful foreword to a recent McWilliams reader (*Fool's Paradise*), "he was a sardonic Galahad, constant to the democratic Grail."(105)

Robinson also does a wonderful job of evoking McWilliams's strength of commitment, but the last word belongs to the *Nation*'s former editor himself: "What it comes down to is that I am the rebel-radical I have always been (for reasons I have never fully understood) and that I still take a generous view of the future and remain basically an optimist despite much evidence that I could be wrong. On balance, however, my brand of indigenous radicalism and idealism has stood the test of time as well as or better than some of the apocalyptic ideologies of the right and left."(104)

(September 19, 2006, *The Nation*)

FORTY-FOUR

RIOT NIGHTS ON SUNSET STRIP

From shortly before the Watts rebellion in August 1965 until late October 1966, I was the Los Angeles regional organizer for Students for a Democratic Society. My assignments from the national office in Chicago were to build a core of draft resistance in the city (I had burned my own draft card the previous March and was waiting to see whether or not I would be prosecuted) and to assist two eloquent and charismatic local SDSers—Margaret Thorpe at USC and Patty Lee Parmalee at UC Irvine—in raising hell on local campuses. The most wonderful hell was generated by a group of 16- and 17-year-old SDS kids from Palisades High School. Hanging out with them, we soon became participants in some of the events described below (although with a crew cut and a phobia about recreational drugs, I was hardly a representative "teenybopper"). I left Los Angeles in 1967 to briefly work for SDS in Texas, returning to Southern California late in the year to begin real life as an apprentice butcher in San Diego and later as a truck driver in East L.A. I missed the 1967 riots on the Strip, but was on the scene for the culminating protest in 1968. So what follows is an alloy of research and memory. It is also the first small installment in a projected history of L.A.'s countercultures and protesters (Setting the Night on Fire).

A moment in rock-and-roll dreamtime: Saturday night on Sunset Strip in early December 1966. Along that famed twelve blocks of unincorporated Los Angeles County between Hollywood and Beverly Hills, the neon firmament blazes new names like the Byrds, the Doors, Sonny and Cher, the Mamas and Papas, and Buffalo Springfield. But the real spectacle is out on the street: two thousand demonstrators peacefully snaking their way west along Sunset into the county Strip then circling back to their starting point at Pandora's Box Coffeehouse (8180 Sunset) just inside the Los Angeles city limits. On one side the boundary are several hundred riot-helmeted sheriffs' deputies; on the other side, an equal number of Los Angeles police, fidgeting nervously with their nightsticks as if they were confronting angry strikers or an unruly mob instead of friendly fifteen-year-olds with long hair and acne.

"There's somethin' happening here"

The demonstrators—relentlessly caricatured as "Striplings," "teeny boppers," and even "hoodlums" by hostile cops and their allies in the daily press—are a cross-section of white teenage Southern California. Movie brats from the gilded hills above the Strip mingle with autoworkers' daughters from Van Nuys and truck drivers' sons from Pomona. There are some college students and a few uncomfortably crew-cut servicemen, but most are high-school age, fifteen to eighteen, and, thus, technically liable to arrest after 10:00 pm when dual county and city juvenile curfews take effect. Kids carry hand-lettered signs that read "Stop Blue Fascism!," "Abolish the Curfew," and "Free the Strip."

The demonstration has been called (but scarcely organized) by RAMCOM (the Right of Assembly and Movement Committee), headquartered in the Fifth Estate Coffeehouse (8226 Sunset). The coffeehouse's manager, Al Mitchell, acts as the adult spokesman for the high-school students and teenage runaways who cluster around the Fifth Estate and Pandora's Box, a block away. This is the fifth in a series of weekend demonstrations—perhaps more accurately, "happenings"—that have protested a year-long campaign by sheriffs and police to clear the Strip of "loitering" teenagers. In response to complaints from local restaurateurs and landowners, the cops trawl nightly at 10:00 pm for under-eighteens. They target primarily the long-haired kids in beads, granny glasses, and tie-dyed shirts.

It has become the custom to humiliate curfew-violaters with insults and obscene jokes, to pull their long hair, brace them against squad cars, and even choke them with billy clubs, before hauling them down to the West Hollywood sheriffs or Hollywood police stations where they will be held until their angry parents pick them up. This evening (December 10), however, has so far passed peacefully, with more smiles exchanged than insults or blows. The high point was the appearance of Sonny and Cher, dressed like high-fashion Inuit in huge fleece parkas, waving support to adoring kids. (Later, after photographs have appeared on front pages across the world, the city of Monterey Park will ban Sonny and Cher from their Rose Parade float for this gesture of solidarity with "rioting teenyboppers.")

By midnight the demonstration has returned to Pandora's and a happy Al Mitchell has officially declared the protest over. As the crowd begins to disperse, LAPD officers enter Pandora's to check IDs. Eason Monroe, head of the Southern California chapter of the American Civil Liberties Union, complains that the police are acting illegally: Pandora's doesn't serve alcohol and the curfew ordinance exempts teenagers inside licensed businesses. The response of the cops is to handcuff and arrest Monroe. When Michael Vossi, a PR agent for the Beach Boys, who is acting as a legal observer for an entertainment industry support group, speaks up in Monroe's defense, he is pummeled by another officer. The few hundred remaining demonstrators outside of Pandora's shout at the police to leave their adult supporters alone. Riot-equipped police reinforcements converge from all sides.

Paul Jay Robbins, another adult supporter from CAFF (Community Action for Facts and Freedom Committee) whose members include *Gilligan's Island* star Bob Denver, Sonny and Cher manager Brian Stone, and Woolworth heir Lance Reventlow, will a few days later in the *Los Angeles Free Press* (lovingly known as the *Freep* to its devotees) describe the unprovoked fury of the LAPD's attack on panic-stricken and fleeing protesters. After Robbins himself is hit by a police baton, he watches in horror as police flail away at a helpless teenager.

I saw a kid holding a sign in both hands jerk forward as though struck from behind. He fell into the path of the officers and four or five of them immediately began bludgeoning him with clubs held in one hand. I stood transfixed watching him as the officers continued beating him while he attempted to alternately protect himself and crawl forward. Finally he slumped against a wall as the officer continued to beat him. Before I was spun around and set reeling forward again, I saw him picked up, belly-down, by the officers and carried away. Later legal representatives of CAFF measured a trail of blood 75 yards long leading from this spot to the point where he was placed in a car. Where is he now?

The night's peaceful demonstration had been wantonly turned into another of the those police "massacres" for which Los Angeles is becoming justly notorious. The two daily newspapers—the Chandler-owned *Los Angeles Times* and the Hearst-owned *Herald-Examiner*—as usual characterize the unwarranted police aggression as a teenybopper-inspired "riot." Al Mitchell and the other adult supporters, meanwhile, are so appalled by the LAPD violence that they call off next weekend's planned demonstration out of fear that the police may yet kill or seriously injure one of the kids. After two months of political debate, litigation, and frustrating negotiations, the protests will resume massively in February 1967 and continue episodically through the autumn of 1968. Thousands of kids will be arrested for curfew violations and American International Pictures will immortalize the "riots" in a camp film (*Riot on Sunset Strip*, 1967) with a famous soundtrack.

"Battle lines being drawn"

This legendary Battle of the Strip, 1966–68, of course, was only the most celebrated episode in the struggle of teenagers of all colors during the 1960s and 1970s to create their own realm of freedom and carnivalesque sociality within the Southern California night. There were other memorable contestations with business and police over Griffith Park "love-ins," beach parties, interracial concerts, countercultural neighborhoods (like Venice Beach), "head" shopping districts (like L.A.'s Haight-Ashbury on Fairfax), cruising strips (Whittier, Hollywood, and Van Nuys boulevards), street-racing locales, and the myriad local hangouts where kids quietly or brazenly defied parents, police, and curfews.(38)

Of course such battles were not a new story (Los Angeles had passed its first juvenile curfew in the 1880s), nor unique to Southern California. But postwar California motorized youth rebellion. A culture of cars, high-speed freeways, centrifugal sprawl, and featureless suburbs generated a vast ennui among bored but mobile teenagers. Any hint of excitement on a weekend evening might draw kids from anywhere in the hundred-odd-mile radius of local AM radio. Thus when one rock station incautiously advertised a party at Malibu Beach in 1961, nearly twenty thousand teenagers showed up and then rioted when sheriffs ordered them to leave. Nor is it surprising that once the Strip "riots" were celebrated in song (by Stephen Stills in 1966), as well as in *Time* and *Life*, that the 8000 and 9000 blocks of Sunset Boulevard would become an even more powerful magnet to alienated kids from the valleys and flatlands. Indeed, decades later, to claim that you had been busted on the Strip in '66 or '67 was the Southern California equivalent of boasting that you had been at Woodstock, at the Creation.

But why the Strip? The parents of many Southern California teenagers in 1966 had their own lustrous memories of a night—returning from a Pacific War in 1943 or after college graduation in 1951—when they had dined, danced, and rubbed shoulders with celebrity in one of the famed Sunset Boulevard nightclubs, such as Ciro's, Mocambo, or the Trocadero. The Strip, one of those strange "county holes" in the Los Angeles urban fabric, was for a generation the major center of movie colony nightlife, and thus the epicenter of tabloid scandal and romance. It was also a city-state run by famed gamblers and their gangster allies in league with a corrupt Sheriff's Department. During its most glamorous years, from 1939 to 1954, the Strip's informal mayor was the indestructible Mickey Cohen, prince of gamblers and king of survivors. Operating from a haberdashery on the 8800 block of Sunset, Cohen defied all odds by emerging unscathed from an incredible series of Mob ambushes and bombings that took the lives of half a dozen of his bodyguards.

But by the late 1950s Cohen was cooling his heels in the pen and the Strip was in steep decline. Las Vegas, thanks to Bugsy Siegel, had usurped the lucrative symbiosis of movie stars and mobsters that the Strip had pioneered, and hijacked its star chefs and famous entertainers. Yet precisely as urban decay was taking a huge bite out of its golden mile, the popular television show *77 Sunset Strip* was generating a new mythology. Ed "Cookie" Byrnes—the program's Elvis-like costar who played a parking-lot jockey who was also a part-time sleuth—briefly became the biggest youth celebrity in the country. The Strip was portrayed as a dazzling nocturnal crossroads for a handsome Corvette-and-surfboard set.

In fact, the Strip, like the larger (west and east) Hollywood community, was in transition between its golden age and two competing strategies for reusing vacant nightclub and entertainment space. The "Times Square" option was to reopen clubs with topless or, later, nude dancers. The Bodyshop was the exemplar of successful neo-burlesque. The other option was to cater to juvenile audiences with rock music. Music producers and PR people, especially, liked the idea of a geographically centralized youth club scene to talent-scout new bands and develop those already under contract. The success of *77 Sunset Strip* moreover established a national cachet and name recognition for groups weaned on the Strip. In 1965 the county reluctantly acceded to club-owners' and record companies' pleas and created a tiered licensing system that allowed 18- to 21-year-olds inside clubs where alcohol was served, while creating special liquor-less music venues for younger 15- to 18-year-olds. The youth club scene promptly exploded.

For older teenagers and young adults the premier clubs were the Whiskey, Gazzarri's, and the Galaxy. The newly baptized "teenyboppers" favored It's Boss (formerly the renowned Ciro's), The Trip (formerly Crescendo), and Sea Witch, as well as cheap, atmospheric coffee houses like Pandora's (owned by former tennis star Bill Tilden) and the Fifth Estate (owned by teen magazine mogul Robert Peterson). As the clubs inexorably hiked their cover charges, younger and poorer kids preferred simply to be part of the colorful street scene, wandering in groups down Sunset or hovering near club entrances for a glimpse of Jim Morrison or Neil Young. As the nightly teen crowds grew larger, however, the Strip's upscale restaurant owners and their wealthy adult clientele began to protest about the lack of parking and the increasing sidewalk congestion. Beverly Hills matrons and Century City lawyers recoiled from contact with the beatified throngs.

"Moreover, at this point," wrote Edgar Freidenburg and Anthony Bernhard later in the *New York Review of Books*, "the good behavior of the 'teenyboppers' had become a problem." Because the kids were generally "not hostile, aggressive nor disorderly," there was no obvious pretext for driving them off the Strip. Eventually, the Sunset Strip Chamber of Commerce and the Sunset Plaza Association, representing landlords and restaurant owners, cajoled the Sheriff's Department to stringently enforce a youth curfew. During the 1940s, when teenage "B-girls" were a national scandal, both the city and county had adopted parallel curfew regulations that forbade anyone under eighteen from loitering in public after 10:00 pm. "Loitering," Freidenburg and Bernhard noted, "is defined as 'to idle, to lag, to stand idly by or to walk, drive, or ride about aimlessly and without purpose'—a definition that may well make the entire solar system illegal."(57)

"Young people speaking their minds..."

During the summer of 1966, the sheriffs on the Strip, soon joined by the LAPD in the adjacent Hollywood and Fairfax districts, escalated their pressure on the under-eighteens. Curfew arrests soared into the thousands, with three hundred hauled away from the sidewalks outside Canter's Restaurant on Fairfax on a single July evening. "It was just like shooting ducks in a duck pond," boasted one deputy. When the city's largest newspaper needed a dramatic image for a story about the teenage hordes, the deputies obligingly arrested ten kids and stood them handcuffed in a line "for the direct accommodation of the *Los Angeles Times.*"(57) "Throughout the spring and summer," reported Renata Adler in a later *New Yorker* article, "licenses permitting minors to be served anything at all were revoked at one place after another: several of these places reluctantly went adult and topless—a change that seemed to cause the authorities no distress." Indeed it was widely rumored that the kids were being cleared off the Strip to make way for the return of Mob-connected sex entertainment and "for more serious, less conspicuous forms of vice than lingering after curfew."(1)

Shortly after Halloween, a couple of angry teenagers decided it was time to organize a formal protest against the arbitrary arrests and police abuse of kids on the Strip. They printed a flyer—"Protest Police Mistreatment of Youth on Sunset Blvd.—No More Shackling of 14 and 15 year olds"—calling for a demonstration on Saturday night, the 12th of November. Al Mitchell, the leftist ex-merchant sailor and filmmaker who managed the Fifth Estate for Robert Peterson, became their informal sponsor. Cans were soon being circulated around the coffeehouse to raise money for additional leaflets. Rock stations began to luridly warn that a "major riot" was brewing, and cautioned kids away from the Strip on the 12th. Of course, this was irresistible publicity for a demonstration whose urgency was underlined by the arrest of eighty kids for curfew violations on Friday night.

The next evening, according to the *Freep*, more than three thousand teenagers, flanked by adult curiosity-seekers and hostile servicemen, gathered in front of Pandora's by 9:00 pm. Aside from a handful of placards hastily painted at the Fifth Estate a few hours before the demonstration, there was no apparent organization or leadership whatsoever. In the spirit of the times, the protest had been conceived as a spontaneous "happening" and the overwhelming majority of the crowd complied with its peaceful purpose. At one point the police called a fire company to the scene, and some of the kids nervously asked the firefighters whether they were going to hose them. A bemused fire captain replied: "Have a good time and let me go home." The engine left.

The overflow of protesters onto Sunset and Crescent Heights boulevards created a traffic jam; several bus drivers angrily honked and screamed at the kids. In response, demonstrators climbed up and danced on the roofs of the buses. One youth scrawled "Free the 15 Year Olds!" on a windshield; another broke a window with a fire extinguisher. On the fringe of the crowd there was a brief scuffle between long-haired protesters and some young sailors and marines. Shortly after 10:00 pm, a hundred cops roughly used their nightsticks to clear the sidewalks. Police with drawn revolvers chased kids into Pandora's. Panicky protesters who tried to retreat westward down Sunset collided with a wall of riot-ready sheriffs, and about fifty were arrested.

The next evening, the LAPD declared a "tactical alert" and closed Sunset from Fairfax to Crescent Heights. State Highway Patrol officers and private Pinkerton guards reinforced the sheriffs' side of the line. Thanks to lurid rumors in the station houses, the atmosphere was irrationally tense, and the *Freep* reported that "many of the officers seemed to be in a state of panic." While Al Mitchell shot footage for his documentary *Blue Fascism*, the three hundred or so protesters jeered "Gestapo, Gestapo!" at the police line and then dispersed after they were declared an "unlawful assembly." They vowed to return the following weekend.

On Monday morning, it was the turn of the Establishment to riot. Although a handful of protesters had been involved in the bus incident (total estimated damage: $158), the *Herald-Examiner*'s headline screamed: "Long Hair Nightmare: Juvenile Violence on Sunset Strip." A *Times* editorial likewise warned of "Anarchy on Sunset Strip," and blamed the teenagers and their "senseless, destructive riot" for a "sorry ending for the boulevard that was once Hollywood's most dazzling area." The *Times* also gave much space to the melodramatic claims of Captain Charlie Crumly, commander of the LAPD's Hollywood Division, that "left-wing groups and outside agitators" had organized the protest. Crumly also asserted that "there are over a thousand hoodlums living like bums in Hollywood, advocating such things as free love, legalized marijuana and abortion."

Los Angeles suddenly seemed like an embattled patriarchy. Holly-wood councilman Paul Lamport demanded a full-scale investigation into Crumly's charges of a subversive plot, while his county counter-part, Supervisor Ernest Debs, ranted that "whatever it takes is going to be done. We're going to be tough. We're not going to surrender that area or any area to beatniks or wild-eyed kids." The Sunset Plaza Associa-tion, representing Strip restaurant owners, called for a city crackdown on such "kid hangouts" as Pandora's and the Fifth Estate that offered sanctuary to protesting teenagers across the county/city border.

Only the *Freep* challenged the daily press's characterization of the previous weekend's police disturbance as a "teenybopper riot." "To the editorial writers of the *Times*, sitting in their bald majesty on First Street, entirely isolated from the events, unable to properly evaluate or analyze them, it is only possible to say: 'You are stupid old men who make reckless and irresponsible statements that can only make a bad situation worse.'" According to the *Freep*, the kids were actually caught in the middle of an economic conflict between the Sunset Strip Chamber of Commerce with its ties to adult-entertainment industry, on one hand, and the Sunset Strip Association, representing the youth venues, on the other. "The police, in effect, have been cooperating with one very wealthy group of property owners on the Strip against a less powerful group of businessmen."

The lopsidedness of the battle was further demonstrated when the Los Angeles City Council unanimously acceded to the Sunset Plaza Association's request and voted to use eminent domain to demolish Pandora's Box. At the same time, Sheriff Peter Pitchess and Supervisor Debs lobbied the County Public Welfare Commission to prevent the renewal of the permits allowing Strip clubs to admit under-twenty-ones. When the Commission balked, the supervisors themselves re-scinded the offending ordinance and effectively banned teenagers from the clubs. Suddenly, Los Angeles's celebrated rock renaissance it-self was under threat, and this quickly galvanized the younger genera-tion of music producers and agents into unexpected solidarity with the next wave of protests on the Strip.

"There's a man with a gun over there…"

Although the second weekend of protests (November 18–20, 1966) again pitted thousands of flower children against huge phalanxes of police and sheriffs , the still leaderless protesters broadcast enough seductive warmth, as well as carnival-like mirth, to take the grim edge off the evening. As they marched down the Strip, they handed out flowers and blew bubbles and kisses. The cops seemed disarmed by the happy mood, although at 10:00 pm a sheriffs' sound truck began warning under-eigtheens to clear the street or be arrested. Hundreds of kids resolutely faced off a cordon of deputies, police, and Navy Shore Patrol around the Crescent Heights and Sunset triangle. Although several score curfew violaters were ultimately arrested, there were no baton charges, and the crowd, still in surprisingly good humor, dispersed by 2:00 am. There were widespread rumors, however, that the business interests were upset with the evening's outcome, and that the sheriffs were under pressure to use more aggressive tactics the next weekend.

To forestall the expected violence against their fans, a group of concerned celebrities and music-industry executives went into a huddle the following Friday. The meeting was called by Jim Dickson, the manager of the Byrds, who took full-time leave to organize the awkwardly titled CAFF. Its initial membership included Dickson's partner Ed Ticker, the Fifth Estate's Al Mitchell, Whiskey's co-owner Elmer Valentine, Sonny and Cher manager Brian Stone, television star Bob Denver, millionaire sportsman Lance Reventlow (a member of the Sheriff's Aero Squadron), and Beach Boy Enterprises' Michael Vossi and David Anderle. The meager political clout of the club owners was now dramatically augmented by support from the top bands and music-industry leaders. CAFF decided to mobilize its members and friends to attend the next evening's demonstration as legal observers in yellow armbands. A group of sympathetic Hollywood ministers and the local chapter of the ACLU also promised to turn out to support the right of peaceful protest.

In the event, amok sheriffs' deputies gave CAFF and some thirty clergy people a shocking exhibition of the abuse that the kids had been complaining about all year. "People were viciously clubbed and beaten," wrote the *Freep*'s Brian Carr. "There was no plan or purpose evident in the beatings or the subsequent arrests. It seemed the hand-iest people, with no regard given to age, sex or social position were clubbed, punched and/or arrested." Bob Denver—one of television's most popular stars (*Gilligan's Island*)—could only mumble "unbe-lievable…just unbelievable" as deputies spit on a woman in his group, then charged down the street to baton some harmless teens. Peter Fonda, who was filming outside the Fifth Estate with actor Brandon de Wilde, was arrested with twenty-seven others, mainly adults, as they watched the LAPD's emulation of the sheriffs. ("Man, the kids have had it," Fonda later told reporters.)

Meanwhile inside the lobby of the West Hollywood sheriff's sta-tion, Brian Stone—who was already a legend for creating Sonny and Cher as well as Buffalo Springfield—was arrested for refusing to pro-duce identification upon demand. His business partner, Charlie Green, was in turn busted for protesting Stone's arrest. Before the night was over, the sheriffs and LAPD together had made enemies of one of the most powerful, if unconventional industries in Los Ange-les. As the Mamas and Papas later explained to reporters, even mil-lionaire rock stars could no longer "drive down the street with any feeling of safety from harassment."

The even more promiscuous police violence at the December 10 protest (described at the beginning of this essay) solidified CAFF's ap-prehension that "blue fascism" posed a direct threat to Los Angeles's billion-dollar rock culture. As the city council and board of supervi-sors forged ahead with their plans to bulldoze Pandora's and gut the Strip club scene, CAFF joined with the club owners and the ACLU in an ultimately successful legal defense of the status quo ante. If the *Los Angeles Times* red-baited the long-haired protesters as dupes of the "the left-wing W.E.B. DuBois Clubs," AM stations fought back with a dramatic recording of a defiant teenager saying "it's our constitutional guarantee to walk unmolested on Sunset Strip" as he was being bundled into a sheriff's car. And with a few weeks, tens of millions of teenagers across the world were listening to the haunting words— "Stop! Children, What's That Sound?"—of Stephen Stills's Strip battle anthem, "For What It's Worth."

Al Mitchell and CAFF, supported by the *Freep*, suspended demonstrations over the Christmas holiday while they held "peace talks" with county officials. Verbal progress on that end, however, was undercut by what was widely seen as an escalation of police pressure on youth and adult countercultures throughout the Los Angeles area. In mid-December, for example, Pasadena Police raided the popular Catacombs art gallery and arrested one hundred young people on a variety of drug charges, many of them utterly bogus. On New Year's Eve, the LAPD vice squad rampaged through the gay bars in the Silver Lake district, roughing up and arresting scores of patrons.

The LAPD also increased their illegal harassment of the *Freep*'s salesforce. Despite a city ordinance authorizing their right to sell papers from the curb to passing cars, *Freep* vendors were systematically ticketed and frequently arrested, especially on the Strip and in front of Pandora's. Since local television and the two dailies had blacked out images of police brutality, the *Freep*, together with a few rock stations and the local Pacifica franchise (KPFK-FM), were truly the alternative media. Persecution, moreover, only made the *Freep* vendors into heroes and boosted the paid circulation of the paper above 65,000.

"I think it's time..."

The "phony war" on the Strip lasted until the end of February when Al Mitchell announced that "we must go on to the streets again...police and sheriff's deputies have again and again violated the terms of a 'truce' RAMCOM and other concerned groups negotiated on 16 December with the Los Angeles Crime and Delinquency Commission." Indeed, Captain Victor Resau of the West Hollywood sheriffs humiliated the commission when he publically renounced the truce or any other constraint on the vigorous enforcement of the curfew law. The county's earlier attempt to outlaw teenagers from rock clubs by ordinance had been ruled unconstitutional, so sheriffs and police were once more under terrific pressure from property-owners to use brute force to drive the kids off the Strip. Mitchell was particularly outraged at repeated raids on the Fifth Estate and other alcohol-free coffeehouses. Some eighty thousand leaflets calling for a demonstration on Saturday night, February 11, 1967, saturated the clubs and made their way clandestinely through every high school in the county.

For the first time there was strategic planning to broaden the base of the protests to incorporate the grievances of gays and people of color. As the *Freep* noted, "one of the most interesting and pace-setting reactions to the call to demonstrate came early this week from homosexual organizations who are currently up in arms about New Year's Eve's police raids on a number of Silver Lake area gay bars." Two leading gay groups, PRIDE and the Council on Religion and the Homosexual, endorsed the February 11 demonstration and added plans for their own simultaneous march along Sunset in Silver Lake. Mitchell's loosely knit RAMCOM group also plotted actions in Watts, East L.A., and Pacoima in the hope that angry Black and Chicano youth would be drawn to participate. The self-concept of the Strip movement was shifting from an amorphous "happening" to an all-embracing coalition of outcast and police-persecuted street cultures.

A crude attempt was made to frame the movement's principal adult leader. Ten days before the scheduled demonstrations, Mitchell—an old veteran of harassment arrests for such offenses as allowing singing in the Fifth Estate and obscene antipolice graffiti in its lavatories—was arrested (but not booked) on suspicion of 150 counts of statutory rape. The fortyish leftist, whom the *Times* had caricatured as the "muezzin of the teenyboppers," was now unmasked as a sinister sex criminal preying on his teenager followers—or so it was claimed on radio and television news. In fact, Mitchell's seventeen-year-old accuser quickly confessed that her allegations were lies told in anger after she had been thrown out of the Fifth Estate for drug use. The *Freep* pondered why Mitchell had been so brazenly arrested and demonized in the media before the LAPD had even checked out the teenager's preposterous story.

In any event, the hubbub around Mitchell did not deter more than three thousand teenagers, along with unprecedented numbers of college students and adults, from once again assembling in front of Pandora's on Saturday night. For the first time, there was an organized rally—with speeches by Mitchell, civil liberties lawyer Marvin Chan, and ACLU counsel Phil Croner—as well as an ingenious tactical plan. Every hour new contingents of protesters were sent west in the county Strip where sheriff's deputies, impassive for the most part, allowed them to march without harassment. The demonstrators, carrying signs that read "Stop Beating the Flower Children" and "Stop Blue Fascism," were both exuberant and disciplined: vivid refutation of the hoary myth of "wild-eyed, drug-crazed rioters."

Meanwhile five hundred protesters in front of the Black Cat Bar at the corner of Sunset and Hyperion were urged by speakers to make "a unified community stand in Silver Lake against brutality." In L.A. history, this was the less dramatic counterpart to the Village's Stonewall Riot, the birthday of an activist gay rights movement. Unfortunately the other protest venues were unhistoric flops. Only a desultory crowd turned out in Venice, where most residents had preferred to join the main action on the Strip, and in Pacoima a small group of hapless RAMCOM kids with good intentions but poor communications skills were set upon and beaten by local gang members. The *Freep* could find no evidence of any protests in either Watts or East L.A.

This did not mean, however, that the Strip protests had no impact upon the ghettos and barrios. Black and Chicano flower children were beginning to integrate the Strip in small numbers, despite frequent racist treatment from club bouncers and, of course, cops; and some Black leaders, both moderate and radical, were rallying to the idea, pushed by Al Mitchell and New Left groups, that there really was new ground for a broad, anti–police-abuse coalition. In March, after another large protest on the Strip, Georgia legislator and civil rights hero

Julian Bond spoke to admiring teenyboppers at the Fifth Estate while cops loomed threateningly on the periphery in riot gear. From February onwards, moreover, every protest on the Strip self-consciously identified itself with the victims of far more deadly police brutality in South Central L.A. Radical groups, especially SDS and the International Socialists, began to play more prominent roles in the protests and actively recruited high-school-age memberships.

But many Angelenos had no inkling that mass protests, larger than ever, were continuing on the Strip. In April, the latest addition to the local alternative media, *Los Angeles Underground*, bannered the huge headline: "STRIP WAR: News Blackout Conceals Struggle, Police Sabotage Truce Agreement." The paper excoriated the *Herald-Examiner*, but even more the *Times*, for their refusal to print a word about the huge but now disciplined demonstrations on the Strip. The *Times*, however, did continue its vilification of youth culture ("teenyboppers" had now metamorphosed into "hippies") with constant stories and editorials of the ilk, "Hippies Blamed for Decline of the Sunset Strip." Furthermore, the *Times* warned, the bell-bottomed hordes were now posed to "invade" and presumably destroy Hollywood as well. Much attention was given to a speech that a local real-estate appraiser, Robert Steel, had made in May 1967 charging that long-haired teens had done more damage than the Watts rioters two years earlier. Steel claimed that under-eighteen youth had reduced property values along the Strip by 30 percent and scared away potential major investors, including a large savings-and-loan company.

The *Times*, at least, was accurate in pointing out a new hot spot in Hollywood where property owners were squaring off against new youth venues, especially Hullabaloo, a vast rock emporium that sometimes staged a dozen popular bands in all-night marathons. On July 28, 1967, the LAPD, using elaborate decoys and commando tactics, had swept down upon the ticket lines at Hullabaloo and arrested two hundred fans for curfew violations, although their IDs were only checked at the station. As usual the incident went unreported in the *Times,* but it sent shockwaves through the music world and revived CAFF-type interest in defending the industry's local fandom.

1968 was year three of the struggle and the Strip War threatened to become as protracted as the Civil War, with the baby sisters and brothers of the original protesters now on the front line. No one could much recall what a "beatnik" was, but hippie-phobia was reaching a crescendo, with the *Times*, as usual, providing a rich diet of innuendo and stereotyping. Yet the immense engines of the culture industry were slowly turning the great ship of mainstream taste around. Straight young adults, from secretaries to longshoremen, were quietly letting their hair grow and putting on bell bottoms. The young sailors and marines who a few years before had waylaid unwary teenyboppers in the Strip's back alleys were now happily trading drugs with their hippie connections. Storeowners and restaurateurs who once had apoplexy at the sight of a madras-clothed teenybopper now couldn't distinguish them from the palm trees.

As the mainstream went countercultural, much of the counterculture, including its music, moved, however temporarily, to the political left. The LAPD and the sheriffs had to shift deployments to deal with the new specters of the Black Panther Party in South Central and high-school unrest on the Eastside. Curfew enforcement on the Strip became a less urgent law-enforcement priority. Although police harassment would continue for another decade or more, the Strip War came to a climax on September 28, 1968, the day after Huey Newton had been sentenced to prison.

The protest this time was organized by the new Peace and Freedom Party, which gave equal billing to three demands: "Free the Strip. End Police Brutality. Free Huey Newton." Although the *Times*—what else could one expect?—gave the protest only a few sentences, claiming that there were about six hundred participants, I can testify that the number was at least four times larger. It was, in fact, one of the most memorable demonstrations of a lifetime, as the same kids, so frequently scorned and physically abused by the deputies, now boldly shoved "Fuck the Sheriffs" and "No More Murder of Black People" placards in their faces.

For the first time the shoe was on the other foot. The West Hollywood sheriff's station was surrounded by protesters, besieged by "revolutionary hippies" no less. In a tense, hour-long confrontation, the kids showed superb courage and good humor. In the end, everyone simply walked off, back into the rock-and-roll night, while some of the girls threw kisses to the thoroughly vexed and defeated sheriffs.

(2007, *Labour/Le Travai*)

DID THE POOR WEEP FOR ROME?

Not at all, according to the great classical historian, G. E. M. De Ste. Croix. In his magnum opus, *The Class Struggle in the Ancient Greek World (from the Archaic Age to the Arab Conquests)*, he documents innumerable examples of how the barbarians were greeted with "positive pleasure and co-operation" by the Empire's lower classes. For example, "during the first siege of Rome by Alaric the Visigoth, in the winter of 408–9, virtually all the slaves in Rome, totaling 40,000, escaped to the Gothic camp." "Other sources, both Greek and Latin," De Ste. Croix continues, "speak of the inhabitants of the Roman empire as actually desiring the coming of the 'barbarians.'"

Moreover, "against all the evidence set out...for discontent, rebellion, and defection to the 'barbarians' on the part of humble Greeks and Romans, I have come across very little sign of spontaneous resistance to 'barbarian incursions on part of either peasants or townsmen.'" Since barbarian conquest tended to reduce the rate of exploitation by large landowners and tax collectors, as well as allowing broader religious tolerance, there were few incentives to fight heroically to the last ditch for one's masters. ("There are clear indications that the regime the Vandals set up on their conquest of Roman North Africa in 429 and the years following was less extortionate than the Roman system existing there, from the point of view of the *coloni*.")

In De Ste. Croix's opinion, those "vampires," the Roman and

Byzantine upper classes, not the maligned "barbarians" (Goths, Vandals, Huns, and Arabs), were the true looters and destroyers of Classical civilization. "As I see it, the Roman political system (especially when Greek democracy had been wiped out) facilitated a most intense and ultimately destructive economic exploitation of the great mass of the people, whether slave or free, and it made radical reform impossible. The result was that the propertied class, the men of real wealth, who had deliberately created this system for their own benefit, drained the life-blood from their world and thus destroyed Graeco-Roman civilization over a large part of the empire..."

It remains to be seen who will cry for the new Rome on the Potomac.

BIBLIOGRAPHY

1. Adler, Renata. "Fly Trans-Love Airways." *New Yorker* (February 25, 1967).
2. Alberts, David S., John Garstka, and Frederick Stein. *Network Centric Warfare: Developing and Leveraging Information Superiority* (second edition) Washington D.C.: National Defence Universty Press, 1999.
3. Allen, Michael. "Americans Fuel Yucatan Land Grab." *Wall Street Journal* (April 18, 2006).
4. Arnesen, Eric. *Waterfront Workers of New Orleans: Race, Class, and Politics, 1863–1923.* Urbana, Il: University of Illinois Press, 1994.
5. Asbury, Herbert. *The Gangs of New York.* New York & London: A. A. Knopf, 1928.
6. Associated Press. "Harsh Urban Renewal in New Orleans" (October 12, 2005, Canizaro quote).
7. Barnes, James. "It's the Suburbs, Stupid." *National Journal* (July 11, 2004).
8. Barry, Ellen. "Power Shifting with Population." *Los Angeles Times* (November 17, 2005).
9. Barry, John M. *Rising Tide: The Great Mississippi Flood of 1927 and How it Changed America.* New York: Simon and Schuster, 1997 (chapter 17, "The Club," is essential reading, an extraordinary portrait of New Orleans's historical elite).
10. Bartels, Larry. "What's the Matter with *What's the Matter with Kansas?*" paper presented to annual meeting of the American Political Science Association, Washington D.C., September 1–4, 2005.
11. Bell, Gertrude Lowthian. *The Letters of Gertrude Bell.* New York: Boni and Liveright, 1927.
12. Benson, Lee. *The Concept of Jacksonian Democracy; New York as a Test Case.* Princeton, NJ: Princeton University Press, 1961.
13. Berkowitz, Bill. "Heritage Foundation Capitalizes on Katrina." www.media transparency.com, September 15, 2005.

14. Boaz, David. "Did Big Government Return with Katrina?" *Cato Policy Report* (November–December 2005).

15. Boia, Lucien. *The Weather in the Imagination.* London: Reaktion Books LTD, 2005.

16. Bonacich, Edna and Richard Appelbaum. *Behind the Label: Inequality in the Los Angeles Apparel Industry.* Berkeley: University of California Press, 2000.

17. Bring Back New Orleans Urban Planning Committee. *Action Plan for New Orleans: The New American City* (January 11, 2006).

18. Brooks, David. "Katrina's Silver Lining." *New York Times* (September 8, 2005).

19. Burnham, Walter Dean. *The Current Crisis in American Politics.* New York: Oxford University Press, 1982.

20. Bumiller, Elisabeth. "Trying on Reagan's Mantle." *New York Times* (June 14, 2004).

21. Bureau of Government Research (New Orleans). *Wanted—A Realistic Development Strategy.* New Orleans (December 22, 2005).

22. Calmes, Jackie, Ann Carns, and Jeff Opdyke. "As Gulf Prepares to Rebuild, Tensions Mount Over Control." *Wall Street Journal* (September 15, 2005).

23. Campanella, Richard. *Time and Place in New Orleans: Past Geographies in the Present Day.* Gretna, LA: Pelican Pub. Co., 2002 (p. 58 on study by Joseph Suhayda).

24. Cardona, Gabriel y Juan Carlos Losada. *Weyler, nuestro hombre en la Habana.* Barcelona: Planeta, 1997.

25. Carr, Martha. "Rebuilding Should Begin on High Ground, Group Says." *Times-Picayune* (19 November 2005).

26 ——— "What will New Orleans look like five years from now?" *Times-Picayune* (25 December 2005).

27. Catherwood, Christopher. *Churchill's Folly: How Winston Churchill Created Modern Iraq.* New York: Carroll and Graf Publishers, 2004.

28. Center for Responsive Politics. *Long-Term Contribution Trends* (1990–2006), www.opensecrets.org/industries.

29. Chamberlain, Samuel E. and William Goetzmann ed. *My Confession: Recollections of a Rogue.* Austin: Texas State Historical Association, 1996.

30. Choe, Sang-Hon, Martha Mendoza, and Charles Hanley. *The Bridge at No Gun Ri: A Hidden Nightmare from the Korean War.* New York: Henry Holt and Co., 2001.

31. Churchill, Winston. *Papers,* as cited in Companion Volume 4, Part 1, of the

official biography by Martin Gilbert, *Winston Churchill* (London: Heinemann, 1976).

32. Civil Rights Project. *Confronting the Graduation Rate Crisis in California.* Harvard University, 2005.

33. Confessore, Nicholas. "Welcome to the Machine." *Washington Monthly* (July/August 2003).

34. Cooper, Christopher. "Old-Line Families Escape Worst of Flood and Plot the Future." *Wall Street Journal* (September 8, 2005).

35. Coover, Robert. *A Political Fable.* New York: Viking Press, 1980.

36. Curtius, Mary. "Image Problem Is Costing Louisiana." *Los Angeles Times* (December 3, 2005).

37. Danner, Mark. "How Bush Really Won." *New York Review of Books* (January 13, 2005).

38. Davis, Mike. "Worse than an H-Bomb." *Dead Cities and Other Tales.* New York: New Press, 2002.

39. De Ste. Croix, G. E. M. *The Class Struggle in the Ancient Greek World: From the Archaic Age to the Arab Conquests.* Ithaca, NY: Cornell University Press, 1981.

40. Dewan, Shaila and Anne Kornblut. "In Key House Races, Democrats Run to the Right." *New York Times* (October 30, 2006).

41. Drew, Christopher and Jim Dwyer. "Fear Exceeded Crime's Reality in New Orleans." *New York Times* (September 29, 2005).

42. Dunham, Richard and Eamon Javers. "The Politics of Change." *BusinessWeek* (November 20, 2006).

43. Dunn, Walter Jr. *Soviet Blitzkrieg: The Battle for White Russia, 1944.* Boulder CO and London: Lynne Rienner, 2000.

44. Eaton, Leslie and Ron Nixon. "Federal Loans to Homeowners Along Gulf Lag." *New York Times* (December 15, 2005).

45. *The Economist.* "Old Dogs; Few Tricks." (November 11, 2006).

46. Edsall, Thomas. "The GOP's Brownout." *National Journal* (September 2, 2006).

47. ——— "Building Red America." *National Journal* (September 23, 2006).

48. Erickson, Jon. *The Road to Berlin: Continuing the History of Stalin's War with Germany.* Boulder, CO: Westview Press, 1983.

49. Faux, Jeff. "Bait and Switch." *American Prospect* (February 25, 2002).

50. Filosa, Gwen. "Former Mayor Rejects Idea of a New Orleans Reduced in Size." *Times-Picayune* (January 8, 2006).

51. Fischetti, Mark. "Drowning New Orleans." *Scientific American* (October 2001).

52. Fleming, James Roger. *Historical Perspectives on Climate Change*. New York: Oxford University Press, 1998.

53. Fletcher, Michael and Spencer Hsu. "Storms Alter Louisiana Politics." *Washington Post* (October 14, 2005).

54. Foner, Philip S. *The Industrial Workers of the World, 1905–1917*. (Volume 4 of *History of the Labor Movement in the United States*). New York: International Publishers, 1987.

55. Foreman, Jonathan. "How Mel Gibson Helped to Turn Us into Nazis." *Guardian* (July 10, 2000).

56. Frank, Thomas. *What's the Matter with Kansas?: How Conservatives Won the Heart of America*. New York: Metropolitan Books, 2004.

57. Friedenberg, Edgar and Anthony Bernhard. "The Sunset Strip." *New York Review of Books* (March 9, 1967).

58. Friel, Brian. "Splits of Their Own." *National Journal* (September 9, 2006).

59. Gebauer, Matthias. *Der Spiegel* (interview with Finis Shellnut).

60. Garzon, Baltasar. "The West Shares the Blame." *Financial Times* (October 3, 2001).

61. Gill, James. *Lords of Misrule: Mardi Gras and the Politics of Race in New Orleans*. Jackson, MI: University Press of Mississippi, 1997.

62. Glassman, James. "Back to the Future." *Wall Street Journal* (January 12, 2006).

63. Gordon, Meghan. "Quick Sell." *Times-Picayune* (December 1, 2005).

64. Greenberg, Stanley. *The Meltdown Election: Report on the 2006 Post-Election Surveys*. Washington, D.C., 2006, www.greenbergresearch.com.

65. Gunwald, Michael and Susan Glasser. "The Slow Drowning of New Orleans." *Washington Post* (October 9, 2005).

66. Hauser, Christine. "Its Work Force Scattered, New Orleans Wrestles with Job Crisis." *New York Times* (October 26, 2005).

67. Hayden, Tom. "Analysis of 2006 Election." Handout to Sociology 178, Pitzer College, November 2006.

68. Hayes, Christopher. "The New Democratic Populism." *Nation* (December 4, 2006).

69. Heather, Peter J. *The Fall of the Roman Empire: A New History of Rome and the Barbarians*. New York: Oxford University Press, 2006.

70. Helfand, Duke. "Nearly Half of Blacks, Latinos Drop Out, School Study Shows." *Los Angeles Times* (March 24, 2005).

71.   Hersh, Seymour. "Uncovered." *New Yorker* (November 10, 2003).

72.   Hoeg, Peter. *Smilla's Sense of Snow.* New York: Farrar, Straus and Giroux, 1993.

73.   Hsu, Spencer. "$29 Billion Approved for Gulf Coast Storm Relief." *Washington Post* (December 23, 2005).

74.   ——— "Post-Katrina Promises Unfulfilled." *Washington Post* (January 28, 2006, Coburn quote).

75.   Iritani, Evelyn. "Mexican Resorts Show No Sign of Catching U.S. Housing's Cold." *Los Angeles Times* (August 26, 2006).

76.   Kabler, Phil. "Manchin Wins by Wide Margin." *Charleston Gazette* (November 3, 2004).

77.   Karol, K. S. *Between Two Worlds: The Life of a Young Pole in Russia, 1939–46.* New York: Henry Holt and Co., 1987.

78.   Kaufmann, Karen. "The Gender Gap." *PS* (July 2006).

79.   Kelber, Harry. *LaborTalk,* www.laboreducator.org.

80.   Klein, Ezra. "Spinned Right." *American Prospect* (online edition, November 8, 2006).

81.   Klinenberg, Eric. *Heat Wave: A Social Autopsy of Disaster in Chicago.* Chicago: University of Chicago Press; New edition, 2003.

82.   Koerner, Brendan. "The Security Traders." *Mother Jones* (September/October 2002).

83.   Kotkin, Joel. "Ideological Hurricane." *American Enterprise* (January–February 2006).

84.   Kraul, Chris and Kenneth Weiss. "Baja Marinas Project OKd." *Los Angeles Times* (November 8, 2003).

85.   Kriz, Margaret. "Reserving Front Burner." *National Journal* (September 9, 2006).

86.   Krugman, Paul. "Not the New Deal." *New York Times* (September 16, 2005).

87.   Kuttner, Robert. "The Road to Enron." *American Prospect* (March 25, 2002).

88.   ——— "How the Democrats Lost Their Fast Ball." *BusinessWeek* (March 11, 2002).

89.   Lampert, E. *The Apocalypse of History; Problem of Providence and Human Destiny.* London: Faber and Faber, 1948.

90.   Larsen, Janet. "Setting the Record Straight: More than 52,000 Europeans Died from Heat in Summer 2003." Earth Policy Institute release (June 28, 2006).

91.   Levi, Primo. *The Reawakening: A Liberated Prisoner's Long March Home Through East Europe.* Boston: Little, Brown, 1965.

92. Lichtenstein, Nelson. "Wal-Mart and the New World Order." *New Labor Forum* (Spring 2005).

93. *Los Angeles Times.* "State Blaming WA for Budget Woes." (February 15, 2005).

94. Luke, Mike. "St. Thomas Redevelopment." *Where Y'At* (Kabacoff quoted).

95. Maggs, John. "Grover at the Gate." *National Journal* (October 11, 2003).

96. Maginnis, John. "Small Business Waiting for Relief." *Times-Picayune* (January 4, 2006).

97. Malaurie, Jean. *Last Kings of Thule; A Year Among the Polar Eskimos in Greenland,* London: G. Allen and Unwin, 1956.

98. Mann, James. *The Rise of the Vulcans: The History of Bush's War Cabinet.* New York: Penguin Books, 2004.

99. Marshall, Bob. "Corps Never Pursued Design Doubts." *Times-Picayune* (December 30, 2005).

100. Marshall, Joshua. "Kerry Faces the World." *Atlantic Monthly* (July/August 2004).

101. Martin, Hugo. "GOP Looks to Inland Empire." *Los Angeles Times* (May 10, 2004).

102. McCash, Douglas. "New Urbanism Dominates Rebuilding Chatter." *Times-Picayune* (November 14, 2005).

103. McQuaid, John and Mark Schlcifstein. "Washing Away" (five part series). *Times-Picayune* (June 2002).

104. McWilliams, Carey. *The Education of Carey McWilliams.* New York: Simon and Schuster, 1979.

105. McWilliams, Wilson. Foreword, *Fool's Paradise: A Carey McWilliams Reader.* Berkeley, CA: Heyday Books, 2001.

106. Miller, T. Christian. "Riding Shotgun on a Pipeline." *Los Angeles Times* (May 16, 2004).

107. Monsiváis, Carlos. *Entrada libre: crónicas de la sociedad que se organiza.* Mexico, D.F.: Ediciones Era, 1987.

108. Moore, James and Wayne Slater. *Bush's Brain: How Karl Rove Made George W. Bush Presidential.* New York: Wiley, 2003 (on steel tariff: pp. 294–95).

109. Nadel, Stanley. *Little Germany: Ethnicity, Religion, and Class in New York City, 1845–80.* Urbana, IL: University of Illinois Press, 1990.

110. Nevin, Alan (CBIA chief economist). *California Home Equity Analysis.* California Building Industry Association. Sacramento, CA, June 2005.

111. Editorial. "Mr. Bush in New Orleans." *New York Times* (September 16, 2005).

112. ———— "Death of an American City." (December 11, 2005).

113. Nicholson, Peter. "Hurricane Katrina: Why Did the Levees Fail?" testimony

on behalf of the American Society of Civil Engineers, U.S. Senate, Committee on Homeland Security and Governmental Affairs, November 2, 2005.

114. Omissi, David. *British Air Power and Colonial Control in Iraq: 1920–1923*. Manchester, 1990.

115. Overpeck, J., et al. "Arctic System on Trajectory to New, Seasonally Ice-Free State." *EOS* 86:34 (August 23, 2005).

116. Paige, Jeffery M. *Agrarian Revolution: Social Movements and Export Agriculture in the Undeveloped World*. New York: Free Press, 1975.

117. Perry, Tony. "For Marine Snipers, War is Up Close and Personal." *Los Angeles Times* (April 19, 2004).

118. Peters, Major Ralph. "Our Soldiers, Their Cities." *Parameters* (Spring 1996).

119. Pew Research Center. "Religion and the Presidential Vote," (December 6, 2004).

120. Plotnick, Robert, et al. "The Twentieth Century Record of Inequality and Poverty in the United States." Institute for Research on Poverty Discussion, Paper no. 1166-98, 1998.

121. Popkin, Susan, et al. "The HOPE VI Program: What About the Residents?" *Housing Policy Debate* 15:2 (2004).

122. Porch, Douglas. *The Path to Victory: The Mediterranean Theater in World War II*. New York: Farrar, Straus and Giroux, 2004 (see chapter 12 for account of Churchill's 1941 invasion of Iraq).

123. Puzzanghera, Jim. "Pelosi Likely to Speak Up for Tech Industry." *Los Angeles Times* (November 13, 2006).

124. Rathke, Wade. "A New Orleans for All." (January 12, 2006) www.TomPaine.com.

125. Rauch, Jonathan. "The Loss of New Orleans Wasn't Just a Tragedy. It Was a Plan." *National Journal* (September 17, 2005, Corps commander quoted).

126. Richardson, Peter. *American Prophet: The Life and Work of Carey McWilliams*. Ann Arbor: University of Michigan Press, 2005.

127. Rivlin, Gary. "Divisions Appear Within a Storm Recovery Commission." *New York Times* (October 30, 2005).

128. Russell, Gordon and James Varney. "Blue Tarps." *Times-Picayune* (December 29, 2005).

129. Russell, Gordon and Frank Donze. "Officials Tiptoe Around Footprint Issue." *Times-Picayune* (January 8, 2006).

130. Safire, William. "After the Thumpin'." *New York Times* (November 9, 2006).

131. Sallah, Michael and Mitch Weiss. *Tiger Force: A True Story of Men and War*. New York: Little, Brown, 2004.

132. Schiermeir, Quirin. "The Power of Katrina." *Nature* 437 (September 8, 2005).

133. Schwartz, John. "'Malfeasance' Might Have Hurt Levees, Engineers Say." *New York Times* (November 3, 2005).

134. Semenza, J., et al. "Heat-Related Deaths During the July 1995 Heat Wave in Chicago." *New England Journal of Medicine* 335(2), 1996.

135. Shukrallah, Hani. "Shrouded in Darkness." *Al-Ahram Weekly* (September 20–26, 2001).

136. Silverstein, Ken. "Top FEMA Jobs: No Experience Required." *Los Angeles Times* (September 9, 2005).

137. Simon, John. "The Achievement of Malcolm X." *Monthly Review* (February 2005).

138. Simon, Richard. "Green Laws No Slam-Dunk in New Congress." *Los Angeles Times* (December 18, 2006).

139. Simons, G. L. *Iraq: From Sumer to Saddam*, New York: St. Martin's Press, 1994.

140. Solomon, Burt. "Bush and Clinton's Urban Fervor." *National Journal* (May 16, 1992).

141. Stern, Andy. *A Country That Works: Getting America Back on Track*. New York: Free Press, 2006.

142. Starr, Kevin, "Saving California Centrism." *Los Angeles Times* (September 19, 2004).

143. Taw, Jennifer M. and Bruce Hoffman. *The Urbanization of Insurgency: The Potential Challenge to U.S. Army Operations*. Santa Monica, CA: Rand Corp., 1994.

144. Teixcira, Ruy. "Cultural Alien." November 11, 2004, www.alternet.org/election04/20464/.

145. Thevenot, Brian. "Returning New Orleanians Ponder City's Future." *Times-Picayune* (October 1, 2005).

146. Tidmore, Christopher. "Groundbreaking Begins at St. Thomas Site." *Louisiana Weekly* (November 24, 2003, Kabacoff quote).

147. Travis, John. "Scientists Fears Come True as Hurricane Floods New Orleans." *Science* 309 (September 9, 2005).

148. Thomas, Captain Troy. "Slumlords: Aerospace Power in Urban Fights." *Aerospace Power Journal* (Spring 2002).

149. Tunnel, Ted. *Crucible of Reconstruction*, Baton Rouge, LA: Louisiana State University Press, 1984.

150. Turse, Nick and Deborah Nelson. "Vietnam: The War Crimes Files." *Los Angeles Times* (August 6, 1996).

151. UN Human Settlements Program. *The Challenge of Slums: Global Report on Human Settlements 2003*, London 2003.
152. Vonnegut, Kurt. *Player Piano*. New York: Scribner, 1952.
153. Walsh, Bill. "Louisiana Feeling Shortchanged." *Times-Picayune* (January 20, 2006).
154. Walters, Jonathan. "Solidarity Forgotten." *Governing* (June 2006).
155. Webb, James. "Class Struggle: American Workers Have a Chance to Be Heard." *Wall Street Journal* (November 15, 2006).
156. Wilke, John and Brody Mullins. "After Katrina, Republicans Back a Sea of Conservative Ideas." *Wall Street Journal* (September 15, 2005).

ALSO FROM HAYMARKET BOOKS

Welcome to the Terrordome: The Pain, Politics, and Promise of Sports
Dave Zirin • This much-anticipated sequel to *What's My Name, Fool?* by acclaimed sportswriter Dave Zirin breaks new ground in sportswriting, looking at the controversies and trends now shaping sports in the United States—and abroad. Always insightful, never predictable. ISBN 978-1-931859-41-7.

Beyond the Green Zone: Dispatches From an Unembedded Reporter in Occupied Iraq
Dahr Jamail with a foreword by Amy Goodman • As the occupation of Iraq unravels, the demand for independent reporting is growing. Since 2003, unembedded journalist Dahr Jamail has filed indispensable reports from Iraq that have made him this generation's chronicler of the unfolding disaster there. ISBN 978-1-931859-47-9.

Sin Patrón: Stories from Argentia's Occupied Factories
The lavaca collective, with a foreword by Naomi Klein and Avi Lewis • The inside story of Argentina's remarkable movement to create factories run democratically by workers themselves. ISBN 978-1-931859-43-1.

Between the Lines: Readings on Israel, the Palestinians, and the U.S. "War on Terror"
Tikva Honig-Parnass and Toufic Haddad • This compilation of essays—edited by a Palestinian and an Israeli—constitutes a challenge to critially rethink the Israeli-Palestinian conflict. ISBN 978-1-931859-44-8.

No One Is Illegal: Fighting Racism and State Violence on the U.S./Mexico Border
Justin Akers Chacón and Mike Davis • Countering the chorus of anti-immigrant voices, Davis and Akers Chacón expose the racism of anti-immigration vigilantes and put a human face on the immigrants who risk their lives to cross the border to work in the United States. ISBN 978-1-931859-35-3.

A Little Piece of Ground

Elizabeth Laird • Growing up in occupied Palestine through the eyes of a twelve-year-old boy. ISBN 978-1-931859-38-7.

The Communist Manifesto: A Road Map to History's Most Important Political Document

Karl Marx and Frederick Engels, edited by Phil Gasper • This beautifully organized and presented edition of *The Communist Manifesto* is fully annotated, with clear historical references and explication, additional related texts, and a glossary that will bring the text to life. ISBN 978-1-931859-25-7.

Subterranean Fire: A History of Working-Class Radicalism in the U.S.

Sharon Smith • Workers in the United States have a rich tradition of fighting back and achieving gains previously thought unthinkable, but that history remains largely hidden. *In Subterranean Fire*, Sharon Smith brings that history to light and reveals its lessons for today. ISBN 978-1-931859-23-3.

Soldiers in Revolt: GI Resistance During the Vietnam War

David Cortright with a new introduction by Howard Zinn • "An exhaustive account of rebellion in all the armed forces, not only in Vietnam but throughout the world."—*New York Review of Books.* ISBN 978-1-931859-27-1.

Friendlly Fire: The Remarkable Story of a Journalist Kidnapped in Iraq, Rescued by an Italian Secret Service Agent, and Shot by U.S. Forces

Giuliana Sgrena • The Italian journalist, whose personal story was featured on *60 Minutes*, describes the real story of her capture and shooting in 2004. Sgrena also gives invaluable insight into the reality of life in occupied Iraq, exposing U.S. war crimes there. ISBN 978-1-931859-39-4.

The Meaning of Marxism

Paul D'Amato • A lively and accessible introduction to the ideas of Karl Marx, with historical and contemporary examples. ISBN 978-1-931859-29-5.

Revolution and Counterrevolution: Class Struggle in a Moscow Metal Factory

Kevin Murphy • Murphy's wealth of research and insight deliver an exciting contribution to the discussion about class and the Russian Revolution. ISBN 978-1-931859-50-9

The Women Incendiaries: The Inspiring Story of the Women of the Paris Commune Who Took up Arms in the Fight for Liberty and Equality

Edith Thomas • *The Women Incendiaries* tells the often over-looked story of the crucial role played by women during the Paris Commune of 1871, one of history's most important emxperiments in working-class democracy. ISBN 978-1-931859-46-2.

Vive la Revolution: A Stand-up History of the French Revolution

Mark Steel • An actually interesting, unapologetically sympathetic and extremely funny history of the French Revolution. ISBN 978-1-931859-37-0.

Poetry and Protest: A Dennis Brutus Reader

Aisha Karim and Lee Sustar, editors • A vital original collection of the interviews, poetry, and essays of the much-loved anti-apartheid leader. ISBN 978-1-931859-22-6.

The Bending Cross: A Biography of Eugene Victor Debs

Ray Ginger, with a new introduction by Mike Davis • The classic biography of Eugene Debs, one of the most important thinkers and activists in the United States. 978-1-931859-40-0.

What's My Name, Fool? Sports and Resistance in the United States

Dave Zirin • What's My Name, Fool? offers a no-holds-barred look at the business of sports today. In humorous and accessible language, Zirin shows how sports express the worst, as well as the most creative and exciting, features of American society. ISBN 978-1-931859-20-5.

Literature and Revolution

Leon Trotsky, William Keach, editor • A new, annotated edition of Leon Trotsky's classic study of the relationship of politics and art. ISBN 978-1931859-16-5.

ABOUT HAYMARKET BOOKS

Haymarket Books is a nonprofit, progressive book distributor and publisher, a project of the Center for Economic Research and Social Change. We believe that activists need to take ideas, history, and politics into the many struggles for social justice today. Learning the lessons of past victories, as well as defeats, can arm a new generation of fighters for a better world. As Karl Marx said, "The philosophers have merely interpreted the world; the point however is to change it."

We take inspiration and courage from our namesakes, the Haymarket Martyrs, who gave their lives fighting for a better world. Their 1886 struggle for the eight-hour day, which gave us May Day, the international workers' holiday, reminds workers around the world that ordinary people can organize and struggle for their own liberation. These struggles continue today across the globe—struggles against oppression, exploitation, hunger, and poverty.

It was August Spies, one of the Martyrs who was targeted for being an immigrant and an anarchist, who predicted the battles being fought to this day. "If you think that by hanging us you can stamp out the labor movement," Spies told the judge, "then hang us. Here you will tread upon a spark, but here, and there, and behind you, and in front of you, and everywhere, the flames will blaze up. It is a subterranean fire. You cannot put it out. The ground is on fire upon which you stand."

We could not suceed in our publishing efforts without the generous financial support of our readers. Many people contribute to our project through the Haymarket Sustainers program, where donors receive free books in return for their monetary support. If you would like to be a part of this program, please contact us at info@haymarketbooks.org.

Order these titles and more online at www.haymarketbooks.org or call 773-583-7884.